DOMESTIC MURDER IN NINETEENTH-CENTURY ENGLAND

For Sally and Micky:
'Love has occasioned it all'

Domestic Murder in Nineteenth-Century England

Literary and Cultural Representations

BRIDGET WALSH

Hills Road Sixth Form College, UK

Routledge

Taylor & Francis Group

LONDON AND NEW YORK

First published 2014 by Ashgate Publishing

Published 2016 by Routledge
2 Park Square, Milton Park, Abingdon, Oxfordshire OX14 4RN
711 Third Avenue, New York, NY 10017, USA

First issued in paperback 2016

Routledge is an imprint of the Taylor & Francis Group, an informa business

British Library Cataloguing in Publication Data
A catalogue record for this book is available from the British Library

The Library of Congress has cataloged the printed edition as follows:
Walsh, Bridget, 1964–
  Domestic murder in nineteenth-century England : literary and cultural representations /
    by Bridget Walsh.
    pages cm
  Includes bibliographical references and index.
  ISBN 978-1-4724-2103-6 (hardcover: alk. paper)
  1. English literature—19th century—History and criticism. 2. Popular literature—Great
Britain—History and criticism. 3. Murder in literature. 4. Family violence in literature.
5. Social values in literature. 6. National characteristics in literature. 7. Social values—
Great Britain—History—19th century. 8. Murder—Press coverage—Great Britain—
History—19th century. I. Title.
  PR468.M85W35 2014
  820.9'355—dc23

                                                                          2013043332

ISBN 13: 978-1-138-25297-4 (pbk)
ISBN 13: 978-1-4724-2103-6 (hbk)

Contents

List of Figures

Acknowledgements

The idea for this book originated with my dear friend, the late Sally Ledger. It was Sally who gave me the original impetus to undertake the research, and whose relentless good humour, encouragement, kindness, intellectual rigour and sense of fun carried me through. Without her, I would never have written this book and my only sadness about this entire project is that she won't be with me to celebrate.

My deepest thanks also go to Professor Hilary Fraser and Dr. Matt Cook, both of Birkbeck, who provided endless enthusiasm and encouragement. The Birkbeck 'family' made me feel it wasn't too late to return to academic study, and the generous funding from the AHRC made that a possibility. Professor Michael Slater shared his knowledge of the Victorian theatre, particularly 'The Colleen Bawn'. Professor Rohan McWilliam offered valuable guidance and pointed me in the direction of Ashgate, where thanks must also go to Ann Donahue, whose kind words and positivity encouraged me to push forward with the project.

The staff of the following libraries, archives and museums were always friendly and knowledgeable: Birkbeck library; the British Library; the British Library's Newspaper Library at Colindale; the Public Record Office at Kew; the Radzinowicz Library, Institute of Criminology, University of Cambridge; the Bodleian Library, Oxford. Alex McWhirter from St. Edmundsbury Heritage Service, Moyse's Hall Museum, Bury St. Edmunds provided the image of Corder's hanging (Figure 1.1).

Inevitably, there will be people I should have thanked and have overlooked. Returning to academic study later in life, and trying to balance it with the demands of a full-time teaching career, has not always been easy, but it has been a genuine joy. To my friends and family who have cheered me on from the sidelines, and perhaps feigned an interest they didn't always feel – thank you.

This work is co-dedicated to Sally and to Micky, my lovely husband. He kept me fed, watered and walked me regularly; not dissimilar treatment to that enjoyed by our dog, Pip, although with fewer bones.

Introduction

On 18 May 1827, Maria Marten, a 26-year-old mole-catcher's daughter from the village of Polstead in Suffolk, met her lover William Corder in the Red Barn on Corder's farm. Following the recent death of their baby, Maria was now pressing for marriage, and Corder had promised her that they would elope to Ipswich. The exact sequence of events that occurred that day was never fully explained, even at the trial; all that was certain was that Maria did not leave the barn on 18 May. Corder did, however, moving to London and maintaining the fiction with Maria's family that she was still alive. In the meantime he advertised for a wife, and married sometime towards the end of 1827. Almost concurrent with this marriage, Maria's stepmother Ann was visited by the first of several dreams that Maria was buried in the Red Barn; on investigation, the body was found and Corder was arrested, tried and hanged for the murder.

On the face of it, Maria Marten's murder (or 'The Murder in the Red Barn', as it came to be known) was nothing exceptional. A cursory perusal of nineteenth-century newspapers reveals any number of such murders of sweethearts or spouses, committed for social or financial expediency, or as an act of revenge or thwarted desire. But this particular case triggered something in the nineteenth-century cultural imagination; so much so that, in the weeks leading up to Corder's trial, an estimated 200,000 people visited the scene of the crime, over 1,000,000 broadsides featuring the case were sold by one broadside producer alone, and the murder was the subject of puppet shows, ballads and re-enactments at county fairs. Seven thousand people were present at Corder's hanging, a further 6,000 viewed his corpse after the execution, and the case provided material for various published accounts of the trial, a novel, and several melodramas which were performed throughout the nineteenth century.

Why were the public so fascinated by this crime? And why, throughout the nineteenth century, did certain murders and the subsequent trials achieve similar levels of notoriety, while others received only a brief mention in the press; particularly given that certain of the more notorious cases verged on the mundane in their motivation or execution, and the level of public interest they attracted therefore seems difficult to understand? Historian Matt Cook has argued that criminal trials help 'to define the boundaries of normality and to rearticulate ideologies of gender, class and nation' ('Law', 74) and J. Carter Wood, speaking of violence in nineteenth-century England, argues that 'attitudes towards violence are inextricably connected to issues of identity, class hierarchy, institutional development, codes of behaviour, views of recreation, the nature of private and public spaces, and societal arrangements' (15). What might such *causes célèbres* as the Corder trial, the trial of Frederick and Maria Manning in 1849, the Madeleine Smith case of 1857 and the conviction of Florence Maybrick in 1889 – to name but a few – reveal about the 'ideologies of gender, class and nation', and the 'nature of private and public spaces' in the Victorian era? This book was prompted, in part, by a desire to find the answer to these questions.

Initially perusing the *Annual Register* for the murder cases which had generated the most publicity (and which, therefore, might be said to offer some sort of cultural barometer), it became apparent that many of these cases could be grouped as 'murders of lovers, spouses or love rivals', but did not all qualify as 'crimes of passion', as they were often planned and executed with a considerable degree of foresight, and were often motivated not by passion but by expediency. Given the somewhat clumsy semantics of the taxonomy 'murders of lovers, spouses or love rivals', I have chosen to label these cases 'domestic murders' for ease of reference. Obviously, the term 'domestic murder' encompasses other forms of homicide – infanticide, parricide and fratricide being the most obvious – but a full and detailed examination of all types of domestic murder lies outside the remit of this book. It is also important to note that not all these crimes took place within the family home, and neither were the two (or more) parties involved necessarily sharing that home, but the *concept* of the home and its attendant domesticity was still a significant feature of the crime coverage and trial proceedings; the home, both physically and symbolically, was crucial to Victorian domestic ideology, as will be discussed later in this introduction. What I am contending in this work is that the media coverage of these murder cases helped to formulate but also, on occasion, to contest ideas of the domestic which were being shaped during the nineteenth century, particularly ideas of masculine identity, the acceptable limits of female behaviour, and the potential for secrecy and deviance afforded by the privacy of the home. I have focused on murders, as opposed to cases of domestic violence or abuse which did not result in murder, because it is the murder cases that attracted the greatest publicity and that publicity might say something to us about the Victorian mindset. I have also chosen not to examine the 'law and literature' school of writing; my focus lies with the media representation and public response to these crimes and their perpetrators rather than the legal technicalities.

In themselves, though, trial transcripts and press coverage do not reveal the 'whole picture'. As will be evident in the chapters that follow, works of fiction often revealed a more troubling domestic sphere than the press was willing or able to show. As such, literature is a crucial means of understanding these crimes and the nature of the domestic. Whilst works of literature can be read and examined for themselves, as cultural historians and the new historicism suggest they are also vital documents for the analysis of social and cultural life, and for the way they can register wider shifts in structures of thought and feeling, often in advance of what might be perceived as the more 'truthful' or 'representative' works of the press. By examining trial coverage alongside the fictional and dramatic representation of domestic murders, a contested and troublesome domestic ideology emerges.

***

The importance of the domestic space to the Victorian idea of self and nationhood is now embedded in our understanding of Victorian history and culture. As Anthea Trodd summarizes: 'the dominant image of the Victorian home is of a sanctuary, a firelit circle enclosed against the hostile and dangerous external world' (1). For Anthony S. Wohl, 'the Victorians regarded it as axiomatic that the home was the foundation and the family the cornerstone of their civilization and that within the family were first learned the moral, religious, ethical and social precepts of good citizenship' (10). Although home ownership was not a realistic goal for most Victorians, it was the *concept* of the home that mattered, as a source of peace and security from the vagaries and stresses of industrial capitalism. Connected to this is another cornerstone of Victorian domestic ideology:

> the fundamental division of the world into "public" and "private" spheres that came to constitute the dominant definition of "reality" in Victorian middle-class culture. The model of a binary opposition between the sexes was used to ground the division between these supposedly "separate spheres", shaping and legitimising this social arrangement according to sexual differences that were apparently fixed and immutable (Waters, *Politics of the Family*, 4).

In her examination of mid-Victorian family magazines, Catherine Waters argues that

> proper maintenance of the home by a successful domestic economist is held to be an essential requirement in the formation of male subjectivity, for without a home the Englishman's identity is incomplete … The hegemonic function of home-worship in family periodicals of the 1840s and 1850s is evident in the frequency with which the domestic ideal is held to transcend differences of class, gender or generation, uniting readers in the veneration of a common object (*Politics of the Family*, 19, 20).

This worship of the home as a place of privacy held within it, though, the potential for problems. A July 1860 edition of the *Morning Post* quoted in Kate Summerscale's *The Suspicions of Mr. Whicher* argued that

> every Englishman is accustomed to pride himself with more than usual complacency upon what is called the sanctity of an English home. No soldier, no policeman, no spy of the Government dare enter it … It is with this thoroughly innate feeling of security that every Englishman feels a strong sense of the inviolability of his own house (37).

It is the 'thoroughly innate feeling of security', and the 'strong sense of inviolability' that gave rise from the mid-nineteenth century onwards to concerns regarding the potential for deviance and criminal behaviour that the privacy of the home afforded. As Summerscale argues:

> though the 1850s had been christened with a great glasshouse – the Crystal Palace of the Great Exhibition of 1851 – the English home closed up and darkened over the decade, the cult of domesticity matched by a cult of privacy … Privacy

had become the essential attribute of the middle-class Victorian family, and the bourgeoisie acquired an expertise in secrecy (109).

The problem of this 'cult of privacy', the sense in which the Victorian domestic ideal was a contentious and often troubled one, is not a new idea. Dating from Mary Poovey's highly influential *Uneven Developments*, much recent work on Victorian domestic ideology has centred on the troublesome nature of the domestic ideal. Trodd argues that 'the essential conditions for domestic crime ... the uneasy relations between respectability, privacy and surveillance' (1) were established during the mid-Victorian period. Catherine Waters, in Sally Ledger and Holly Furneaux's more recent work *Charles Dickens in Context*, argues that

> the transgressive women who so deeply engage Dickens's imagination ... offer other challenges to normative ideology, as do the many plots involving family secrets, which depend upon the supposed inviolability of the home to leverage a narrative effect of sensational exposure. The tenuousness of the familial ideal is also suggested by the readiness with which the boundary between private and public life can be breached (354–5).

Waters uses the example from Dickens's *Dombey and Son* of a broker named Brogley invading the Wooden Midshipman because Sol Gills has failed to meet a payment on a debt, and a similar argument could be made for Rogue Riderhood's invasion of Bradley Headstone's schoolroom in *Our Mutual Friend* (discussed in greater detail in Chapter 4). In her earlier work *Dickens and the Politics of the Family*, Waters argues that the representation of the family in Dickens's work, and in mid-Victorian family magazines, reveals 'fundamental contradictions and instabilities within the ideologies of sexual difference and separate spheres' and that 'the family was often in fact a source of tension and discord' (*Politics of the Family*, 4, 25).

Mary Poovey's definition of ideology, although widely quoted, is worth reiterating as it is central to this work, and remains fundamental to much scholarship on Victorian domestic ideology. Poovey argues for the 'apparent coherence and authenticity' of ideology, on the one hand, and 'its internal instability and artificiality, on the other', resulting in what she defines as 'uneven developments' surrounding the ideology of gender in mid-Victorian England. Poovey argues that

> representations of gender constituted one of the sites on which ideological systems were simultaneously constructed and contested; as such, the representations of gender ... were themselves contested images, the sites at which struggles for authority occurred, as well as the locus of assumptions used to underwrite the very authority that authorized these struggles.

For Poovey, 'the middle-class ideology we most often associated with the Victorian period was both contested and always under construction; because it was always in the making, it was always open to revision, dispute, and the emergence of oppositional formulations' (2, 3).

This book builds on Poovey's ideas, arguing that the representation of domestic murder reveals how far the ideology of the domestic sphere was a troubled and contested one, closer to the 'uneasy cauldron of bliss' that Chase and Levenson identify (14). Whilst the concept of a contested domestic sphere is not a new one, this book focuses on how such an ideology was contested across different genres; in particular, the representation of domestic murder on the Victorian stage which is examined in detail in Chapter 2. Examining the portrayal of domestic murder in a variety of cultural forms across a period of more than sixty years reveals not merely a conflict or inconsistency in portrayal across different genres, but also within those genres. Essentially, this book shows how these 'uneven developments' identified by Poovey can also be witnessed generically.

***

Richard D. Altick's *Victorian Studies in Scarlet* (1970) formed the starting point for my early research. Moving from the 1820s to the early years of the twentieth century, Altick traces 'the crimson thread that runs through the fabric of Victorian social history' (9) and adopts an impressive, broad-brush approach which encompasses drama, prose, the popular press and visual culture, alongside potted histories of fifteen notorious crimes. Altick's cross-genre analysis, exploring the interplay between trial coverage and the fictional representation of domestic murder, offered the potential for a fuller insight into the public perception of such crimes. As part of this cross-genre analysis, I was particularly interested in examining the representation of domestic murder on the Victorian stage; although there has recently been significant research undertaken on Victorian drama, including the University of Worcester's Lacy's Plays Project and the work of cataloguing the Lord Chamberlain's Collection in the British Library, the representation of domestic murder on the stage is relatively under-researched, particularly in relation to representations in other genres.[1]

Other work within this field has tended to focus on developments in criminal policy (Wiener, *Reconstructing*; Rodensky) or to present a more populist account of notorious crimes (Wilson, Hartman). Work which does examine the cultural mediation of murder has tended to draw a distinction between fictional and 'real' crime, whereas my work examines the relationship between the two. Beth Kalikoff's *Murder and Moral Decay in Victorian Popular Literature* focuses on the representation of murder across a range of genres from 1830 to 1900, but her analysis of non-fiction deals only fleetingly with trial transcripts, and does not examine them in any great detail. Lisa Rodensky's *The Crime in Mind* examines the interplay between literary and legal texts, focusing on *Oliver Twist*, *Adam Bede*, *Felix Holt*, *Middlemarch* and *Daniel Deronda*, and also the writings of James Fitzjames Stephen, the nineteenth-century judge and legal historian, but her analysis is restricted to the novels mentioned and pertinent legal issues, with no examination of the press coverage of crime, or its depiction on the Victorian stage.

---

[1]   Juliet John's essay, 'Melodrama and Its Criticism' in the journal *19* provides a fuller overview of recent work in the field of melodrama.

Judith Knelman's *Twisting in the Wind* is one of the few recent works to examine the interplay between the press coverage of murder, and its fictional representation. Knelman contrasts the press coverage of the murderess as a 'monster' with the fictional murderess who can be an 'attractive, passionate, sympathetic' figure. She argues that this is made possible as 'literature, because it fleshes out its characters, tends to look into the circumstances that triggered peculiar behaviour' (20), an argument partly echoed in Rodensky's and Kalikoff's work. Interestingly, she seems to argue that fiction is more true to life, because it allows for some exploration of motivation, whereas journalism does not, a claim I am not entirely convinced by. As this book will reveal, the motivation of the individual perpetrator was unraveled in different ways across different genres, and proves to be more complex than the simplistic juxtaposition of 'fiction' and journalism is able to reveal. Knelman's argument that the Victorian press 'tended to treat crime as a fiction while presenting it as a fact' (40) is certainly borne out by my own research. However, her focus is on the motivation for the crimes, what the women were like and how they were treated, whereas my interest lies less with why or how they did it, and more on the public reception and the representation of the act. Restricting her focus to female murderers, Knelman adopts a feminist argument which hinges on patriarchal analyses of gender relations, rather than one which also considers the potential impact of other factors such as class and age. Knelman argues that the press 'by and large, made murderesses seem inhuman', depicting them as 'ugly, "masculine", old-looking' (4, 20), a claim supported by Wilson who argues that the *Newgate Calender* stereotyped all women murderers as 'either raucous harridans or pure girls led astray by a false step in youth' (14). Knelman elucidates such press coverage by arguing that

> a murderess had to be presented as other than human so as to preserve the social norm of acquiescent inferiority. For not only had she flouted the human taboo against killing another human being, but she had also challenged the social stereotype of femininity: gentle, submissive, passive, self-sacrificing, delicate (20).

My research does not fully support Knelman's claims; whilst there were, undoubtedly, instances where the female murderer was masculinized or demonized, there were equally many examples where the press seemed somewhat bewildered by the incongruity between the accused woman's crimes and her appealing demeanour (see Chapter 5 for further details). Knelman also argues for the financial oppression of these women, but fails to apply this line of reasoning to the significant numbers of middle-class, relatively affluent women who committed murder. The class aspect of these domestic murders is important to my work, not least because the cases that attracted the greatest notoriety and press attention were often committed by middle-class men and women. In addition, the importance of the 'home' was very much tied up with the construction of a Victorian middle-class identity.[2]

---

[2]   See Chase and Levenson for a fuller discussion of the construction of the Victorian middle-class 'home'. Also Deborah Cohen, *Household Gods: The British and Their*

Much academic work in this field, then, focuses largely on either fictional crime or trial coverage, with a strong emphasis on transgressive women in particular. Given more recent work on Victorian masculinity by historians such as John Tosh and Martin Wiener, this book broadens the analysis to explore the gendered representation of domestic murder for both male and female perpetrators. In addition, the book interrogates the cultural significance of domestic murders as mediated by trial transcripts, medico-legal documents, novels, broadsides, criminological and scientific writing, illustration and, notably, popular Victorian melodrama, a genre that has been neglected in any analysis of domestic murder. Such an oversight is partly explained by the relative paucity of extant melodramas featuring such crimes; my research only unearthed seven such plays for the entire period under examination in this book. Kalikoff and Altick do touch on the presentation of murder on the stage, with Kalikoff arguing that, within melodrama and street literature, 'because the criminal and his crime are not closely related to a particular social environment, we are not implicated or endangered by our enjoyment' (52). Kalikoff seems here to be aligning herself with Michael Booth, who regards the action of melodrama as taking place in a dream-like, idealized world. Such arguments have been refuted by other work, most notably that of Peter Brooks, which has tended to highlight the social criticism inherent in the action of melodrama, an approach pursued in Chapter 2 of this work.

Moving between these various discursive fields, this book examines why certain murders fired the public imagination, how the perception of the domestic murderer changed across the century, and how the public appetite for such crimes was representative of wider social concerns. The work argues that the portrayal of domestic murder reflected not a consensus of opinion regarding the domestic space, but rather significant discontent with the cultural and social codes of behaviour circulating in society, particularly around the issues of gender and class. As the press representation of domestic murder and the concept of melodrama are two threads which run throughout the book, they are examined in some detail in the first two chapters. Thereafter, the book adopts a more chronological approach for Chapters 3 through 5, to explore the shifting representations over time.

Chapter 1 opens with an examination of the importance of the domestic space to Victorian ideas of nationhood and national health, and then moves on to examine the coverage of the more notorious domestic murder trials in street literature and in the newspaper press between 1828 (with the murder of Maria Marten by William Corder) and 1890 (Eleanor Pearcey's murder of Phoebe Hogg and her child). The chapter's primary source material includes murder and execution broadsides, the *Times*, *Lloyd's Weekly London Newspaper*, *Reynolds's London Newspaper* and the *Illustrated Police News*. The diverse social, political and cultural 'reach' of this body of texts enables an examination of the representation of domestic murder in

---

Possessions and John Tosh, *A Man's Place: Masculinity and the Middle-Class Home in Victorian England*.

both populist and more high-brow publications, and demonstrates the fascination with domestic murder amongst the Victorian readership.

The chapter argues that the crime of domestic murder was a particularly threatening one to the Victorian public, given that it undermined the sanctity of the home. To counteract this threat the newspaper press and street literature contained it within certain tropes of melodrama: namely, the visibility of good/evil on the body, the inevitable triumph of justice and suffering of the guilty, and the aestheticization of the trial into a piece of theatre. Even with the waning popularity of the melodramatic mode within the Victorian theatre, the theatricalization of domestic murder trials continued through to the end of the century, although the 1870s onwards saw a growing lack of certainty as regards the visibility of good/evil on the body.

The chapter also examines how far changing class and gender expectations were played out in nineteen cases of domestic murder from 1828 to 1890. Whilst *Reynolds's* was the only publication examined for this book to identify any class bias in the judging of these cases, the extent of coverage afforded to some cases and not to others itself implied a class distinction. In terms of gender, the chapter demonstrates not a demonizing of the female killer (as suggested by Knelman), but rather a degree of bewilderment at the incongruity between gender and action. Linked to the representation of gender as the century progressed was an increasing gulf between public opinion and the newspaper press as regards sexual impropriety (as demonstrated through public agitation for more lenient treatment of the accused, an attitude often not mirrored in the press coverage of such cases).

Chapter 2 focuses on domestic murder on the Victorian stage where, by a rigid system of containment and censorship, the theatre was enlisted in the depiction of an idealized domestic sphere. Although the theatre offered the potential for disruption and dissent with regard to political and social inequality, when it came to the portrayal of the domestic space, the censorship of plays by the Lord Chamberlain effectively meant that no such discontent was permitted. Focusing on five plays that feature domestic murder, or attempted murder, I argue that the domestic myth was so powerful that these plays were effectively sanitized and stripped of any theatrical power or potential for disruption. I then move from an examination of the heavily regulated theatres to the 'theatre of the streets', which was less easy to control, as evidenced by the public disorder at the 1828 trial of William Corder for the murder of Maria Marten. Through a detailed examination of this trial, I argue for a public discontent with the constraints imposed within the confines of both the theatre, and the ideology of the domestic sphere.

Chapter 3 engages with the debate surrounding the Newgate novel of the 1830s and 1840s. Firstly, the Newgate controversy is contextualized by a brief examination of the content and generic features of *The Newgate Calendar*, which provided source material for the Newgate novelists. Setting this alongside contemporary news and street literature coverage of murder, the chapter then gives an explanatory account of the controversy surrounding the Newgate novel, before examining two novels central to the debate – Charles Dickens's *Oliver Twist* (1838) and William Makepeace Thackeray's *Catherine* (1840) – both of which have, at their heart, domestic murders: Sikes's murder of Nancy, and Catherine Hayes's murder of her husband. The two authors' treatment of this disruption of the domestic sphere differs radically. Dickens allied himself firmly with contemporary ideology in regarding domestic murder as the ultimate crime, and one for which Sikes must be seen to suffer. However, although appearing to position Sikes firmly within the melodramatic mode, Dickens actually created something of a transitional figure in him; Sikes exhibits elements of the psychological realism which sees fuller development in the character of Bradley Headstone from *Our Mutual Friend*, examined in greater detail in Chapter 4. Thackeray, on the other hand, by making the motive for the murder more domestic and sexualized than its source in *The Newgate Calendar*, actually mitigates Catherine Hayes's offence, and engenders a degree of sympathy for her. In his ambivalent treatment of his heroine, Thackeray foreshadows the more engaging figure of the sensation fiction villainess.

Chapter 4 examines the male domestic murderer in the middle decades of the century, arguing that unstable and contested models of masculinity were refracted through the cultural texts of trial transcripts and novels that concern themselves with domestic violence and murder. The chapter assesses how contemporary debates on models of male behaviour were played out in the murder trials of Frederick and Maria Manning for the murder of Patrick O'Connor (1849), the Reverend Watson for the murder of his wife (1871) and Louis Staunton and others for the murder of Staunton's wife, Harriet (1877). The chapter also examines the models of male behaviour offered in five novels featuring sexually motivated acts of extreme violence or murder: Wilkie Collins's *Basil* (1852), Thomas Hardy's *Desperate Remedies* (1871) and *Far From the Madding Crowd* (1874), and Charles Dickens's *Our Mutual Friend* (1865) and *The Mystery of Edwin Drood* (1870). The relationship between desirable male behaviour and the domestic sphere in these novels is shown to be a contested one, ultimately remaining unresolved.

Chapter 5 argues that the ambivalent portrayal of the female domestic murderer at the fin de siècle was a manifestation of developments in psychology and criminology, and the changing relationship between women and the domestic space. The chapter focuses on the trials of Adelaide Bartlett (1886), Florence Maybrick (1889) and Eleanor Pearcey (1890), and the representation of female domestic murderers in Mona Caird's *The Wing of Azrael* (1889) and Thomas Hardy's *Tess of the d'Urbervilles* (1891). In determining the shifts in portrayal of the key protagonists in each case, the chapter examines the interplay that took place at this time between the discourses of psychology, criminology, criminal trials and works of fiction.

In 1828 the press were almost unanimous in their portrayal of William Corder as some sort of monster in league with the devil. In 1890 the case of Eleanor Pearcey took on a very different complexion and complexity. Found guilty of murdering her lover's wife and baby child, Pearcey was, nonetheless, treated with a degree of sympathy by both the press and the public. She was, by turns, vilified and portrayed almost as the heroine of the story, often within the same publication. An explication of the distance travelled between these two cases – but also the threads which connect them – forms the core of this work.

Fig. 1.1   The execution of William Corder. Source: Moyse's Hall Museum, Bury St. Edmunds

Chapter 1
'The Demon in the Dock':
Domestic Murder in Street Literature and the Newspaper Press[1]

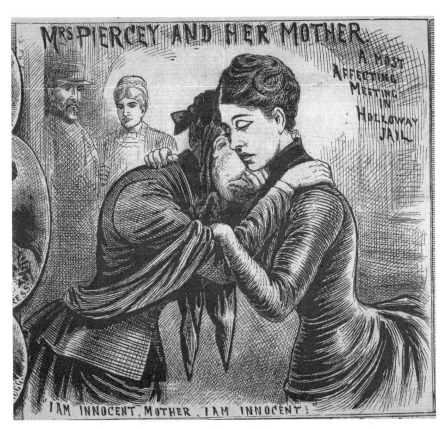

Fig. 1.2   'Mrs. Piercey and her mother'. *Illustrated Police News*, Saturday, 22 November 1890, 1. Source: The British Library

---

[1]   The phrase 'the demon in the Dock' is from Dickens's *Household Words* article, 'The Demeanour of Murderers'.

The two illustrations that open this chapter are separated by 62 years, and an ideological shift of immense proportions. The first represents the execution of William Corder in 1828 for the murder of his lover, Maria Marten, as discussed in the Introduction to this work, and in greater detail in Chapter 2. Although the provenance of the illustration is unknown, it is representative of broadside illustration in its portrayal of the isolation of the accused, displayed before a crowd of onlookers, but removed from such community because of the crime committed. Corder is afforded no individuality or humanity – indeed, he is barely detectable in the melee; and, by virtue of the situation in which he is depicted, the inevitable consequence of domestic murder is conveyed.

The second illustration is from the *Illustrated Police News*, 22 November 1890. The attractive woman portrayed on the right hand side of the illustration is not, as might be surmised, the victim of the crime, but the perpetrator. Her name was Eleanor Pearcey (sometimes referred to as Eleanor Piercey, Eleanor Wheeler or Mary Wheeler), and she was hanged on Christmas Eve 1890 for the brutal murder of her lover's wife and child. Not only is Pearcey afforded an individuality lacking in the earlier broadside, she is presented to the reader as an attractive woman, in a state of genuine distress at the visit of her mother. The caption for the illustration declares it 'a most affecting meeting', and Pearcey's words appear to reinforce her professed innocence. Pearcey is also at the foreground of the illustration, unlike in the broadside where the figure of the hanged man is at some distance from the reader. The positioning of Pearcey and the focus on her distress invite the reader to a greater degree of empathy than could ever be afforded the anonymous figure of the hanged William Corder. Although, like Corder, Pearcey is the subject of some scrutiny (from the two figures to the rear of the illustration) these observers are drawn with a lighter touch than Pearcey and could easily be overlooked. Their surveillance could also be viewed as oppressive, with the viewer invited to identify with Pearcey rather than with her warders.

These two illustrations are suggestive of a shift in perception and portrayal of the domestic murderer across the period under examination. But the shift is not as simple as one from vilification to empathy. Modes of depiction change over the period, and also conflict with one another, illustrating the cultural tension over the meanings of domestic murder. These tensions and uncertainties are evident in the visual and verbal representations of the crimes, the relationship between these two modes, and the relationship between the press, the Victorian stage, and the novel.

This chapter examines the representation of domestic murders and murderers in street literature and in the newspaper press between the years 1828 and 1890. Given the number of domestic murders which occurred during this time period, some selection of cases was necessary. The *Annual Register* for each of the years in question carried details of the most notorious cases; this formed the starting point for my research, as the level of publicity generated by a particular murder might be seen as forming some sort of social 'barometer'. With the breadth of printed crime coverage available, the chapter focuses on murder and execution broadsides (in existence throughout the century, but waning in popularity from the 1860s onwards), the *Times*, *Lloyd's Weekly Newspaper*, *Reynolds's Newspaper* and the *Illustrated Police News*.[2] These publications have been chosen as they all devoted considerable space to crime reporting, and covered an extensive readership: the *Times* was marketed at a more middle-class readership, *Reynolds's* and *Lloyd's* were more radical newspapers, and the *Illustrated Police News* was a prototype scandal sheet.

Through an examination of these publications, it will become clear that domestic murder held a huge fascination for all sections of society, but such fascination was tempered in equal parts with genuine concerns that the health of the nation would be undermined by any disruption to the domestic space. As a result of these fears, the earlier decades of the century saw a degree of consensus in how such crimes were reported, regardless of the professed readership of the publication; this consensus was a means not only of preserving the domestic space, but also of minimizing the potential for class unrest that the nature of these crimes, and the subsequent punishment meted out to the perpetrators, might potentially have aroused. The primary means by which an appearance of social consensus was achieved through the reporting of these crimes was by the adoption of melodramatic tropes, which are examined in some detail in this chapter. As the dominant theatrical mode of the first half of the nineteenth century, melodrama operated within a clear moral framework, and seemed to offer a rigidity and moral certainty that could counteract the crime of domestic drama. The dominant tropes of melodrama which found their way into crime reporting were the visibility of good/evil on the body, and the inevitable triumph of justice and suffering of the guilty. More than this, the press coverage of such crimes transformed the trial into a piece of theatre, further reinforcing the links with melodrama.

As the century progressed, however, particularly from the 1870s onwards, an increasing ambivalence and uncertainty was detectable in the press coverage of domestic murder; this was partly the result of a decline in melodrama as the dominant theatrical mode of the century but, more significantly, was a response to the burgeoning disciplines of psychology and criminology, and concerns regarding the nation's health and the putative threat of degeneration. Faced with a prevailing sense of uncertainty, the press coverage of domestic murder offered a mixed response, occasionally attempting to paint what we might now see as a more 'rounded' or psychologically complex portrait of the accused, but equally often harking back to an earlier time of perceived moral certainty by resorting to the familiar tropes of melodrama. This cultural tension concerning the domestic space, and those who transgressed within it, was also evident in the illustrative content of *Lloyd's*, *Reynolds's* and the *Illustrated Police News*, where the illustration frequently belied the written text.

Domestic murder was a particularly disturbing offence for a Victorian readership. Not only did it transcend class and gender boundaries, it also struck

---

[2]   *Reynolds's Newspaper* was titled *Reynolds's Weekly Newspaper* until 1851.

within the home, the one area of life deemed 'safe'. This is not to suggest that 'the home' has a transhistorical meaning. As John Tosh has argued:

> while a consistent strand of domesticity is to be found in both aristocratic and bourgeois circles throughout the eighteenth century, it was only in the 1830s and 1840s that the ideal of home was raised to the level of a cultural norm. For the middle class above all it had become *de rigueur* to practise significant elements of that ideal, while those sections of the working class and the aristocracy which resisted it were often perceived to be at odds with the national character (30).

Karen Chase and Michael Levenson make the point that the Victorians did not invent the family

> and yet the conditions of mid-nineteenth-century English life – the sheer extent of the home fetish, the maturing apparatus of information (newspapers, journals, telegraph), the campaign for legal reform of the family (infant custody, divorce, married women's property), the self-consciousness of modernity – gave it a special claim on its own attention (13)

Particularly during the middle decades of the nineteenth century, as Deborah Cohen argues, 'possession became a way of defining oneself in a society where it was increasingly difficult to tell people apart. Homes ... became flexible indicators of status' (xi).

So central was the importance of the home to Victorian thinking, and so profound was the betrayal occasioned by the crime of domestic murder, it was regarded as 'domestic treason'.[3] In the judge's passing of the death sentence on Sarah Westwood (found guilty of poisoning her husband in 1843), he emphasized the particularity of domestic murder, accusing Westwood of murdering 'one whom it was your duty to have cherished and protected instead of to have injured and attacked. I can scarcely conceive a crime of greater enormity or one of a deeper dye' (*Times*, 30 December 1843, 7). An earlier broadside held in the John Johnson Collection in the Bodleian Library, Oxford University, tells of Margaret Cunningham, alias Mason, who was hanged for the murder of her husband. The broadside highlights the particularly heinous nature of the crime, identifying the deep-seated fear which it unearthed:

> Against the midnight plunderer and assassin we are in some measure guarded by our prudence and ingenuity, and locks, and bolts, and various mechanical instruments, are fabricated for our defence and security: But when a man's enemies are those of his own house – when the wife of his bosom deliberately imagines and compasses his death – no human prudence, ingenuity, or foresight, will be found sufficient to render abortive her diabolical machinations, or avert the direful catastrophe ('Treason and Murder' broadside).

---

[3]   Killing one's husband was first designated as treason in 1352.

Although the broadside is undated, and the typography suggests an earlier date than the nineteenth century, the same principles hold true. The fear of the 'midnight plunderer and assassin', the unknown assailant, is evident here, but is accompanied by a conviction that something can be done to ward off such attacks. No such conviction accompanies the activities of the spouse or sweetheart with murder in their heart; indeed, any defence seems pointless, as nothing 'will be found sufficient to render abortive her diabolical machinations'.

This was, then, a crime against which there was apparently no defence, a crime which (in the case of poisoning, a particularly popular means of domestic murder)[4] required no physical supremacy and could therefore be committed just as easily by a woman as by a man, a crime which did not announce itself and which positively blossomed within the secrecy afforded by the home. Faced with such a threat, the broadside and newspaper coverage of domestic murder in the first half of the century turned to the perceived moral certainties of melodrama as a means of defence.

Readership and the Appetite for Crime

Broadsides were the cheapest, most widely available form of written communication until the mid-1860s, when the advance of cheaper newspapers and periodicals signalled their decline.[5] They were also the first publications featuring illustration during the period under examination. A single sheet of paper detailing the news of the day, costing 1d or ½d, and sold on the streets by 'paper-workers' or 'death-hunters' (broadside sellers who specialized in murder broadsides), such publications were hugely popular, and those dealing with murder particularly so. Murder and execution broadsides generally consisted of a single sheet, with an account of the murder, trial and execution, a poem or song allegedly written by the accused, and sometimes a single woodcut (or more than one for particularly notorious cases). The full murder and execution broadside would generally be preceded by a handbill in quarter-sheet on the fate of the victim, and a half-sheet detailing the particulars of the crime extracted from newspaper reports. More notorious cases might give rise to a 'book' of four, eight or more pages, published after the execution.

The abolition of the newspaper tax in 1855 heralded the decline in broadsides, with the ascendancy of the penny newspaper aimed at a populist market. Both

---

4   'Murder ... is still unfortunately in fashion, and as long as this is the case poisoning will be a favourite variety of it ... chiefly because it seems so easy and so safe' ('The Medical Evidence of Crime', *Cornhill Magazine* 7 [1863]: 338–9).

5   Although, as late as 1889 *Reynolds's* refers to the selling of street ballads, illustrated 'by penny dreadful woodcuts representing a woman on her knees before a chaplain in prison, and a tomb overshadowed by a weeping willow' (25 August 1889, 5). The ballad refers to the reprieve of the death sentence for Florence Maybrick, whose case is examined later in this chapter and also in Chapter 5.

priced at 1d, *Reynolds's Newspaper* and *Lloyd's Weekly Newspaper* were not only cheaper and more populist newspapers than the *Times*, they were also aimed at a more radical readership. *Lloyd's* advocated 'democratic and ... progressive' principles and *Reynolds's* was described in *The Newspaper Press Directory* for 1870 as follows:

> Principles: Democratic. Advocates the widest possible measures of reform. It contains much strong nervous writing, thickly spiced with abuse of the privileged orders, which causes it to be eagerly read by a certain class. The news and literary departments of the paper are respectably conducted; and, but for its violent politics, it might be characterised as a good family paper (23, 27).

The various police gazettes that proliferated throughout the period were aimed at a similarly populist market, but with no overtly progressive agenda. The *Illustrated Police News*, first published in 1864 as a Saturday weekly at a cost of 1d, relied heavily on the visual element to attract readers. A four-page publication, the front page was eventually devoted solely to illustration of the stories contained within, with particular favourites being explosions, mass deaths, carriage accidents, duels, and the dastardly activities of nuns.

Lest we assume that extensive murder coverage was the preserve of these more populist publications it is important to note the coverage devoted to such crimes in the newspapers aimed at a more affluent or aspirational class. The *Times* carried extensive and detailed crime reporting, with the more infamous court cases sometimes meriting an entire page of coverage for the day's proceedings, with details of witness testimony printed verbatim; given the lack of illustration in newspapers until the later decades of the century, one page of coverage constituted a considerable quantity of writing. The *Daily Telegraph*, founded as the first penny daily in 1855 and aimed at a middle-class readership, also featured considerable crime coverage and had achieved a circulation of 200,000 by the early 1870s, clearly showing the success of such an editorial policy.

William Corder's trial for the murder of Maria Marten (1828) and Frederick and Maria Manning's murder of Patrick O'Connor (1849), although more than twenty years apart, exhibit the consistent level of public interest in such crimes, with broadside sales of 1,166,000 and 2,500,000 respectively for James Catnach, one of the most successful broadside producers (Anderson, 25). Such figures should undoubtedly be treated with caution but, even if grossly exaggerated, this was the output of only one printer and such notorious cases provided material for dozens of others. Importantly, these same crimes merited similar levels of interest in the *Times*. The murder of Maria Marten occasioned 21 entries in the *Times* covering the period 23 April to 20 September 1828, and the Mannings warranted 59 separate articles, from 18 August to 22 November 1849. Even as late as 1889, the case of Florence Maybrick (found guilty of the murder of her husband) gave rise to an astonishing 105 entries in the *Times*, from 20 May to 5 September 1889, a melodrama entitled *A Fool's Paradise*, and a figure of Maybrick in Madame Tussaud's. These three cases span a time period of more than 60 years, and yet the public appetite for these crimes remained as strong in the closing decades of the century as in the earlier ones.

Even were we to adopt the simplistic notion, then, that the more affluent classes did not enjoy the vicarious appeal of the broadside or the penny weekly, it is evident that the crime of domestic murder was seen to have a cross-class appeal throughout this period. This interest in domestic murder, and crime in general, seems at odds with the arguments surrounding the Newgate novel and sensation fiction (examined in greater detail in Chapters 3 and 4), where the pernicious influence of working-class literature was seen as sullying the middle- or upper-class home. An interest in the murky underbelly of the criminal world clearly predates both the Newgate novel and sensation fiction.

In their coverage of such crimes, newspapers and broadsides did more than simply pander to the public appetite, but actually went some way towards uniting a potentially disparate and fragmented population by the reporting of such crimes. Domestic murders involving the seduction and murder of young women by their employers, or an evident disparity in the sentencing of the labouring classes and the more affluent, could have ignited considerable class discontent. And yet, with the exception of *Reynolds's* (examined later in this chapter), the class element of almost all these cases was played down, or completely ignored in the sample of publications examined for this book. This is not to say that *Reynolds's* was the only publication drawing attention to class bias; rather that, of the four publications examined for this book, and the particular cases examined, it is notably the only one to focus on class disparity. The one exception to this was William Corder's trial in 1828, where the minimal social disparity between victim and murderer was actually amplified by the press; this case is examined in greater detail in Chapter 2 of this work, and the reasons for the overplaying of the class card are examined therein.

There were numerous cases throughout the period where either the crime itself, or the treatment of the accused, seemed to offer the press an opportunity to highlight class differentials; but, with the exception of *Reynolds's*, the publications examined for this book generally failed to utilize class in their 'explanation' of these crimes. Jael Denny, murdered by Thomas Drory in 1851, was the daughter-in-law of an old servant of Drory's father and had fallen pregnant by Drory; Edmund Pook, Jane Clowson's 'young master', murdered Clowson in 1871; Madeleine Smith, a young middle-class woman almost certainly guilty of the poisoning of her lover, received the verdict of Not Proven in 1857 and walked free. Yet neither the broadsides, nor the majority of newspaper coverage, made any mention of the class disparity inherent in these cases, which is particularly interesting given the subversive element of the canting ballads of the eighteenth century, precursors of the broadsides.

Within the sample of publications that I have examined for this work, it was not until the advent of *Reynolds's Weekly Newspaper* that a clear political reading of these cases emerged. *Reynolds's* advocacy of the 'widest possible measures of reform' explains why cases that appeared to exhibit class injustice were treated with particular venom by this publication. The Watson (1871), Edmunds (1871–72), Maybrick (1889) and Pearcey (1890) cases invited particular censure from *Reynolds's*.[6]

The Reverend T. Selby Watson, a 67-year-old clergyman and former headmaster of Stockwell Grammar School, was found guilty in 1871 of murdering his wife by repeatedly beating her about the head. When Watson was found guilty, an editorial in *Reynolds's* described the murder as 'one of the most barbarous ever perpetrated' (21 January 1872, 5). Flying in the face of much public and press sympathy for Watson, *Reynolds's* was outraged when Watson was reprieved from the death sentence, prompting the following editorial:

> If he had been a poor and friendless man, he would most assuredly have suffered the extreme penalty of the law; but being a clergyman, highly educated, moving in the upper circles of life, overwhelming influence has been brought to save the life of one of the most cowardly, brutal, bloodthirsty, detestable murderers that ever defiled God's earth with his presence (28 January 1872, 5).

Such open avowal of opinion was always confined to an editorial at this point in the century, never appearing in the news coverage of the trial and its aftermath, but the vehemence of the opinion expressed here is still noteworthy. Watson's murder of his wife could hardly make him one of the most 'brutal, bloodthirsty, detestable' murderers ever; 34 years earlier (within living memory of many people at the time of Watson's trial), James Greenacre had cut up the body of his murdered fiancée, and five years after that, in 1842, Daniel Good murdered and dismembered his lover, Jane Jones. For *Reynolds's*, Watson's crime was more reprehensible precisely because he was an educated man, and therefore 'far more deserving of the severest punishment, than the rude, illiterate, ill-conditioned "rough," who, in a moment of tipsy frenzy, commits the crime for which he suffers death'. Watson was cast in the light of a religious hypocrite by *Reynolds's*, 'a man who for years has been solemnly warning his congregation every Sunday from the altar to do no murder, and yet he does it in the most cold-blooded manner'.

The editorial draws attention to a comment made by Baron Martin during the trial of Christiana Edmunds the same year, to the effect that 'a poor person is seldom afflicted with insanity, and it is common to raise a defence of that kind when people of means are charged with the commission of crime' (21 January 1872, 5). Christiana Edmunds was charged with one count of murder, one count of attempted murder, and two counts of attempting to cause grievous bodily harm. Thwarted in her desire for the married Dr. Beard, Edmunds tried to poison Dr. Beard's wife with a sweetmeat laden with strychnine. Her attempt failed, and the

---

[6]   These cases were also at the height of the debate surrounding the Contagious Diseases Acts of 1864, 1866 and 1869, where the 'professional' middle-class abuse of prostitutes was central to the debate. Josephine Butler's campaign for the repeal of the Acts saw her 'indignation … directed … at the moneyed youth of the middle and upper classes who thought nothing of preying on those with nothing to sell but their bodies' (Tosh, 154).

Beards cut off all communication with Edmunds; in an effort to re-establish the friendship, she tried to lay the blame for the poisoning at the door of Mr. Maynard, the local sweetshop owner. She bought several boxes of sweets, laced them with strychnine and then returned them to the shop as unwanted; she also offered poisoned sweets to children on the streets, thereby causing the death of a young boy, Sidney Albert Barker.

The commutation of Edmunds's death sentence on the grounds of insanity invited a scornful response from *Reynolds's*, suggesting that '*she* is a genteel murderess, and the gallows is not for such as her.' Far from seeing her behaviour as evidence of 'mental imbecility', the paper regarded it as 'suggestive of extreme shrewdness', and portrayed her as an 'artful and subtle-minded woman' who 'played her part accordingly' when placed under medical examination (28 January 1872, 5). The mental state of the accused played an increasingly important part in their defence from the 1870s onwards, and is examined further in Chapter 5. What is significant here is *Reynolds's*' apparent attempt to counteract the prevailing sympathy exhibited for both Edmunds and Watson; in an effort to highlight the inequalities within the legal system, the newspaper was driven to dispute Edmunds's insanity.

Even more than 20 years later *Reynolds's*' coverage of the Florence Maybrick (1889) and Eleanor Pearcey (1890) cases exhibited similar condemnation of a justice system it viewed as decidedly partisan. Both women were found guilty of murder: Maybrick poisoned her husband with arsenic extracted from fly-paper, Pearcey murdered her lover's wife and child. Maybrick's death sentence was commuted, Pearcey was executed. Again, *Reynolds's* went to extremes to make its point, depicting Pearcey as 'poor and unfortunate' and Maybrick as 'a criminal of deeper dye than Mrs. Piercey [*sic*] ... one of the vilest characters that has ever figured in the criminal courts' (7 December 1890, 4). Such a juxtaposition is difficult to accept; although both women were found guilty of murder, Pearcey's crime involved a far greater degree of physical violence, and also involved the murder of a young child. More recent critics have argued the class aspect of the Maybrick case with equal vigour, George Robb drawing a parallel between Maybrick and Margaret Higgins. Both women poisoned their husbands with arsenic extracted from fly-paper but, as Robb points out, whilst working-class Higgins was hanged for the crime in 1884, Maybrick had her sentence commuted. What Robb fails to mention is that Higgins was also found guilty of the murder of her stepdaughter and, along with her sister Catherine Flanagan, the murder of Flanagan's son, and one Margaret Jennings. Whilst the class element should not be overlooked, there were often other circumstances which might justify a particular sentence.

Whilst, with the exception of *Reynolds's*, there was a lack of overt class bias in the coverage of these cases, the issue of class was dealt with more covertly, simply through the selection of cases and the amount of coverage they excited. Alongside the extensive newspaper coverage generated by certain domestic murders was the comparative lack of interest aroused by others, and the distinguishing factor here was generally the social class of the protagonists. Working-class domestic murder merited some attention, but generally no more than a paragraph, particularly if the case involved abuse of alcohol. There were, obviously, exceptions to this rule, but such cases often had some other distinctive characteristic: the dismemberment of the body, the revenge murder of one or more children, or exceptional violence or deviousness in the execution of the crime. Whilst the press coverage often said little or nothing regarding the class of the protagonists, some of the most notorious cases of the period, those which received the most attention from the press, were committed by middle-class men and women. Implicit within the reporting of such cases is the argument that working-class murder was seen as less of a threat; they were, after all, often only killing 'their own'. Middle-class murder, particularly domestic murder, presented what was perceived as a genuine threat to domestic security.

Within the sample of publications examined for this book, and taking the exception of *Reynolds's* into account, it is reasonable to posit the argument that the avoidance of explicit reference to class in the coverage of domestic murder worked as a means of uniting a disparate readership, and reinforcing the supremacy of the (implicitly middle-class) domestic space for all classes. The other means whereby the potential to highlight class tensions was minimized and a consensus of opinion regarding the domestic sphere was encouraged, was the portrayal of domestic murder trials as a type of melodrama.

The Courtroom as Theatre

> Let the reader imagine the dingy, undignified *mise-en-scène* we have described, and which represents the famous Old Bailey, by Newgate; filled with hosts of "privileged" people. Let him imagine the Bench covered with gaily-dressed "distinguished" lovers of the sensational; and then, fronting the glittering row of holiday aspect, let him mark a pale, a livid, hard-set face of a solitary woman in a box, arraigned to be tried for her life! Only last week, in this same "square well with a lid on the top of it," an old, tottering man was the point of attraction in that same box. There has been a change of performances. A Grandfather Whitehead has been removed, and to-day the star is a little, careworn, hard-featured woman. Every eye is fixed upon her, so that no twitch of the mouth, no flash of the eye, no clenching of the hand, no quivering of the bosom, shall be lost. It is a hard, cruel, deliberate scrutiny, most repulsive, as it is directed from the privileged spectators of holiday aspect. Each spasm, every movement of the hand and head, is reported (*Lloyd's*, 21 January 1872, 1).

This description of the trial of Christiana Edmunds in 1871–72 illustrates perfectly the theatricalizing of court proceedings. The Old Bailey is the '*mise-en-scène*' and Edmunds is in the leading role, the 'star' of the proceedings. 'Grandfather Whitehead' refers to the trial only a few weeks earlier of the Reverend Watson. Drawing attention to the artifice and theatricality of the proceedings, and effectively presenting it as a form of narrative painting or tableau, distances us from what is actually taking place here: a woman is being tried for the murder of a young child, and attempted murder of several other individuals. Theatricalizing the proceedings means the 'audience' do not have to deal with the disturbing, and perhaps unsavoury fact that a middle-class, middle-aged woman was in the grip of a passionate affection for a married man, and was willing to place any number of lives at risk in order to fulfill that passion. *Lloyd's* was also taking a swipe at the audience for flocking to such entertainments, particularly the number of 'ladies' who would constitute a significant part of the courtroom audience.

It is important to note, however, that this theatricalized, visual portrayal of events was reserved for editorials, the initial appearance of the prisoner in the dock, or the passing of sentence. The business of witness testimony and medical evidence was delivered with relatively little authorial comment or theatrical flourish, and was marked by a distinctly prosaic style until the advent of the 'new journalism', evidenced in the 1889 trial of Florence Maybrick discussed below. When first encountering the trial coverage of the nineteenth century, it is striking how detailed the witness and medical testimony is, and the level of medical knowledge implied therein. For example, the *Times'* coverage of John Connor's murder of Ann Tape in 1845 revealed that 'the surgeon found a deep and wide gash in the central part of the back of the neck, which penetrated directly through to the front, and had separated the jugular vein, and probably the carotid artery' (2 April 1845, 6).

Even where the witness lacked medical knowledge, the testimony was still explicit. Greenacre's trial in 1837 for the murder of his fiancée Hannah Brown offered the following testimony from the Regent's Canal lock-keeper:

Mr. Rawlinson: In what state was the head?

Witness: It appeared fresh, but it seemed as if it had had a violent blow from a stick, or some other instrument.

Mr. Rawlinson: Why do you think so?

Witness: Because an eye was knocked out, the left jaw broke, and the bones protruded through the skin (3 April 1837, 7).

While the evidence was gruesome, there was no theatricalizing or signposting on the part of the newspaper. This may have been the means whereby the *Times* and similar 'respectable' publications avoided accusations of sensationalism, as they could simply argue that they were including relevant medical testimony, no matter how gory.

Such was the case for most of the century; it is only when we encounter the Florence Maybrick trial in 1889 for the murder of her husband that there is any deliberate sensationalizing of the witness testimony in *Lloyd's*. The shocking nature of the evidence offered by Mr. Edward Davies is signposted for the reader as 'one of the greatest sensations of the trial', and then embellished with instructions for the delivery of Davies's 'lines' and further techniques of suspense:

> He gave his evidence as coolly and calmly as if he was delivering a scientific exposition to a chemical class of students. When he had exhausted his statement as to his analyses, Mr. Addison asked him, "Have you anything else to say? What did you find else?" Turning to a tin box he produced a dressing-gown of a fashionable type and cut, and, holding it in his hand, showed it to the judge and jury and those in court. The word went through the court and among the members of the bar "This is new evidence." So it was. It had not been adduced at the coroner's inquest or at the hearing before the magistrates. It came as a surprise upon the defence, and Mr. Davies's narration of the circumstances connected with it was followed by almost breathless excitement (4 August 1889, 3).

Davies's lines are delivered 'coolly and calmly', and the comparison with the delivery of a 'scientific exposition' provides further elucidation, and lends gravitas to Davies's testimony. The delivery of the new evidence is deliberately delayed by the writer dwelling on the appearance of the dressing-gown, before its significance is unveiled, and by the use of such brief sentences as 'so it was'. The supposed reaction of the court and members of the bar is also speculated on, another new departure in the coverage of trials, before the final hyperbolic flourish of the 'breathless excitement' which accompanies Davies's explanation.

The return of the verdict on Maybrick provides the reader with a clear stage setting, directions for delivery of lines, and authorial embellishment of the proceedings:

> At three minutes to four, the dark curtain which fell over the outer-door which opened on the jury box was suddenly shaken; there then appeared the red-coated officer to whom had been entrusted the conveyance of the jury to "some safe and convenient place," and, after him, came the jury. During the time occupied in the calling of the roll of jurors, Mrs. Maybrick's face – she had meanwhile been brought back to the dock – wore an imploring aspect. "Have you agreed upon your verdict, gentlemen?" said the Clerk of Arraigns, and the prompt reply was "We have." "And do you find the prisoner guilty of murder or not guilty?" was the further question in the terrible formula, and after a brief pause, the foreman of the jury spoke the word "Guilty," whereupon a prolonged "Ah!" sounded through the court, and Mrs. Maybrick, still seated, suddenly started and buried her head in her hands, while her frame quivered (*Lloyd's*, 11 August 1889, 3).

The visual juxtaposition of the 'dark curtain' and 'red-coated officer'; Mrs. Maybrick's 'imploring aspect', and quivering frame; the 'prompt' reply from the foreman of the jury; the 'brief pause' before the delivery of the 'fatal' verdict; all of this is highly unusual for the newspaper coverage of any trial up until this point in time.

Such sensationalizing of the material seems to be in accordance with what Matthew Arnold termed 'the new journalism'. The rising cost of newspaper production led to 'increasingly popular styles of journalistic reporting', which 'sought to establish an emotional relationship to the audience by drawing upon personalized narration, vivid language, evocative detail, and, most important of all, sensational subjects' (Ed Cohen, 130).

The Courtroom and Melodrama

The depiction of a courtroom trial as a piece of theatre was hardly surprising: the trial followed a clear structure, with a suspenseful denouement at the close; the court was peopled with familiar types; and the proceedings told an exciting, often shocking tale. Nineteenth-century melodramas themselves often featured trials, where the battle between good and evil could be played out within a ritualized setting.

The marriage between crime and melodrama was firmly established on the Victorian stage, with newspaper stories often providing fodder for the plots of plays. Michael Booth quotes from Henry Arthur Jones, making the explicit connection between newspaper crime coverage and melodrama:

> in melodrama we find that those plays have been most successful that have contained the most prodigious excitement, the most appalling catastrophes, the most harrowing situations, and this without reference to probability of story or consistency of character. The more a play has resembled a medley of these incidents and accidents which collect a crowd in the streets, the more successful it has been. On the whole, a melodrama has succeeded much in proportion as the general impression left by it is the same as the general impression left by the front page of the *Illustrated Police News*.[7]

Jones's words would suggest that the theatre was not so much an escape from the 'real world', but more an attempt to work out the incomprehensible and inchoate events of such a world within a stylized and ritualized setting. Although melodrama was a theatrical mode that gave a voice to the working classes and the oppressed, it did not necessarily do so to stir up political discontent, and this was certainly not the case in the portrayal of the domestic space on the Victorian stage. As is discussed in much greater detail in Chapter 2, the Victorian theatre was a highly regulated space that resisted almost all subversive portrayal of the domestic, to the extent that virtually no plays featuring domestic murder are now extant. Rather, the Victorian stage can be read as a means of redirecting discontent, because any political unrest could be played out on stage, and the labouring classes could witness their reward at the end of the performance.

The relationship between melodrama and the domestic was firmly established by 1828 (the starting point of this work), and remained reasonably firm throughout the period under examination. Even in the latter half of the century, although gothic melodrama had largely disappeared, the domestic melodrama reigned supreme. The adoption of a domestic setting enabled the exaggerated excesses

---

[7]　　Booth, *English Melodrama*, 51, quoting from Henry Arthur Jones, *The Renascence of the English Drama*, 1895, 9. In a footnote to p. 51 of *English Melodrama*: 'Owen Davis recalls that "if a particularly horrible murder excited the public, we had it dramatized and on the stage before any one knew who had been guilty of the crime."'(Owen Davis, *I'd Like To Do It Again*, 1931, 85).

of the melodramatic mode to become rooted in a more realistic setting; what Booth regards as 'the curious paradox of ... a dream world disguised as a true one' (Booth, *Melodrama*, 120).

What was taking place in the press coverage of domestic murder up until the 1870s at least was, I believe, the inverse of this: a true world was being disguised as a dream one, much as Arthur Jones suggests with his view that the closer to events from the *Illustrated Police News*, the more a play was likely to succeed. The threat posed by domestic murder was of sufficient gravity to render it necessary to 'contain' it in some way. By adopting the familiar tropes of melodrama, by turning a real act of atrocity into a piece of theatre, the crime became limited within known parameters and thus its horror was more contained. By the same token, crimes were also located firmly within a topographical location, such as 'The Bayswater Murder' or 'The Pimlico Poisonings'. By placing the atrocity within a known and specific location it perhaps became particular; it could not happen 'anywhere', as it had occurred in a named location and, by implication, remained confined to that location. The topographical element also made the crime *sound* like a work of fiction, like the title of a play or a short story. Of course, given our lack of knowledge as to how individuals would have consumed this material, the converse may also have been true: the naming of the location could have suggested that it could happen in *any* street, including that of the reader.

The world of melodrama embodied a moral certainty that justice would ultimately be done; it offered the audience

> a world of certainties where confusion, doubt, and perplexity are absent; a world
> of absolutes where virtue and vice coexist in pure whiteness and pure blackness;
> and a world of justice where after immense struggle and torment good triumphs
> over and punishes evil, and virtue receives tangible material rewards.

Operating within such a world, melodrama was able to provide 'a logical moral philosophical coherence' for what appeared on the surface to be 'a wildly chaotic and exceedingly trivial drama' (Booth, *Melodrama*, 14). Hardly surprising, therefore, that this theatrical mode offered a blueprint for the portrayal of domestic murder, a crime which threatened to make chaos of the world and portrayed the sanctity of the home as little more than a 'trivial drama'.

One means whereby such moral coherence was established in the world of melodrama was that good and evil were instantly made manifest on the stage by means of costume, make-up and props. As Booth makes clear, 'moral position is identifiable with character type; audiences could know at once, by the initial appearance and first speeches of any person in melodrama, his or her character and forthcoming role in the play' (Booth, *Melodrama*, 15). Peter Brooks, in *The Melodramatic Imagination*, argues that this polarization of good and evil 'works toward revealing their presence and operation as real forces in the world. Their conflict suggests the need to recognize and confront evil, to combat and expel it, to purge the social order' (13). Thus, a villain always looked like a villain and, once recognized, evil could be expelled.

Similar techniques were at work within the press portrayal of domestic murder cases in the first half of the period under examination. If we look first at broadsides, the limited space afforded to the written coverage of crimes and the formulaic content of such material meant that any physical portrayal of the accused tended to be achieved through illustration. Given the speed and relatively low cost of production, broadside woodcuts tended to be somewhat repetitive, regularly reused for a whole variety of cases. Except in cases of particular notoriety these woodcuts could not be said to form an illustration of any particular murder, and they lacked sufficient detail to render them a replacement for the verbal depiction of the scene. In terms of artistry, they were simple and undeveloped, and remained so long after the technology had advanced.

However, more notorious cases sometimes merited new, individualized woodcuts, particularly so if the case involved dismemberment of some sort, which offered full and gruesome flight for the illustrator's imagination. James Greenacre and Sarah Gale's murder of Hannah Brown in 1837 was one such case. Brown was Greenacre's fiancée; when he learned that she had no money, he called off the engagement, killed her, and chopped up her body. Greenacre was executed for the crime, Gale transported for life. Broadsides covering the case would often show Greenacre and Gale dismembering the body, and Greenacre holding Hannah Brown's severed head with her legs in a sack.

Daniel Good's murder and dismemberment of Jane Jones in 1842 offered similar scope for the illustrator's art. A unidentified newspaper cutting, dated Sunday, 1 May 1842 and held in the John Johnson collection, features two gruesome drawings, one in which Good cuts off Jones's leg (with some conveniently exposed breast), and another in which the victim's head, foot and hand are being burnt (Folder 3, Murder and Execution Broadsides). In these cases, the crime became the focus of attention, and both the victims and the murderers were afforded a degree of individuality. Simply by virtue of what they are illustrated as doing – murdering and cutting up a body – it was unlikely that there could have been any ambivalence about how these texts would have been read; but, lest there should be, the villains clearly looked like villains and the victims invited our sympathy, sometimes by gazing directly at us. On occasion even the devil was lurking in the background to ensure an appropriate reading. The visual element of broadsides lacked any moral ambiguity, and the woodcuts offered a repetition and a reinforcement of the visceral nature of the text, with both verbal and visual revelling in the gruesome details of the murder. The broadside text for Good's murder of Jane Jones provides a suitable example of this, with the grisly illustrations of the dismemberment reinforced by the following verse:

Alas! The doom that 'waited her she little did foresee –
That him she loved so dearly, her butcher soon would be. –
He struck her head with violence, which fell'd her to the earth;
Then in a fit of frantic rage, loud laugh'd with manic mirth.
The villain then cut off her head, and burnt it in the fire;
And likewise cut off all her limbs, to satisfy his ire;

The trunk alone remained to tell her lamentable fate.
'Twas chopped and cut; the entrails gone; how awful to relate
('Apprehension of Daniel Good', Murder and Execution Broadsides, John Johnson Collection).

There was one way of 'reading' these woodcuts: murderers were bad people and would die for their crimes.

Gatrell suggests that we view these images as 'ideograms rather than as failed or clumsy representations'. By so doing,

> their meaning opens up at once … Just as woodcuts of demons or monsters in chap-books and prints, drawing on the cultural codes of people who believed in magic, had long had the power to electrify their perusers, so, in their starkly simplified black and white contrasts, the figure dangling in grotesque disproportion, scaffold prints drew on an 'image magic' which had fuelled the graphic imagination for centuries (177).

If we look at the woodcuts in the light of Gatrell's analysis, they not only reinforce the formulaic content of the broadside text, but work independently of it, providing a shorthand whose meaning was already known to a visually literate readership. In addition, they encapsulate the 'story' for individuals unable to read the actual text.

The somatic quality of wrongdoing was also emphasized in the newspaper coverage of domestic murder, certainly up until the 1870s. Just as, in the theatre, costume, make-up and props were signifiers of virtue or vice, so in the courtroom it was the body language and outward appearance of the accused that offered a clear signpost as to their guilt, innocence or repentance. The countenance of Daniel Good was 'rather unpleasant', with sunken eyes and long black hair (*Times*, 19 April 1842, 7). William Dove, who poisoned his wife with strychnine and was hanged for the crime in 1856, had a 'slight spasmodic twitching of the eyelids, which imparts to his appearance a sinister and unfavourable expression' (*Reynolds's*, 20 July 1856, 9).

In the majority of cases leading up to the 1870s, any outward calmness on the part of the accused was generally regarded as evidence of an inhuman indifference to the crime, whereas bodily agitation or distress was indicative of repentance, or at least an awareness of the gravity of the situation. Daniel Good was described in 1842 as 'cool and collected' (*Times*, 19 April 1842, 7). Christiana Gilmour, found innocent in 1844 of the crime of murdering her husband with arsenic, was initially reported in the *Times* as manifesting little concern about the position in which she was placed: 'the impression left generally … was, that she was callous and unconcerned about her position' (19 September 1843, 6). When Gilmour was declared innocent, there was a complete *volte-face* on the part of the *Times*: Gilmour's callous indifference was now translated into a manner 'as unaffected as a child' (20 January 1844, 3).

When Harriet Parker was brought before the magistrate for the murder of her lover's two children in 1848, we are told that 'the wretched woman when brought into the court walked boldly into the dock, and having coolly surveyed the numerous assemblage in the crowded court, seated herself in the seat provided for her' (*Times*, 10 January 1848, 6). The use of 'coolly' and 'boldly', the delivery of her statement in a 'firm' voice were all damning judgements on Parker's demeanour. When the death sentence was passed on Catherine Foster in 1847 for the murder of her husband, she responded 'with a slight quivering of the lips: but beyond that expression of feeling, which was momentary, she exhibited not the least emotion from the first to the last moment of the enquiry which was fraught with such awful consequences for her' (*Times*, 29 March 1847, 7). Reporting the details of sentencing on 31 March, the *Times* commented that

> the prisoner was removed, as on Saturday, without any apparent appreciation of the position in which she stood. Not a single tear glistened in her eye, which was unobservant and inattentive – not a single contraction of the facial muscles betokened the inward workings of suppressed feelings; but calm and composed she received the sentence as she had listened to the overwhelming evidence adduced against her, and she descended from the dock to the dark cell beneath with as light a step as if she had been convicted of an ordinary larceny (31 March 1847, 7).

To ensure an appropriate reading of Foster's situation, we have the repetition of 'not a single' to emphasize her lack of remorse, and the dramatic image of her descending to the 'dark cell' (with its connotations of a descent into hell) contrasting with her 'light', unrepentant step.

Even if all outward control were maintained, the visit of the accused's family was guaranteed to bring about an outbreak of emotion. Scenes between defendants and parents were always 'affecting' and always gave rise to extreme outbursts of feeling. This not only reinforced the supremacy of the family unit within the melodramatic mode, but also acted as a means of restructuring the domestic unit that these murders appeared to destroy; ultimately, the domestic unit remained robust and indestructible. When Ann Kennet (charged in 1831 with the murder of her lover's wife but subsequently acquitted) was visited by her father 'the prisoner burst into tears and threw herself into his arms' (*Times*, 15 December 1831, 5). The 'agonizing' scene between William Dove and his family (Dove poisoned his wife in 1856) enabled the writer to create a moving tableau, reminiscent of contemporary melodrama:

> The aged mother threw her arms around the wretched son's neck, and unable in words to give expression to her grief, she sobbed convulsively for several minutes. The sisters, kneeling at his feet, were equally overpowered ... The prisoner was deeply moved. He fell down on his knees, and with up-lifted hands, earnestly prayed for forgiveness of his sins, but he avoided making any direct confession of the murder (*Lloyd's*, 10 August 1856, 12).

The importance of the family is here made manifest, and the fearful consequences of destroying or fragmenting it. It was only with the visit of his mother and sisters that Dove starts to display any emotion, and is moved to any expression of contrition (although, tellingly, no direct confession of the murder).

Keeping entirely within the melodramatic mode, defendants' parents were invariably elderly, honest, and capable of arousing the strongest emotion in the defendants. During the trial of John Connor in 1845 (Connor was executed for the murder of Ann Tape) Connor's father, 'the afflicted parent of the murderer', offered his evidence in an 'open and candid' manner,

> the result purely of a strong and honest conviction that if his son were guilty of the horrible crime imputed to him, it was no part of a father's duty to protect him, by a misrepresentation of facts essential to the inquiry, from the just penalty of the law.

His father's appearance in the box caused Connor to 'become wholly unnerved … his whole frame seemed agitated' whereas prior to this he had 'continued firm' (*Times*, 7 April 1845, 6).

Christiana Edmunds's mother, during her 1871–72 trial, was 'weeping, wailing, heart-broken', her testimony giving rise to the following comment in *Lloyd's*: 'the appearance of the aged mother of Christiana Edmunds in the witness-box, is a scene from the real tragedy of life, the pathos, the terror of which the imagination of the dramatist could not surpass' (21 January 1872, 1). Note here the explicit connection the writer draws between the courtroom scene, and a scene from a play; this, however, is 'the real tragedy of life', yet still constrained within a theatrical mode.

Children were invariably used as a moral counterpoint to their guilty parents. Prior to Sarah Westwood's execution in 1843 for the murder of her husband she was visited by her two youngest children 'and on their parting a scene presented itself of a most affecting character, such a one as not to be wished for again to occur within the walls of this prison' (*Times*, 30 December 1843, 7). Sarah Gale, James Greenacre's accomplice in the 1837 murder of Greenacre's fiancée Hannah Brown, was led away to a lock-up room, with her child by her side 'holding tightly her hand, and, in happy ignorance of its mother's fearful situation, smiling as it tripped along' (*Times*, 6 April 1837, 5).

The point with all such poignant scenes was that the family was central to genuine repentance on the part of the murderer; consciousness of the gravity of the crime became apparent when faced with parents, siblings or children. In this way, the presence of the family acted as a counterpoint to the threat to the family posed by the act of domestic murder; it showed that the family unit remained intact and healthy, operating as the means whereby a murderer could find repentance and, ultimately, forgiveness.

Even more than the outward evidence of guilt, the outward visibility of suffering and repentance was exaggerated throughout the coverage of these cases. Ann Kennet, charged in 1831 with the murder of her lover's wife but eventually acquitted, fainted several times during the religious service on the morning of her planned execution. Sarah Gale was 'downcast and agitated', holding her head down during the trial as if mindful of the 'awful situation' in which she stood (*Times*, 6 April 1837, 5). Thomas Drory, executed in 1851 for the murder of Jael Denny, betrayed 'fearful emotion, every muscle quivering, and his face assuming a ghastly look' (*Reynolds's*, 30 March 1851, 6). Daniel Good, found guilty in 1842 of the murder and dismemberment of Jane Jones, exhibited a demeanour and gestures which read like an extract from a contemporary actor's manual:

> he clasped his hands together sometimes, and sometimes he raised them up and pressed them against his breast in great agony, the tears streaming from his eyes whilst he endeavoured to catch a glimpse of some old acquaintance or friend amongst the surrounding multitude. So strong was the expression of horror in his face and demeanour, that a respectable female … shrieked and fainted. The culprit looked with evident anxiety towards the spot from which the alarm proceeded; but, finding that a stranger was the cause of it, he seemed to retire within the awful circle of his own meditations, and to struggle with feelings beyond the power of any human being to describe (*Times*, 23 May 1842, 6).

Good here evinces all the exaggerated movements of a melodramatic performance, clasping his hands together, raising them up to the heavens and pressing them against his breast. The 'great agony' he labours under, and the 'awful circle of his own meditations', which conveniently defy description, act as a clear warning to any reader contemplating similar acts.

Even when the murderer appeared untroubled, they were betrayed by a closer examination. Greenacre appeared to bear the weight of the case with fortitude, 'but from an inspection of his eyes, it was evident that he had gone through considerable suspense and anxiety of mind: they were inflamed, and a gloom seemed to pervade his countenance.' John Connor, found guilty in 1845 of the murder of Ann Tape, revealed himself as

> a man with whose troubled spirit a desire to look bold and fearless was in fierce contest. Now and then he would betray a semblance of agitation, the existence of which he would seem to deny by a subsequent affectation of firmness, which only exhibited more clearly the true state of his mind (*Times*, 7 April 1845, 6).

Regardless of the efforts of the murderer the message was clear: the ultimate transgression that murder constituted would inevitably lead to extreme suffering on the part of the murderer, and would be written on the body for all to see. Such moral certainty was not, however, to remain consistent throughout the century, as will be shown later in this chapter.

In his analysis of broadsides (and the argument could hold equally true of much newspaper coverage) Gatrell argues that the trade

> reflected as much as it constructed a set of common ethical postures which all social classes shared – a fragile consensus (always capable of being broken, however, as particular cases dictated) that villainy, especially against others' bodies, must be punished (175).

This shared ethical position – that villainy must be punished – enabled broadsides and newspapers to sidestep the issue of class bias regarding the treatment and punishment of the perpetrators. It is also worth noting that these totemic broadside images tended to focus on the punishment, and not the crime. Again, this was partly for economic reasons; crimes differed sufficiently to warrant new woodcuts, punishment remained the same. But the stark silhouette of a body on a gibbet might also have been intended as some sort of deterrent; the lack of individuality attached to the hanged man or woman meant it could be anyone, including you, the reader, should you transgress in such a way. Very often these figures were strikingly isolated, as if their crime had effectively cut them off from society (see the illustration of Corder's execution, Figure 1.1). The mob may have been present in the form of an audience for the execution, but the convicted murderer was removed from any form of community. Again, this was a means of containing the threat of domestic murder; by disrupting the micro-community of the domestic space, the individual would find themselves expelled from any wider community, much as Sikes does after the murder of Nancy in *Oliver Twist* (examined in greater detail in Chapter 3).

Changing Times

Analysis of the *Annual Register* for 1871 reveals a number of quite remarkable domestic murder trials: the Reverend Watson was found guilty of murdering his wife; Christiana Edmunds, a middle-class woman of forty-three was charged, and later found guilty of one count of murder, one count of attempted murder, and two counts of attempting to cause grievous bodily harm, all engendered by her passionate and misguided love for a married man; Edmund Pook was charged with the brutal murder of his servant's daughter, who was beaten about the face and head with a weapon resembling a slater's hammer; and Flora Davy was jailed for eight years for the stabbing of her lover, Frederick Moon. All of this took place close to or alongside one of the most notorious trials of the nineteenth century, that of the Tichborne Claimant's attempt to establish his inheritance.[8] Commenting solely on the Watson, Edmunds and Tichborne trials, *Lloyd's* was compelled to speculate whether 'the most passionate lover of the startling and enthralling drama [could] desire more' than 'three sensation trials in a bunch!' (21 January 1872, 1).

These murders would seem to lend themselves beautifully to a melodramatic rendition of events, with very little artifice or embellishment required on the journalists' behalf. And yet these cases mark the beginning of an increasing ambivalence in the portrayal of the domestic murderer and the court proceedings. There are instances at work in these final decades of the century which demonstrate a tenacious desire to hold onto the certainties of melodramatic rhetoric, a desire which sits uncomfortably with a decline in moral certainty. At times, clearly, the

---

[8]   For a full exploration of the Tichborne Claimant trials see McWilliam, *The Tichborne Claimant*.

press response is at odds with the public view of events, and there is everywhere a shifting of representation, as the professed moral certainties of the earlier decades give way to a moral ambivalence. This change in representation is discussed in much greater detail in Chapters 4 and 5, with an examination of the shifting models of masculinity in the 1850s to 70s, and the growth of psychology and criminology in the closing decades of the century. For now, this chapter will focus on instances within the press coverage which showed a conflicted response in terms of how to portray such misdemeanours.

Roger Luckhurst has identified 'one of the most marked features of the fin de siècle ... [as] the authority given to science' and recognizes the early 1870s as the point when workers in science 'finally moved into positions of power' (Ledger and Luckhurst, 199). This, coupled with the developments in psychology and criminology in Britain and the rest of Europe, the perceived decline in the health of the nation (linked to prevailing concerns regarding degeneration and neurasthenia) and the increasing destabilization of gender roles and the sanctity of the domestic space, goes some way to explaining the changing responses to domestic murderers; much that had formerly been regarded as 'evil' was now increasingly viewed as 'ill', with the attendant potential for sympathy on the part of the public.

Alongside such developments within science and gender relations, the latter decades of the century witnessed the demise of melodrama within the theatre, and as a cultural mode more generally. This is not to say that melodrama disappeared within the Victorian theatre, but changes were evident. The middle and upper classes started patronizing West End theatres in greater numbers in the second half of the century, facilitated in large part by the Bancrofts' gentrification of the Haymarket Theatre in the 1870s and 80s, and the boom in West End theatre building, which started in the 1860s and continued till the end of the century. West End melodrama made appropriate adjustments to meet perceived changes in the audience's interests. Dialogue became more natural, plots were more skilfully constructed, and the characters were more believable. More significantly in terms of the relationship between melodrama and crime reporting was what Booth has identified as 'the blurring of the sharp distinctions essential to melodramatic morality and character types' (*Melodrama*, 181). Such a blurring of distinctions is evident in the crime reporting of this period, but there is equal evidence of a desire to hold onto the somatic certainties of the earlier decades.

With increasing frequency from the 1870s onwards the legal system and the public were more alive to the idea that outward demeanour did not equate to inner structures of thought and feeling, and that any emotion could be feigned. In the judge's summing up of the Edmund Pook case in 1871, he drew attention to the fact that Pook's calm demeanour might be an affectation 'put on for the occasion' (*Times*, 17 July 1871, 12). Not merely alive to the possibilities of artifice, an apparent lack of concern (often viewed earlier in the century as evidence of guilt) could now serve as proof of what was dubbed 'moral insanity' (see Chapter 5 for a fuller discussion of this term). Christiana Edmunds, later found insane, was described in the *Times* coverage of the case as 'a self-possessed woman, fair, and well-dressed. She sat in a corner of the prisoner's dock, and not infrequently smiled as the descriptions were given of the pains taken to trace the hand administering the poisons' (1 September 1871, 9). Such responses were later used to support her defence of insanity, whereas earlier in the century they would have pointed to her obvious guilt.

To an extent, the more respectful treatment of Edmunds could simply be attributed to her being a middle-class woman, and the description of her carried within it an element of disbelief that such a person could commit such a crime. But there were aspects of her demeanour that would certainly have been treated differently earlier in the century. Her 'singularly firm' bearing was no longer evidence of an unfeeling nature, but rather 'respectful and becoming'. When addressing the judge after the verdict had been passed, she spoke with 'much modesty and propriety' and heard the sentence with 'fortitude' (*Times*, 17 January 1872, 12). The decision to commute the death sentence on the grounds of insanity was greeted with widespread public approval.

As I have noted, in the first half of the century the press dwelt on the ways in which the appearance of the accused often concurred with their deeds. One of the growing concerns as the century progressed was that quite frequently the villains did *not* look like villains, but like 'ordinary' people. Such concerns were also linked to the anonymity possible in the rapidly growing metropolis. London was 'an immense world-city, culturally and economically important, yet socially and geographically divided, and politically incoherent'; a city represented through images of 'political disorder, urban pathology, and physical degeneration' (Walkowitz, 24, 25). Within such a city, expanding at a rate of 800,000 people every 10 years from 1850 onwards, it was perceived as increasingly easy for an individual to adopt a mask of anonymity, to escape undetected. It was no coincidence that this period witnessed the growing popularity of detective fiction, which 'speaks of mayhem – of criminality, transgression, violence, carnage, and (most usually) death – but which at the same time houses this Dionysian tumult and chaos within parameters of Apolline order, of (social and literary) convention, of rational explanation' (Chernaik, Swales and Vilain, xii).

Whilst crime might no longer be 'written on the body', there was still a desire to cling onto the certainties of the pseudo-science of physiognomy; even as late as the Wilde Trials of 1895, there were repeated attempts on the part of the press to identify Wilde's 'degeneracy' in his face, as much as in his clothes or behaviour.[9] The whole idea of identity as a singular concept was radically called into question from the mid-century onwards, finding fictional outlets in Wilkie Collins's repeated use of doubles, Dickens's twinning of his deviant characters 'with doubles or alter

---

[9]   'The bodies of Wilde ... and others were each interpreted by journalists, and in turn by the reading public. Stereotypes were evoked, clarified and endorsed, rendering the pariah recognisable in a number of forms in the city streets' (Cook, *Culture of Homosexuality*, 61). Wilde's 'physical transformation' during the trial was used to 'signify the "truth" of his position' (Cohen, *Wilde Side*, 186).

egos at the opposite end of the emotional scale to themselves' (John, *Dickens's Villains*, 9) and in the most notable examples of Stevenson's *The Strange Case of Dr. Jekyll and Mr. Hyde* (1886) and Wilde's *The Picture of Dorian Gray* (1891).

If earlier press coverage of domestic murder relied on moral identity making itself manifest through appearance, from the 1870s onwards there was a growing concern with cases where moral identity was in direct conflict with appearance. Some of the more infamous domestic murders of the nineteenth century were committed by young, attractive, middle-class women, with trials such as those of Adelaide Bartlett (1886) and Florence Maybrick (1889) generating enormous publicity. In the case of these female protagonists, the press often expressed bewilderment at the apparent incongruity between appearance and action. Historian Judith Knelman argues that the press 'by and large, made murderesses seem inhuman', depicting them as 'ugly, "masculine", old-looking' (4, 20). My research does not support such a claim; if anything, the press coverage often dwelt on the apparent charms of the women in question, and the bewilderment this gave rise to, and such an approach seems reasonably consistent across the period under examination. *Reynolds's*' coverage of the Christiana Edmunds trial in 1871–72 took pains to counteract any view of Edmunds as ugly; in contrast to the 'hideous' photographs in circulation, *Reynolds's* sought to describe her less sensationally:

> The upper part of the face, with the high narrow forehead, the hazel eyes, the fair brown hair, and clear olive-coloured complexion, is certainly not wanting in feminine charm ... Whatever might be the objections to the face, it is not wanting, so far as expression goes, in either character or intelligence; and one could even fancy that when it is bright and animated, instead of being set and rigid, it might easily enough be deemed attractive (21 January 1872, 6).

The apparent transparency of such a description may, however, have served another purpose. As discussed earlier in this chapter, *Reynolds's* was outraged when Edmunds's death sentence was commuted on the grounds of insanity; the depiction of her as attractive and intelligent may have been deliberate, to support their assertion that she was *not* insane.

By 1889, *Lloyd's* was describing Florence Maybrick (found guilty of the murder of her husband) as 'a woman of exceedingly attractive appearance – slight, graceful, and neat in figure, and in profile at least more than passably pretty' (4 August 1889, 3). As discussed at the start of this chapter, the 1890 case of Eleanor Pearcey occasioned a similar conflict in representation, with illustrations from *Lloyd's* and the *Illustrated Police News* sometimes mirroring the style of illustration in contemporary serialized fiction, and thus seeming to cast Pearcey as the heroine. The *Illustrated Police* News illustration shown at the start of this chapter (Figure 1.2) seems to accord with the growing ambivalence in the portrayal of the female domestic murderer that we witness at the fin de siècle, and which is examined in greater detail in Chapter 5. In this illustration Pearcey does not look like a villain, and so lacks the moral legibility that might have been afforded her fifty years earlier; the illustration concords with much of the press coverage of the crime, which afforded Pearcey a surprising degree of sympathy, given the brutal nature of the murders with which she was charged.

One notorious case of 1877, in which there was a marked disparity between appearance and action, caused particular concern. Louis Staunton, his brother Patrick, sister-in-law Elizabeth, and lover Alice were found guilty of the murder by starvation of Louis's wife Harriet. The case was remarkable for the outward veneer of respectability maintained by the defendants. Indeed the suggestion was even made during the trial that this desire for respectability was one of the contributing causes to Harriet Staunton's death; had Louis Staunton and his lover, Alice Rhodes, been able to live together openly, there might have been no need to murder Staunton's wife Harriet. A *Times* editorial on the case echoed earlier broadsides in its rhetoric, examining the 'revolting narrative' of the Stauntons, the 'baseness' of Louis Staunton and the 'unfortunate' Harriet. The *Times* coverage of this case was one of several instances where there was a harking back to an earlier use of melodramatic rhetoric, presenting the accused and victim within a moral dichotomy that was not borne out by the public's response to the crime. Far from wishing to see Alice Rhodes (Louis Staunton's lover) punished for the murder, public opinion actually turned so far in her favour that the *Times* lamented a feeling 'which it would scarcely be too much to describe as one of sympathy'. The paper was at pains to mark the distinction between the immorality of Rhodes's sexual conduct, and the suggestion that she was complicit in the murder; in seeking to prove her innocent of murder, they argued, the public had somehow condoned her immorality at the same time. For the *Times*, the conduct of Rhodes and Staunton 'cannot be condemned too strongly ... It is nothing less than a misfortune that sentiments of compassion should be wasted upon objects so utterly unworthy of them' (15 October 1877, 9). It was almost as if, in a desperate attempt to convince the public of the Stauntons' moral turpitude, the paper was forced to resort to an earlier, perhaps now outdated rhetoric. The paper was particularly concerned with the 'exterior of seemliness' maintained by the Stauntons, which 'makes the contrast of their actual life more shocking' (27 September 1877, 9). Such concerns for the privacy that the domestic sphere afforded are explored in greater detail in Chapter 4, with an examination of the models of masculinity played out in sensation fiction of the 1850s to 1870s. What had once served as the bastion of domestic and, by extension, national security and health, was now the place likely to conceal all manner of aberrant behaviour.

Flora Davy's murder of her lover Frederick Moon in 1871 is significant for the changing views on sex outside of marriage. Davy had cohabited with Frederick Moon and, in what seems by all accounts to be an accident, she killed him during an argument. Davy was found guilty of manslaughter, and sentenced to eight years in prison. In the first half of the century, sexual conduct such as Davy's was generally used as a cautionary device: a broadside featuring the murder of Ann Tape by Joseph Connor in 1845 contains verses addressed to women, warning them to be wary of falling into immoral conduct, with the implication that such conduct places them in greater danger of physical violence and ultimately murder

('The Trial, Sentence and Execution of Joseph Connor', Murder and Execution Broadsides Folder 2, John Johnson Collection).

There were occasional exceptions to such moral condemnation earlier in the century, largely where it was deemed necessary that a clear distinction be made between victim and perpetrator. The most noteworthy example of this was the case of Annette Myers in 1848. Myers, a 26-year-old Belgian servant girl, shot and killed her lover, Henry Ducker. There were numerous witnesses to the murder, which took place in St. James Park, London, and Myers's guilt was never in question. The case provoked quite phenomenal press coverage and a national outcry when the death sentence was passed. Given the facts of the case, it might seem obvious that Myers should be cast in the role of villainess, and Ducker the wronged innocent. It was, however, the latter who came in for the greatest censure, and with good reason. Ducker was a private in the Coldstream Guards, a handsome man who was described by his comrades as having been 'a good sort of fellow', but 'very racketty'. Ducker was known to have had relations with six or seven other women, chiefly servant girls from whom he extorted money. When Myers was unable to supply him with sufficient funds, he suggested that she prostitute herself to raise the necessary cash; at this point Myers purchased a gun and shot Ducker in the back of the head from a distance of about two yards.

The initial report of the murder in the *Times* opened with details of Ducker's dubious past, and *then* moved on to Myers. The portrayal of Myers in the courtroom revealed her as stylish but not ostentatious, 'dressed more like a mistress than a servant, having a neat blue velvet bonnet, puce Orleans dress, sable boa, etc. and wearing her hair in long ringlets, of decidedly French cultivation.' The description of her looking 'more like a mistress than a servant' may go some way to explaining the great public sympathy generated for Myers. Her demeanour conveyed

> a person of strong determination, wholly abandoned to her fate in the consciousness that she had been justified in the dreadful act which she had committed. She appeared occasionally faint and overcome, but these were rather the results of fatigue than any feeling of contrition, no manifestation of which once escaped her (*Times*, 7 February 1848, 6).

Her lack of contrition might, at this point in time, have been deemed evidence of a callous indifference, but it merely served to provoke greater public sympathy, perhaps because she was seen as being something better than the servant class, but more because Ducker was portrayed as such an outright bounder. Her defence undertook a masterful display of rhetoric, and public outcry at the passing of the death sentence was so overwhelming that the sentence was eventually commuted to life imprisonment, a decision which was met with cheers in the House of Commons.

Cases like Annette Myers's were, however, largely the exception until the 1870s, when the case of Flora Davy appeared to mark a distinct change in attitude. In his summing up for the defence (a speech of two hours' duration), Mr. Parry urged that Davy's 'immoral' relations with Moon be regarded without prejudice by the jury, as 'the sin of such a relation was not wholly on the side of the woman'.

Parry then went further, putting the case for 'degrees of immorality', whereby the Davy/Moon relationship was a 'less immoral one than such a relationship would ordinarily predicate'. The concept of 'degrees of immorality' echoes the ideas of 'partial insanity' and the 'borderlands' of insanity that were being promulgated by Henry Maudsley and other key thinkers within the burgeoning field of psychology. The degree of affection exhibited by Davy for Moon, despite her having been 'degraded' by the relationship, suggested that 'there must have been some elements of a better nature both in her and in Mr. Moon' (*Times*, 17 July 1871, 12). Such a shift in opinion may, of course, be partly explained by the timing of Davy's case; public agitation for the repeal of the Contagious Diseases Acts was at its height, with the attendant debates surrounding women's sexual morality, issues of blame and the sexual double standard.

A similar ambivalence concerning sexual (mis)conduct was equally apparent in the 1889 case of Florence Maybrick. Despite being found guilty of the murder of her husband, the real interest of the case centred on Maybrick's open avowal of her affair with a Mr. Brierley. In his summing up for the defence, Mr. Russell did not attempt in any way to deny this adultery, but rather argued

> there was a great chasm between such an offence against morality, grave as it was, and the felonious killing of her husband. Moral faults in a man were too often regarded as venial; but in the case of the woman it was the unforgivable sin. She was regarded as a leper and deprived of all sympathy and comfort. Were the jury, because she had sinned once, to misjudge her always? When woman fell, if all was known, some palliation might frequently be found, though no excuse (*Times*, 6 August 1889, 9).

Mr. Addison, summing up for the prosecution, made an explicit link between Maybrick's adultery and a capacity to commit murder, arguing that her letters to Brierley 'showed that the prisoner was capable of duplicity, deceit, and falsehood', although he conceded that adultery was not automatically evidence of murderous intent. A *Times* editorial, whilst offering no defence of that 'grave misconduct, that desertion on her part of all her duties as a wife and a mother' did argue that 'it must not be assumed that her passion for Brierley was so intense as to lead her to commit murder in order to be free to marry him' (8 August 1889, 7). The case occasioned numerous letters to the editor of the *Times;* one from 'a barrister of six years' standing' argued that Mr Justice Stephen dwelt too much on 'the heinousness of Mrs. Maybrick's admitted immorality' (10 August 1889, 4). A *Times* editorial of 12 August went some way towards supporting the public outcry for a reprieve of the death sentence but, just as with Flora Davy, sought to make a firm distinction between the crime of murder and that of adultery, and deplored

> the hysterical agitation which has made of Mrs. Maybrick a species of heroine. If she is guilty, she is guilty of a deliberate and pitiless crime, and deserves hanging as richly as any human being ever did. If she is not guilty, her treachery as a wife, treachery which reached its summit when her husband lay upon what

she by her own admission thought his deathbed, ought at least to exclude her from the category of ladies who deserve sentimental admiration and bouquets of flowers (12 August 1889, 9).

Public reaction to Florence Maybrick invited a similar response in *Lloyd's*. The paper felt that the guilty verdict was a fair one, and deplored the desire of 'the mob' to make

> a heroine of a wretched woman who has been found guilty of murder, and who has confessed to adultery of a most shameful type ... we object altogether to the morbid sensationalism which has been imported into the case, and we confess that we have no liking for such innovations as Sir Charles Russell's allusion to "the lady in the dock." There is great danger of evoking such a sympathy with criminals as may tend to weaken the popular feeling for the sanctity of life, which, in the interests of society at large, must ever remain the paramount consideration (11 August 1889, 1).

The allusion to the 'lady in the dock' in this editorial is one of the few instances in *Lloyd's* where the class of the defendant was specifically referred to.

What is evident in the Davy, Staunton and Maybrick cases is that sexual misconduct seems to have been viewed by the public with a greater degree of tolerance, perhaps even with a degree of sympathy. If nothing else, there certainly seems to be a mismatch between the 'ideal reader' envisioned by the press and the 'actual reader'. The editorials in *Lloyd's* and the *Times* manifested an increasingly futile clinging to a set of moral absolutes in the face of what seemed to be a changing public consciousness.

This is also evident in the prevailing belief in some form of ultimate justice that these publications were keen to promulgate, despite all the uncertainties generated by developments in science. Whilst the latter decades of the nineteenth century may have witnessed the demise of melodrama on the stage, the 'moral universe' that this theatrical mode created was still evident in the press coverage of domestic murder, albeit partially. Unlike the conflicting responses to sexual misdemeanours, this desire for some form of ultimate justice was, I believe, not just a belief expressed by the press, but the reflection of a genuine need within a public experiencing significant degrees of cultural and economic change. George Robb and Nancy Erber highlight the climate of uncertainty in operation at this point, where 'the need for social stability, law, order and normality never seemed greater' (1). The desire for a clearly ordered moral universe would seem entirely in keeping with such a climate.

Despite all the inconsistencies and uncertainties in the portrayal of the domestic murderer at this period, there was still a resolute clinging to some of the earlier beliefs. One of the most notable instances of this was the persistent desire to present such cases as aberrations, outside the bounds of 'normal' human behaviour. The judge's view of the Stauntons' case (1877) as 'a crime so black and hideous that I believe in all the records of crime it would be difficult to find its parallel' bore no slight similarity to the Recorder's words on James Greenacre's murder of his fiancée in 1837, 40 years earlier, a murder the Recorder felt afforded Greenacre 'an odious notoriety in the annals of cruelty and crime' (*Times*, 27 September 1877, 8; 13 April 1837, 5).[10] Annalee E. Golz detects a similar trend in the Canadian coverage of spousal homicides between the years 1870 and 1915; she comments on the striking extent 'to which they were constructed as relatively isolated acts, for which a plausible and definitive explanation had to be found' and argues that this was the means whereby spousal murder avoided being seen as an attack on the institution of marriage (165).

The desire on the part of the press to emphasize the inimitable nature of domestic murder contradicts Judith Rowbotham and Kim Stevenson's argument that the presentation of crime in the mass media can

> operate as a metaphor for a perceived disorder and decline in society generally, reflecting a feeling of social panic in the community and generating outbursts of morally-justified concern expressed in terms of a desire for more order and security to curb bad behavior (36).

Certainly, there were cases where a single case of domestic murder was taken as evidence of a larger social malaise, but there were also clear attempts by the media to portray certain murders as aberrations that could not and would not be repeated.

Beth Kalikoff has argued that, as the century progressed, crime was increasingly no longer confined to an underworld, but committed by people 'just like us' and that, by the late nineteenth century, 'it is no longer incongruous for anyone to kill' (158). Such a statement may be supported by novels and plays in the latter half of the nineteenth century (and will be examined in later chapters, particularly Chapter 4 focusing on the fiction of the 1850s to 1870s), but newspaper coverage seems to belie this argument. As late as 1890, Eleanor Pearcey's defence attorney argued that

> the crime must have been committed, judging from the wounds, with merciless savagery. The prisoner was a young woman of affectionate and kindly disposition, and he asked if it would not be extremely difficult for them to come to a conclusion that she could have been the person who committed so atrocious a crime (*Times*, 3 December 1890, 13).

There is a clear disparity here between press coverage and fictional accounts of domestic murder. Sensation fiction may have revelled in unveiling the secrets of the middle-class home and suggesting that 'one's kindly comfortable neighbours, male and female, are in fact the Other Victorians; and worse, that we have met the Other Victorians and they are us' (Showalter, 'Desperate Remedies', 2); but even by the closing decades of the century the press coverage of such crimes continued to present domestic murder as an aberration.

---

[10]   This presentation of particular crimes as existing outside the boundaries of 'normal' human behaviour is, of course, a general feature of court discourse, and persists to this day.

Chapter 2
'The Theatre of His Deep Dyed Guilt':
Domestic Murder and the Victorian Stage

> It is almost impossible to separate the melodrama of crime from domestic
> melodrama generally; one can only say that the sensational element in crime
> suited it perfectly to melodrama, that dramatists kept up with the latest crimes
> in their newspapers, and that the public's appetite for crime stories, whetted by
> what they read, was further satisfied by the stage ... Murder then, as now, was
> the most popular stage crime (Booth, *Melodrama*, 139).

Despite Michael Booth's assertion that 'murder ... was the most popular stage
crime', the murders of spouses, sweethearts and love rivals are notable by their
relative absence from the Victorian stage. In a society where trial coverage of such
cases dominated the newspapers and populist periodicals, and where the details
of such crimes would seem to lend themselves readily to a theatrical rendition, it
is surprising how rarely domestic murder featured in Victorian drama. Although
Booth establishes firm links between newspaper coverage of murders and the
portrayal of crime on the stage, he only mentions one play based on a domestic
murder case, *Maria Marten* (1840). Despite the proliferation of cases in the press,
some of them with highly melodramatic content, the only theatrical versions
of actual crimes I have uncovered are two plays based on the 1827 murder of
Maria Marten – *The Red Barn* (1828) and *Maria Marten* (1840) – and a play very
loosely based on the Florence Maybrick case of 1889.[1] When it comes to purely
fictitious stage murder the case is very similar. My research unearthed five plays
which feature domestic murder, or attempted murder: *The Rose of Corbeil* (1838),
Michael Erle the Maniac Lover (1839), *Grace Clairville* (1843), *The Green
Bushes* (1845) and *The Colleen Bawn* (1860). Such research supports Shellard and
Nicholson's assertion that 'licences for plays dealing with murders were refused
outright' (42).

This chapter will attempt to explain why domestic murder featured so rarely
on the Victorian stage. Firstly, I will revisit the centrality of the domestic ideal to
Victorian thinking, and the problems of displaying a disrupted private sphere in
public; secondly, I will argue that, by the exercise of containment and censorship,
the Victorian theatre was enlisted in the portrayal of an idealized domestic sphere.
Although the theatre offered the potential for disruption and dissent with regard to

---

[1]   Sydney Grundy, *A Fool's Paradise*. First performed at the Garrick on 2 January 1892,
the play features the character Beatrice Selwyn who, out of love for Lord Normantower,
attempts to poison her husband Philip Selwyn; discovered by Sir Peter Lund, Beatrice takes
the poison herself and dies.

political and social inequality, when it came to the portrayal of the domestic space no such discontent was permitted; focusing on the five plays that feature purely fictional murders, I will demonstrate that the domestic myth was so powerful that these plays were effectively sanitized and stripped of any theatrical power or potential for disruption. I will then move from an examination of the heavily regulated theatres to the 'theatre of the streets', less easy to control, as evidenced by the public disorder at the 1828 trial of William Corder for the murder of his lover, Maria Marten. A detailed examination of this trial reveals a public unhappy with the constraints imposed on them within the ideology of the domestic sphere.

As the work of numerous cultural historians has shown, the preservation of the domestic sphere was central to Victorian ideas of nationhood, and anything which might threaten the domestic space was a threat to the nation as a whole:

> the regulation of moral behaviour during the nineteenth century was part of a wider formation of class identity, nation and empire. Morality was a central component within the ideology of empire. International leadership and the domination of foreign competition were believed to depend directly on the existence of a stable domestic base, and social stability, it was claimed, was a consequence of moral purity (Nead, 91).

Placing the stable domestic space at the heart of national identity explains why, in the rare examples of stage murder, the villain was often a foreigner. In her study of murderesses on the stage and screen Jennifer Jones discovered occasional representations of the violent husband 'but he was inevitably of the lower class, usually a criminal, probably foreign' (34). Certainly, in my study of original works featuring domestic murder or murderous intent, the murderer is often of foreign extract, thus placing them firmly outside the range of 'acceptable' behaviour and, at times, providing the justification for their crimes. In *The Colleen Bawn*, *The Green Bushes* and *The Rose of Corbeil* the murderer (or attempted murderer) is foreign. In *Michael Erle*, Michael is insane and therefore stands outside the expected range of human behaviour.

Jones's comment that the violent husband is 'inevitably of the lower class' also supports the idea that the idealized domestic sphere was central to the development of the middle classes. This nascent class used the concept of the domestic sphere to formulate their own identity in opposition to both the working and the upper classes. An essential component of the domestic was its separation from the public sphere; the creation of a private space which Ruskin famously defined as

> the place of Peace; the shelter, not only from all injury, but from all terror, doubt, and division. In so far as it is not this, it is not home; so far as the anxieties of the outer life penetrate into it, and the inconsistently-minded, unknown, unloved, or hostile society of the outer world is allowed by either husband or wife to cross the threshold, it ceases to be home (Ruskin, 88).

This obviously presents the first problem in showing the domestic sphere at all on the stage: it was a private space which was being displayed in the public arena.

The problem was overcome by the censoring of plays, which enlisted the stage in the creation of an idealized domestic space; a place where, ultimately and always virtue would reign triumphant and the discordant element would be reformed or expelled. By means of such control, domestic melodrama was 'allowed' to flourish, and became the most popular stage genre of the first half of the nineteenth century. However, for such a vision to work, virtue must indeed reign triumphant, and such an ideology was difficult to promote when the domestic sphere has been disrupted by the ultimate and irrecoverable disruption of murder. The implications of showing domestic murder on the stage were to admit that the heart of the nation was, if not under threat, at least not so idyllic as first suggested. And the public were well aware that the domestic ideal promoted on the stage and, to an extent, through novels was a construct; a cursory glance at the crime pages of any newspaper would reveal the reality.

Enlisting the theatre in the promulgation of the domestic myth was part of what Peter Bailey has identified as 'a new social conformity – a play discipline to complement the work discipline that was the principal means of social control in an industrial capitalist society' (5). The imposition of such a 'play discipline' was not uncontentious, and the theatre, particularly within more working-class areas, was not an uncontested public space; but any disruption or dissent rested on issues of political or social inequality, not in the portrayal of the domestic.

The first means by which the theatre was controlled was under the 1737 Licensing Act, which afforded a patent to Drury Lane, Covent Garden and the Haymarket (summer only) theatres. The Act meant that the performance of legitimate drama – regular comedy and tragedy – was confined in London to these three theatres; other London theatres, now all deemed 'minor' or 'illegitimate' under the 1737 Act, had to rely on 'dumb show, music and spectacle', as they were forbidden to show plays which were unaccompanied by music. In response to this attempt to control the content of theatrical performances, the minor theatres turned to melodrama, a dramatic form whose constant musical interjections satisfied the edicts of the 1737 Act. Although this form of theatre may have been 'created by the law' (Booth, *Melodrama*, 53), it was also a means of subverting the more established theatres, a means whereby the minor theatres were able to occupy 'an institutional position that disrupted and indeed helped to destroy the gentlemanly, decorous world of patent dramatic culture' (Moody, 202).

Going even further in their attempts to subvert the control imposed on them, the minors were also often home to political agitation. The Rotunda in Blackfriars Road was used as a venue for the delivery of political lectures, and was denied a licence under the Theatres Act of 1843, with the Lord Chamberlain justifying his refusal with reference to the 'improper purposes to which the Rotunda has been so long applied' (Earl, 80). The Coburg, also known colloquially as the Blood Tub for its diet of sensational melodramas, staged Henry Fielding's political satire *Tom Thumb* in 1832, with a King and Queen clearly modelled on William IV and his consort. Davis and Emaljanow argue that East End theatres such as the Britannia (located in Hoxton) were often 'ideologically in line with the likely attitudes and aspirations of … [their] local community and many East End melodramas contain passages critical of social injustices' (92).

David Worrall, in his work *Theatric Revolution*, argues that the struggle of the minor theatres against the Royal Patent theatres was a surrogate for parliamentary reform; for Worrall it is no coincidence that the unease manifested by this perceived inequality culminated in the Select Committee on Dramatic Literature in 1832 – the same year that the Reform Bill extended the franchise:

> the political dimension of reform of the Royal Patent theatres was widely understood as a mature cultural metaphor for the more general political Parliamentary reform of the electoral franchise. The reformist discourse of the one was simply mapped onto the reformist discourse of the other. The equation between a monopolistic, unreformed theatre and an unreformed, narrow franchise for Parliament was a ubiquitous political observation and one which increases quite visibly the nearer the 1832 Reform Bill is approached (57–8).

In addition to the perceived injustice of the Royal Patents, the structure of the theatres themselves also reflected the hierarchical nature of society. With the box, pit and lower and upper galleries all enjoying different entrances, and different prices, the economic hierarchy was reinforced, but not without vocal discontent on the part of the poorer element of the audience:

> relegated to the dizzying heights of the sixpenny or one-shilling 'heavens' by their inability or disinclination to pay the higher prices for box, pit or first gallery, these audiences frequently retaliated by making their presence impossible to ignore, by actors and the rest of the audience alike (Donohue, 'Theatres', 295).

The Old Price (or OP) Riots of September 1809 demonstrate the extent to which audiences were unhappy with such stratification within the body of the theatre, and fully prepared to vocalize their discontent. The riots were occasioned by the reopening of the Covent Garden Theatre Royal on 18 September 1809, after a fire the previous year. The refurbishment triggered an increase in ticket prices: boxes increased from 6s to 7s, the pit from 3s 6d to 4s. More significantly for the audience of the theatre, though, were the changes to the internal structure: the lowest-paying spectators were now so distanced from the stage they could barely see or hear the performance, and private boxes for season ticket holders now constituted half the seating in the theatre. Such restructuring was construed by the audience as

> a realignment of social relationships … In addition to imposing segregation, the enlarged theatre made it virtually impossible for those in the dress boxes and gallery to see the same performance as those in the private boxes, as if the new theatre space were institutionalising the social demarcations already associated with the various theatrical genres (Hadley, 40).

The audience were extremely vocal in their protest, holding up banners expressing opposition to this introduction of physical partitions, and drowning out the actors with 'voices, rattles, and cat-calls' (Worrall, 14; Hadley, 38–9). This went on for 67 nights, until agreement was reached on 14 December, 1809. The OP Riots, and the staging of plays deemed contentious, show us that the theatre could be used as the site of vocalized discontent over perceived social or political inequality; yet, within such a space, the portrayal of the domestic sphere remained decidedly uncontentious.

Aside from the restricting of 'legitimate' drama to the patent theatres, other measures were at work to control the content of plays. Until 1843 all plays performed at the Royal Patent theatres and any other theatre within a 20-mile radius of Westminster had to be submitted to the Lord Chancellor for approval. Local magistrates had influence over other theatres, so effectively all were censored. With the passing of the 1843 Theatre Regulation Act, which abolished the patent monopoly, the Lord Chamberlain was afforded the power to scrutinize the texts of plays performed anywhere in London.

The most fundamental principle underlying the Lord Chamberlain's policy on censorship was a belief in the intrinsic power of the play itself, as opposed to a novel or poem. Stottlar, in his article examining the work of William Bodham Donne, Examiner of Plays from 1857 to 1874, explains it thus:

> the foundation of Donne's theory of censorship (it was something of a commonplace in his day) was that a play was potentially a more dangerous work of art than a novel – or than a painting or a musical composition. When a committee member asked him why plays should be subjected to censorship when books were not, Donne answered that a story enacted on the stage by real people appealed "much more strongly" to the senses than did the same story in the pages of a novel (256–7).[2]

The novelist Charles Reade, speaking before the same Select Committee in 1866, argued similarly that

> a play reproduces a story in flesh and blood; it realises the thing in a different way to a book entirely. I do not find it very easy to make that clear; but things might be described in a book which could not be presented in a play, and which could not be even indicated without doing perhaps very considerable harm (Stottlar, 257).

There were clearly class issues at work here. Certainly until the boom in West End theatre building which started in the 1860s, and the Bancrofts' gentrification of theatres in the 1870s and 80s, the theatre was regarded largely as the domain of the working classes, and the calls for censorship were couched in paternalistic

---

[2]   Donne's tenure as Examiner of Plays commenced towards the end of the period under examination in this chapter, but the principles underlying his censorship were already in operation before he took on the role.

terms that suggested an inability on the part of the potential audience to control its own impulses, an almost childlike overwhelming of the senses that might occur if any strong emotion was acted out in front of them.

Alongside these concerns regarding the fundamental power and subversive potential of the theatre were Donne's other principles of censorship; firstly, a play should not be morally ambiguous:

> where there is an obvious intention or a very strong suspicion of an intention to make wrong appear right, or right appear wrong, those are the cases in which I interfere; or in those in which there is any open scandal, or any inducement to do wrong is offered (Stottlar, 259).

Secondly, a play should not concern itself with contemporary events. In 1862 Viscount Sydney, the Lord Chamberlain, was sent *The Gypsy of Edgware*, a play based on the notorious murder of William Weare by John Thurtell in 1823. Sydney refused a licence for the play, arguing that 'all such representations of recent murder on the stage appear to me to be very undesirable. It only gives the Public a morbid feeling and encourages mischievous ideas in their minds' (Shellard and Nicholson, 42). It is Sydney's objection to 'recent murder' that is significant here; the proximity to 'real life' is what causes alarm, much as the reviewer of *Oliver Twist*, commenting on the murder of Nancy, argued that 'bloodshed in midday comes home to our peaceful threshold, it shocks the order of things; it occurs amid life' (*Quarterly Review*, June 1839, 91). Sydney's concern that such a performance would encourage 'mischievous ideas' in the audience again emphasizes the class bias underlying censorship.

Julia Swindells in her examination of the 1832 Select Committee on Dramatic Literature, recounts the testimony of George Colman, Examiner of Plays. Colman objected to plays representing 'adultery, murder, and parricide'; when questioned how he would deal with *Macbeth* in the light of such objections, he argued that *Macbeth* 'represents history, not contemporary matters' (5). Placed within these tenets of the need for moral clarity and a resistance to showing contemporary events, merely showing a domestic murder could, it was argued, be misinterpreted and might lead to copy-cat behaviour. More than that, giving theatrical realization to the disruption of the domestic space offered the potential for such disruption to leak out to the wider public sphere.

That such censorship was effective is evidenced by the paucity of plays featuring domestic murder, and the sanitizing of those that did exist. The playwrights' strategies to evade the censor's pen effectively led to self-censorship, with the resultant dramas so diluted that the potential theatrical impact of the crime was lost, alongside any potential to disrupt. Acknowledging the relationship between the domestic sphere and national identity, various devices were at work in these plays to place the crime outside the realm of everyday British life, either through portraying the murderer as foreign or 'other' (as in *Grace Clairville* and *The Green Bushes*), setting the action in the past, or having the attempted murder fail (as in *The Colleen Bawn*). Where the murderer does succeed, his or her subsequent suffering and ultimate demise place these crimes within a clear moral framework that re-establishes social order. Without exception, all the murderers die at the end of the play, either by their own hand, through a broken heart, or by execution; leading up to their deaths, they all suffer extremes of emotional anguish, and those committing the more cold-blooded murders are portrayed as being in league with the devil, or as bound for hell. Felix, in *The Rose of Corbeil*, declares that 'hell gasps to receive me' (*Rose*, Act I, scene 2, p. 18); Michael Erle addresses Philip D'Arville as a 'dark monster' in *Michael Erle* (Act II, scene 4, p. 27); and Grace refers to Hubert in *Grace Clairville* as a 'demon of hypocrisy' (Act II, scene 4, p. 12).

Of the five plays researched, three were performed at East End or traditionally working-class theatres; *Michael Erle the Maniac Lover* and *Grace Clairville* premiered at the Surrey on 26 December 1839 and 5 March 1843, respectively; *The Rose of Corbeil* at the City of London, November 1838. The Royal Surrey was located just south of the Thames, in Southwark. The area enjoyed a diverse social mix, and good transport links from the West End of London facilitated an audience from outside the immediate environs of the theatre (Davis and Emaljanow, 5, 25). Prior to the 1843 Theatre Regulation Act the Surrey kept 'a relatively popular repertoire', but specialized in 'libertarian modern drama', such as *Black Ey'd Susan* and *The Factory Lad* (Davis and Emaljanow, 23; Bratton, 64). Davis and Emaljanow cite evidence that the audience applauded the radical sentiments of *Venice Preserv'd* (1837), while the anti-Chartist sentiments of *Cinderella or Harlequin and the Little Glass Slipper* (1846) were not well received (25). The theatre therefore enjoyed a reputation for showcasing drama which offered the potential for political dissidence, and yet the sanctity of the domestic sphere was such that neither *Michael Erle* nor *Grace Clairville* achieved any significant impact. These two plays, alongside *The Rose of Corbeil*, received virtually no press attention. Eight weekly or daily newspapers[3] which regularly carried theatre reviews failed to review *The Rose of Corbeil* or *Grace Clairville*, and *Michael Erle* received only one review, in the *Atlas*. This review says more about how the paper wished to portray the audience at the Surrey than about the play itself, and was so dismissive of the work that little attempt was made even to get the title right:

> Here on boxing night the audience were the chief actors. There were several "settings to" in earnest, and more mock brawls in the gallery, accompanied by a running fire of shrill whistling from some hundreds of voices, during the performance, on the stage, of a new drama – of deceit, seduction, madness, and revenge – called *Michael Earle* [sic], *or the Married* [sic] *Lover* (*Atlas*, 28 December 1839, 829).

Regrettably, the critic did not say whether the audience response to the play was in any way out of the ordinary; Davis and Emaljanow assert that the Surrey audiences

---

[3] The *Era*, the *Examiner*, the *Weekly Dispatch*, the *Morning Chronicle*, the *Magnet*, the *Times*, the *Atlas*, the *Illustrated London News*.

were generally well behaved, so the 'shrill whistling' was presumably a comment on the poor quality of the play.

The lack of reviews for productions at East End theatres was another means of controlling the stage and privileging the West End theatres. It was also a comment on the quality of these works; productions at the Surrey were reviewed in the press, but not *Michael Erle* or *Grace Clairville*.

The only two plays featuring domestic murder that were shown at a West End theatre – *The Green Bushes* and *The Colleen Bawn*, both premiering at the Adelphi on 27 January 1845 and 10 September 1860, respectively – received extensive press coverage, most of it very positive. Undoubtedly the reputation of the playwrights, J. B. Buckstone and Dion Boucicault respectively, partly explains the press response; but it was the location of the Adelphi on the Strand, geographically and ideologically closer to the likes of Drury Lane and Covent Garden that accounted for the press interest.

The Adelphi enjoyed a reputation for 'sensational' drama, with impressive 'Adelphi effects' that provided 'a "nucleus" of enjoyment to those who seek for excitement, startling incidents and pictures of life, from the highest to the lowest degree, in dramatic representations' (*Examiner*, 15 September 1860, 582–3; *Era*, 2 February 1845, 6). This was exactly what *The Green Bushes* and *The Colleen Bawn* provided, albeit in very different ways. Both plays were regarded as being particularly appropriate for the Adelphi: *The Green Bushes* was seen as bearing 'the "veritable" Adelphi stamp' and *The Colleen Bawn* was pronounced 'a real "Adelphi hit"' (*Era*, 2 February 1845, 6; 30 September 1860, 19).

First performed at the Adelphi in 1845, with Madame Celeste in the starring role of Miami, *The Green Bushes* was a huge success, and was performed in 1846, 1849, 1872, 1873, 1874 and 1886, with a final run in 1890. The success of the play even spawned an anonymous novel *The Green Bushes; or, A Hundred Years Ago, A Romance* (1847). The play opens with Connor O'Kennedy fleeing Ireland to escape capture for his part in nationalist activities. On arrival in America, Connor takes Miami, a Native American Indian, as his lover; the arrival of Connor's wife and child inflames Miami's jealousy and she kills Connor. After a lengthy period of suffering, she makes financial reparation to Connor's wife and child, and dies in the final moments of the play.

Reviews for the initial run of the play were positive, but it was the audience and critics' response to the character of Miami that is particularly interesting.[4] The *Times* referred to 'the romantic and extraordinary character of Miami', and the *Era* declared the 'fascinating huntress' as one 'whose winning grace and faultless form would seduce a stoic from his plighted troth, either in the backwoods or a boudoir' (*Times*, 28 January 1845, 5; *Era*, 2 February 1845, 6). Madame Celeste's interpretation of Miami's 'wild love and jealousy ... and the quick and sudden

---

[4]   *Weekly Dispatch*, 2 February 1845, 56; *Morning Chronicle*, 29 January 1845, 5; *Illustrated London News, Atlas*, 1 February 1845, 73.

promptings of her passion' were met with 'storms of approbation' according to the critic of the *Magnet* (3 February 1845, 6).

What is notable about all the reviews of Madame Celeste's performance was the sympathy she engendered in the audience: sympathy for the character of a non-English woman who kills her lover when she sees him in the arms of his wife. The pity engendered by the portrayal of such a character cannot rest solely with Madame Celeste's acting ability, impressive though it may have been. The most significant element of Miami's character, and the one which permitted the audience to feel pity for her, but not empathy, was her 'otherness'. Not only was she not British, she was not even wholly European, having a Native American Indian mother, and a French aristocratic father; as such, she was a novelty, an individual entirely removed from the everyday experience of the theatre audience and, thus, one whose actions could be explained away in the light of her cultural identity. Her actions were not offered as a blueprint for British behaviour, and could in no way be seen as posing a potential threat to the domestic stability of the nation. The *Era's* analysis of Madame Celeste's performance mentioned her attire first, and then her acting, and the *Illustrated London News* (1 February 1845, 73–4) carried two illustrations from the play, one of them showing Madame Celeste in full Indian costume with a rifle slung over her back and a feather in her hair. There is little doubt that a huge part of the play's appeal lay in this whimsical portrayal of a Native American Indian. To highlight this 'otherness' even further Miami frequently speaks of herself in the third person, and exhibits a childlike simplicity as when, seeing Connor and Geraldine embrace, she mimics their actions.

Miami's killing of Connor seems almost to happen in spite of herself and is explained by her exotic parentage. Although confessing that 'there is mischief in my blood, that I fear – an Indian never forgives an injury' – again emphasizing her cultural difference – she does resolve to leave Connor (Act II, scene 1). However, chancing upon Connor and Geraldine kissing, the blood of her 'royal Indian mother's race' mounts in her veins, and 'in her paroxysm she fires', killing Connor (Act II, scene 3).

A review in the *Atlas* summarizes the appeal of *The Green Bushes*, and exhibits clearly the formulaic quality of the disrupted domestic sphere on the stage:

> An Adelphi audience requires that crime should be an ingredient of the serious pieces submitted to its judgement, and Mr. Buckstone … has introduced a sufficiency to satisfy the morbid craving of the multitude, without shocking the good taste of the more refined play-goer. A double infidelity is revenged by the murder of the offender, and a broken heart is, in conformity with strict poetical justice, the ultimate reward of the homicide (1 February 1845, 73).

The play offered just enough to interest the audience, but nothing to shock, and any moral wrongdoing was ultimately punished.

The Colleen Bawn (1860) had already been a hit in America before it premiered in London, and proved equally successful at the Adelphi. All the reviews were glowing, and spoke of the huge audiences and enthusiastic response to the play.

The play was based on a hugely popular Gerald Griffin novel *The Collegians* (1829), set in the 1770s, but based on events in 1819 when the body of 15-year-old Ellen Hanley was washed up near Kilrush, County Clare. John Scanlon, the son of one of the leading local families, had married Ellen, and killed her, afraid of his family's opposition. Scanlon's boatman, Stephen Sullivan, was also indicted. Both were found guilty and hanged in 1820. Boucicault lifted all the characters straight from Griffin's novel, with the exception of Myles-na-Coppalleen, a new character played by Boucicault himself when the play premiered in London.

The action of the play centres on Hardress Cregan's secret marriage to Eily O'Connor (the Colleen Bawn). Persuaded by his mother to pursue Anne Chute, a wealthy heiress, Hardress regrets his union with Eily, a poor working-class girl. Hardress's mother learns of the marriage and tricks Hardress's best friend, Danny Mann, into murdering Eily. Danny throws Eily off the edge of a cliff and believes her dead, but she is secretly rescued by Myles-na-Coppalleen. Danny subsequently dies from a gunshot wound, Hardress's mother's machinations are revealed, and Eily and Hardress are happily reunited at the end of the play.

In the original novel, Eily dies; the fact that she does not die in *The Colleen Bawn* is, of course, highly significant. Boucicault not only sidesteps the unpleasant issue of a dead young woman, he also frees Hardress from censure by having his mother instigate the attempted murder. Indeed, Hardress is ultimately forgiven for his disloyalty to Eily, and the final scene of the play sees him reconciled to her.

More than any changes to the original novel, though, was the sensation caused by the attempted drowning of Eily and her rescue by Myles at the end of Act II. Almost every review mentioned this set piece,[5] with the *Atlas* helpfully providing a detailed account:

> The process of drowning Eilie [*sic*] is the most powerfully graphic picture of a stage murder we ever saw. The mechanist, however, must here share the honour with the author and the actors. The girl having been decoyed by her destroyer to a small island in the midst of a gloomy lake, is, after the preliminary dialogue on such occasions, pushed backwards into the water, and is seen gradually sinking through the waves. Rising to the surface, half immersed in the stream, she clings to the ruffian's knees – "spare me – let me live Danny" – a fierce crash, another push, a smothered scream, she sinks to rise no more, and the patience of the audience is urged to the edge of endurance (15 September 1860, 749).

The reviewer's comment that 'the mechanist ... must here share the honour with the author and the actors' is significant. The Adelphi was known for staging sensational

---

[5]   '[T]he most novel and ingenious achievement in the way of scenic illusion that has been seen for a considerable time', 'nightly arouses the enthusiasm of the spectators, and brings the set-drop down amidst bursts of vigorous applause' (*Era*, 16 September 1860, 10; 30 September 1860, 19); 'strikingly effective' (*Morning Chronicle*, 11 September 1860, 6); 'singularly effective' (*Weekly Dispatch*, 16 September 1860, 10); 'the illusion provokes rounds of applause' (*Examiner*, 15 September 1860, 582–3).

dramas, with elaborate stage effects. Boucicault overcame the troublesome issue of depicting an attempted murder on stage by creating a theatrical sensation; the audience were absorbed in wonder at how the effect was achieved, rather than questioning the morality of such an act – and, of course, the girl did not die. Added to this was the fact the play was based in Ireland. Just as in *The Green Bushes*, the criminal activities of these characters could in no way be seen as threatening the British domestic sphere.

Of the seven plays featuring domestic murder examined for this book, the remaining two – *The Red Barn* (1828) and *Maria Marten* (1840) – were based on the murder of Maria Marten by her lover William Corder in 1827, and his trial the following year. The case was remarkable not only for the vehement public response, or for the fact that it formed the basis of some of the most popular and long-running melodramas of the nineteenth century, but also because the case itself was viewed as a 'living' melodrama by the public and the press. The public response to the murder and the trial revealed a discontent with the idealized version of the domestic space portrayed on the stage, and a desire for agency which was denied them in everyday life.

On 18 May 1827, Maria Marten, a 26-year-old mole catcher's daughter from the village of Polstead in Suffolk, went to meet her lover, William Corder. Corder, 24 and also from Polstead, was the son of a farmer. Following the recent death of their baby, Maria was now pressing for marriage, while Corder was keen to extricate himself from the relationship. Corder instructed Maria to meet him in the Red Barn, dressed in male attire to ensure secrecy; once in the Red Barn, Maria was to change into her own clothes and they would take a gig to Ipswich and be married.[6]

When Maria arrived at the barn the sequence of events is unclear: unable to determine the exact cause of Maria's death, the prosecuting counsel at Corder's trial indicted him with shooting her in the face, stabbing her several times with a sword, choking her with a handkerchief and finally burying her body in a shallow grave (to avoid any legal loop-holes Corder was charged with all these means of murder, both singly and in every possible combination). Corder moved to London, maintaining the fiction with Maria's family that she was still alive. In the meantime, he advertised for a wife, and married some time towards the end of 1827, himself and his wife (Mary Moore) then establishing a school for young ladies in Brentford. Almost concurrent with this marriage, Maria's stepmother Ann was visited by the first of several dreams that Maria was buried in the Red Barn; on investigation, the body was found. Mr. Lea, an officer of Lambeth Street Station, was dispatched to arrest Corder; on gaining entry to Corder's house, 'he found the object of his search sitting at breakfast with four ladies. He was in his

---

[6]   The Red Barn was rented by the Corder family from Mrs. Cooke of Polstead Hall. It was named thus long before the murder, perhaps because part of the roof was covered in red tiles.

dressing-gown, and he had his watch before him, with which he was minuting the boiling of some eggs' (Pelham, 149).

The first mention of the case in the *Times* was on 23 April 1828, with the discovery of the body. The following day Corder was charged with the crime, and two days later was conveyed to Colchester, where the jury at the inquest returned a verdict of wilful murder against him. On 27 April he was taken to the County Gaol in Bury St. Edmunds, Suffolk. The trial took place over two days, 7 and 8 August, and the jury took just 35 minutes to reach a Guilty verdict. Corder finally confessed to the crime on 10 August, although alleging that he and Maria had struggled during a quarrel and the resultant gunshot was an accident; he maintained to the end that he had not stabbed her. He was hanged on 11 August 1828, with the watching crowd estimated at 7,000. After the execution Corder's body was taken to the Shire Hall in Bury St. Edmunds, where it was cut open and viewed by approximately 6,000 people, before being taken for dissection to West Suffolk Hospital.

The excitement roused by the case was momentous, and was generated well in advance of the trial. Shortly after his arrest in April, Corder was transported to Colchester Gaol. The crowds awaiting him on his arrival in Colchester were so great that it was deemed necessary to secure Corder in a private room at a local inn while Mr. Lea, the arresting officer, requested permission from Mr. Smith, the governor of Colchester Gaol, for Corder to be held there. Permission was refused, presumably arising from concerns regarding public safety.

In the weeks leading up to the trial visitors to the Red Barn were estimated at 200,000. Figures such as this, the 7,000 who attended the hanging, and the 6,000 who viewed Corder's corpse, are all the more remarkable when we consider that Polstead and Bury St. Edmunds would not have been easily accessible by the majority of people who attended these events; one account of the trail suggested that many individuals 'travelled fifty miles and upwards; and one gentlemen came all the way from Carlisle' (Curtis, 56). The public were responding to a very public exhibition of a disrupted private sphere, a view of the domestic situation that conflicted so strongly with that propagated on the stage and, simply by virtue of their presence, were perhaps indicating a discontent with this idealized vision of the domestic sphere. Historian Matt Cook has argued that 'trials helped to define the boundaries of normality and to rearticulate ideologies of gender, class, and nation' ('Law', 74). The crowd's response might be an articulation of the discontent surrounding ideologies that the nascent middle classes were imposing on them.

So many sought souvenirs of their visit to the Red Barn that a supervisor was appointed to prevent further desecration of the site (Curtis, 56). The conduct of individuals once inside the barn was significant in terms of the transformation of the crime into a work of melodrama; Curtis, in his account of the case, noted:

> it is creditable to the feelings of human nature that whenever the barn has been
> visited, a silence has reigned among the spectators, as though they had been
> viewing the receptacles of the dead in a funeral vault, but it was sometimes, yea

not infrequently, broken by a sigh or a mournful exclamation of "Poor Maria," "poor thing," "ill-fated girl," &c. At other times the thoughts of the murderer gave rise to expressions such as these, "Cold-blooded villain," "Cruel wretch," and sometimes epithets opprobrious, in reference to this deliberate butcher of a fellow-creature, were uttered (56).

What is significant here is not merely that Corder was already guilty of the crime in the eyes of the public, but the exclamations of 'poor thing' and 'cold-blooded villain' suggest that the public were instrumental in establishing a clear moral dichotomy between murderer and victim. Right from the start, too, the general public drew on the lexicon of melodrama well in advance of the press coverage and theatrical adaptations of the crime, if we are to believe Curtis's account of events.

The public appetite for the crime reached its zenith with the commencement of the trial. Crowds of several thousand started gathering at 5.00 am on the first day, and conduct outside the courtroom resulted in 'nearly one hour and a half of tumult and confusion'.[7] After nearly an hour of attempting to gain entry, the members of the jury were 'brought over the heads of the crowd into the passage leading into the Hall; some with their coats torn, their shoes off, and nearly fainting'.[8] Individuals desperate to witness the proceedings balanced on the window ledges resulting in several windows being broken from the pressure of the crowd. Ladders were also raised to hoist individuals up onto the roof of the courthouse, where a circular aperture enabled them to lie flat on the joists and to 'peep over the edge of the cornice' (Curtis, 179). Arrangements were better managed on the second day, presumably to prevent a repeat of the ignominious sight of the Lord Chief Baron being 'carried off his legs in endeavouring to pass from his carriage to the door of the Shirehall' (Foster, 47).

What this shows is that the public were responding to the dramatic potential of the case before the trial actually commenced, and well in advance of any theatrical adaptations. They were also responding to this very public exhibition of a disrupted private sphere, a view of the domestic situation that conflicted so strongly with that propagated on the stage. The vehemence of their response is worth some consideration. Julia Swindells examines how theatricality was used to bring about a more democratic social order in the decades leading up to the 1833 Emancipation Act, which abolished slavery throughout the British colonies. Swindells uses the term 'theatrical' as 'embracing a consciousness of performance involving actor, audience, and setting in a staged event, whether rehearsed or not' (xi). The behaviour of the crowd on the first day of Corder's trial would certainly seem to suggest a 'consciousness of performance' and, if they regarded themselves as participants in a theatrical event, their behaviour becomes more explicable.

---

[7]   *An Accurate Account of the Trial of William Corder for the Murder of Maria Marten ... etc.* (London: George Foster), 9. Hereafter referred to in the text as Foster.

[8]   *The Trial of William Corder for the Wilful Murder of Maria Marten ... etc.* (London: Dean and Munday), 11–12. Hereafter referred to in the text as DM.

The vehemence of nineteenth-century working-class theatre audiences, and their level of participation in the performance, has been well documented.[9] Arguing against the common misconception of East End audiences as uncouth, Davis and Emaljanow suggest that such audiences were in fact 'generally self-regulating, more lively, and also more engaged than their West End equivalents' (94); it is this level of engagement that could be misinterpreted as alarming by outsiders observing the action of an East End theatre audience. A description of the audience at the Britannia Theatre in 1870 reveals the level of engagement:

> The noise was tremendous, particularly from the gallery, where people were passed back and forward over the heads of those already seated. Throughout the first act of the play the noise continued ... throughout the play the audience kept up a running commentary ... At the end of the play the crowd went wild, their cries, however, being overwhelmed by shrill and piercing whistles, which seemed to be the normal mode of applause at the Britannia (Davis and Emaljanow, 42).[10]

Audiences such as this clearly saw themselves as active participants in the drama. Such participation and vocalizing of the audience response is partly explained by the mechanics and architecture of the theatre. Until 1881, when Richard D'Oyly Carte's Savoy Theatre was lit entirely by electricity, the lights stayed on throughout the performance, therefore 'audience members remained aware of themselves as a live, responsive and often audible presence. Conversely, actors could see their auditors and so had the same conscious awareness of them'. As a result the audience was 'always aware of their identity as a community-in-little and likely to register immediate approval or disapproval' (Donohue, 'Theatres', 293, 294).

More significant was the extent to which melodramas were written and modified in direct relation to audience response. As Hadley points out:

> its emphasis on the visual, the emotive, and the audience aside were structural signs of the audience's importance, not merely as an observer of the action but, most significantly, as a participant in the plot. Michael Harvey guesses that as much as sixty to eighty percent of a script was spoken directly to the audience. In contrast to an exclusive drama composed in secret, written with pen, ink, and paper in a private room, melodrama systematically and spectacularly unfolded its private subplots before the gaze of its inclusive audience (68).[11]

Peter Brooks, commenting on the exaggerated oratory and gesture of melodrama, argues that 'such a non-naturalistic, irreal style of acting allowed the actor to call upon moments of direct communication with the audience, face to face

---

[9]   Davis and Emaljanow; Donohue, 'Theatres'; Earl; Hadley; Moody; Worrall.

[10]   The account was published in *L'International* on 11 and 12 May 1870.

[11]   Hadley refers to Michael Harvey, 'The Actor-Audience in Performance of Nineteenth-Century Melodrama', a paper presented at the Conference on Melodrama, Riverside, California, 1990.

confidences and asides' (47). Modification of the material in the light of audience response continued well into the nineteenth century. The 1860s and 1870s saw the rapid expansion of music halls, where the audience often altered the words of songs to include reference to the topics of the day. The music hall audience was one 'for whom demonstrative involvement in the performance was a fundamental and powerful attraction' (Bailey, 160).

If the audience for Corder's trial saw themselves in the light of a theatre audience, then the mania induced on the first day of the trial makes more sense: outraged by the crime itself, the public were attempting to influence the outcome by the vehemence of their presence. They were also afforded the means to 'act out' their feelings in the uncontested public space of the streets. At the very least there seems to have been a degree of collective consciousness which was aroused by the case, and culminated in the trial. It is understandable that the apparently supernatural elements of the case (Maria Marten's stepmother being allegedly visited by dreams revealing the presence of Maria's corpse) would have provoked interest, but that does not explain the need on the part of so many individuals to witness the court proceedings and/or the actual scene of the crime. The key to the public's response lies in their transformation of a brutal murder into a piece of theatre reflecting the reality of the domestic sphere, and over which they felt they had some control; this transformation is effected by the public themselves and echoed in written accounts, not the other way around.

It was also no coincidence that the public responded so vehemently to a crime that took place in the midst of political agitation for electoral reform, culminating four years later in the 1832 Reform Bill. Placed within this perspective, the distortion of Corder's social status to portray him as an aristocratic villain (examined in the following pages) makes sense. If, as Peter Brooks suggests, melodrama is an inherently democratic form, creating a world where class domination can be destroyed and 'a poor persecuted girl can confront her powerful oppressor with the truth about their moral conditions' (44), then it is necessary for both the 'poor persecuted girl' and her 'powerful oppressor' to be clearly polarized. In actual fact, Corder's family rented the land they farmed, and he was scarcely more educated than Maria.

Richard W. Schoch has argued that

> in the melodramas performed by the working-class audiences, social injustice was personified in the individual villain and not depicted as the dark underside of capitalism itself. In consequence, these plays resolved problems of crime and exploitation by eliminating individual perpetrators, thereby preserving intact the prevailing social and economic structures ... these immensely popular plays were not conducive to radical social change or protest (344).

The 'audience' for Corder's trial was, I believe, doing the reverse of this. It was elevating the social status of the 'individual perpetrator' to make him representative of social injustice and inequality. By bearing vocal witness to his 'elimination' they were, in fact, expressing their support of 'radical social change'.

Interest in the case extended well beyond the confines of the courtroom and its immediate environs. Various accounts of the events tell us of puppet shows, ballads, and re-enactments of the crime at country fairs, all of them implicating Corder in the murder even before the trial commenced. In Curtis's account of the proceedings, he tells us how

> the annual fair at Polstead on 16th and 17th July 1828 featured two shows exhibiting theatrical representations of "THE LATE MURDER OF MARIA MARTEN," which of course attracted considerable attention, and insured to the proprietors a rich harvest.
>
> In one of these exhibitions, there was the scene in "the RED BARN," where the mutilated body was lying on a door on the floor, surrounded by the coroner and the gentlemen of the jury, as they appeared on Sunday the 20th of April, the day after the fatal discovery took place, and the representations are said to be extremely correct (70).

It is interesting how the discovery of the body is here transformed into a dramatic tableau, with all the necessary players present.

Even members of the clergy were not above profiting from Maria's unfortunate demise. The first day of the trial witnessed a conversation between Mr. Brodrick (defence) and the Lord Chief Baron about a dissenting preacher (possibly named Young) who had been preaching about the murder in the Red Barn itself 'to a congregation of several thousand persons' (Foster, 32). Brodrick questioned Mr. Chaplin, the churchwarden of Polstead, about these events:

Mr. Brodrick. – Did you hear the parson preach in the barn?

Witness.   – No, certainly not; but I heard of the occurrence.

Mr. Brodrick. – And you never interfered to prevent it?

Witness.   – I did not.

Mr. Brodrick. – Are there not exhibitions going round the neighbourhood, representing Corder as the murderer?

Witness.   – I have heard so.

Mr. Brodrick. – And you've not interfered to prevent them? Is there not a camera obscura near this very hall at this moment, exhibiting him as the murderer?

Witness.   – There is a camera obscura, I believe, about the streets, but I don't know its nature (Foster, 33).

A sermon was delivered and published by one Charles Hyatt (minister of Ebenezer Chapel, Shadwell) in the Red Barn following Corder's execution. In the published version of the sermon, Hyatt comments on the numbers present:

although the afternoon was unfavourable, the crowd, as was expected, was too large for any walls near the spot to contain them, and the congregation were therefore assembled with all the impressive objects around them, with which are associated the horrible facts here narrated.

The appetite for written accounts of the murder, trial and its aftermath was huge. Publications varied in price from 6d for a 30-page small hardback book to a more lavish edition costing 2s 6d.[12] Authorship of these works is unclear. Only one cites an author on the title page – J. Curtis – but certain recurrent phrases were repeated in more than one of the accounts. Curtis was a writer for the *Times*, which explains some duplication of material.[13] The Knight and Lacey edition of the trial allegedly sold 500 copies in Bury St. Edmunds within a few hours of its arrival from London, and James Catnach estimated that 1,166,000 broadsides were circulated featuring the case.[14] Curtis's version has an index, suggesting it may have been used as some sort of reference work, and this is clearly what Curtis hoped for: giving an exact copy of the 10 counts with which Corder was indicted, Curtis footnotes that 'the exact copy of it here given has cost much labour, time, and trouble, but it is a document of too much value to be withheld from the public in a work like this, which aspires to permanent utility' (footnote to Curtis, 111). The case also appeared regularly in the pages of *The Newgate Calendar*, and was the subject of a novel entitled *The Red Barn: A Tale Founded on Fact*.[15] The ostensibly factual accounts of the crime which were published in the weeks immediately following the trial had much in common with newspaper and street literature coverage of this and other domestic murders. All were at pains to stress the author's reluctance to undertake the task in hand, and the moral intent of the work, stressing the gradations of vice from minor misdemeanours to more heinous crimes. Other familiar motifs from street literature and the popular press recurred: the murder was depicted as lacking a precedent in the criminal annals; the supposition that murder will always be detected was emphasized throughout; and similar stress was placed on the notion that society was united in excluding this individual from its ranks.

---

[12]   The British Library holds five accounts of the trial: the Dean and Munday version; the Curtis version; the George Foster version; *The Trial of William Corder, at the Assizes, Bury St. Edmunds ... etc.* (London: Knight and Lacey, 1828), hereafter referred to in the text as KL; *The Trial, at length, of William Corder ... etc.* (Bury St. Edmunds: T. C. Newby, c. 1828), hereafter referred to in the text as Newby.

[13]   Haining argues that Curtis 'provided columns of text for *The Times*, and then immediately after the execution reworked the material into book form, adding his own comments and interpretations on much that had happened' (90).

[14]   Figures quoted in Anderson, 25.

[15]   *The Red Barn: A Tale Founded on Fact* (London: Knight and Lacey, 1828). Authorship of this work is unclear. The British Library holds two copies of the text, neither of which gives an author on the title page. The British Library attributes one version to Robert Huish and the other to William Maginn.

These written accounts of the case are important in that they give evidence of the public disorder surrounding the trial, and afford a 'role' to the public that is absent in any later theatrical renditions of the crime. By virtue of their length, these accounts were also able to narrativize the case, providing background detail and fleshing out the 'characters', to satisfy the huge public appetite for such details. Affording extensive coverage to the trial proceedings enabled the private act of murder to enter the public arena for extended exhibition and scrutiny.

The theatricality of the case was evident to all who wrote about it, and both the details of the murder and the court proceedings were fully manipulated for their dramatic potential. The motif of the courtroom as theatre was well established in the newspaper and street literature coverage of trials; coupled with the fact that the details of the case read like a melodrama, the repeated emphasis on theatricality is hardly surprising. References to the Red Barn as 'the very theatre of [Corder's] barbarity' (Curtis, 219), and the village of Polstead as 'the theatre of his deep dyed guilt' set the scene, as it were, for the tone of these accounts (KL, 7). Were that not enough, the writers themselves draw specific attention to the fantastic nature of the events: Curtis comments in the introduction to his work that 'when the mysterious murder of Maria Marten was discovered in April last, the "deed of dreadful note" was echoed throughout the land; and it appeared so much like a romance, that it was but little regarded by thousands, and many were wont to say that a vile hoax had been imposed upon the press' (iv). He goes on to flag up the narrative and theatrical potential of the case:

> The Polstead Catastrophe, or the Mysterious Murder of Maria Marten, may (to pursue alliteration) be called "a Medley" – for such it is – as it exhibits the ferocity of man – the frailty and fidelity of woman – the ruin of families – the municipal authority – the power of conscience – the palladium of British liberty – the blessings of a court of judicature, under the jurisprudence of a humane judge – and, finally, that the "glorious laws, those brightest pearls which gem our monarch's crown," are not to be violated and the violator go unpunished; that "he that sheddeth the blood of a fellow-creature (wilfully), by man shall his blood be shed."
>
> Furthermore, herein will be found mythology, necromancy, biography, topography, history, theology, phrenology, anatomy, legal ingenuity, conjugal correspondence, amatory, epistles, poetry, theatrical representations, affecting anecdotes, etc. etc. (iv–v).[16]

It was no coincidence that Curtis affords the case a title in the style of a play – The Polstead Catastrophe, or the Mysterious Murder of Maria Marten – and presents the astonishing contents of the case as a form of playbill, offering something for everyone. As discussed at some length in Chapter 1, the inherent

---

[16]   The reference to the 'glorious laws, those brightest pearls which gem our monarch's crown' is a line lifted from the Pavilion Theatre production of the crime, first shown four weeks after Corder's execution.

theatricality of trials was acknowledged in the press coverage: the moral polarity of victim and perpetrator, the bodily gestures of all participants, and the dock as a form of stage were all common motifs of newspaper and periodical coverage of notorious trials. Similar awareness of the theatrical potential is exhibited in the Knight and Lacey version, which comments that

> the barbarous deed, which has more the appearance of a melo-dramatic romance, than an occurrence in a civilized country like England, possesses, inherently, so fearful a reality, that it requires no fiction of the imagination to add to its horrors – it needs not any embellishment – it demands not any ideal colouring (KL, 2).

In discussing the apparent interposition of Providence in Ann Marten dreaming of the murder, the Knight and Lacey version compares the crime to 'the imaginative tales of our childhood and the nursery' (2).

The influence of the theatre is everywhere present in these accounts of the trial, with the George Foster version even listing the members of the jury as a prelude to the trial proceedings, rather like a cast list. The rhetoric employed both by the key 'players' and by the authors of these publications could be lifted straight from the Victorian stage. The introduction to Curtis's account recounts his journey to Polstead, and his reflections thereon: 'I could not help exclaiming, "Is it possible that, in the midst of this little Eden, a village swain has imbrued his hands in the blood of his damsel?"' (xii). Later, standing in his bedroom with Maria's family home visible from his window, Curtis reflects

> There, in yon once peaceful abode, Maria's infant prattle greeted the ears of her doting parents; there she grew in – beauty, innocence and stature, – but alas! thither the spoliator came, and nipped the tender blooming hyacinth, and for ever blasted the hopes of an aged, admiring father! (xv).

Such theatrical flourishes were not reserved solely for the authors of these accounts. The Lord Chief Baron's words to Corder, after the delivery of the verdict, contained the following:

> You sent this unfortunate woman to her account without giving her any time for preparation. She had no time to turn her eyes to the Throne of Grace for mercy and forgiveness. She had no time given her to repent of her many transgressions. She had no time to throw herself upon her knees and to implore for pardon at the Eternal Throne (Foster, 67).

The repetition of 'she had no time' suggests the Lord Chief Baron was mindful that his words would be reprinted and was at pains to stress the theatricality of the case; the dramatic potential of gestures such as turning her eyes 'to the Throne of Grace' and throwing herself upon her knees mean we can almost see Maria in tableau, framed for an audience's response.

Corder's wife, visiting him in gaol after the passing of sentence, apparently adopted similar gestures, throwing herself into Corder's arms, sobbing hysterically, and fainting 'several times' (DM, 27). Despite such distress, Mrs. Corder was apparently able to muster sufficient presence of mind to address her husband thus: 'Well, dearest William, this trial is terminated in a manner quite different to that which we all most sanguinely expected' (Foster, 76).

Assuming that these were not Mrs. Corder's actual words, such shaping of the narrative for more dramatic purposes is evident elsewhere. The difficulty of interrupting the witness testimony with Corder's response to it is overcome in one publication by occasional theatrical 'asides' such as '[it was observed here that the accused sighed repeatedly and deeply]' (DM, 14) and another publication ingeniously created a subsection headed 'Demeanour of the prisoner during the summing up of the learned judge, and the sentence', explaining that 'to prevent breaking in too much upon the uniformity of our narrative, we have deemed it right to subjoin to the trial itself an account of his behaviour during the latter part of it' (Foster, 68). The authors of these works were clearly aware of the theatrical potential of the case, and were distorting the presentation of the court proceedings to preserve a coherence to the work and keep the reader's interest.

Lest the events of the trial fail to provide the necessary frisson in the readership of these accounts, the authors were not above a little embellishment, to exaggerate the gothic horror of the proceedings. When Maria's skull was produced in court, a footnote on page 174 of the Curtis version informs us that it produced

> a thrilling sensation throughout the court – indeed, how could it be otherwise with any one who reflected, that a few months ago it exhibited the features of the beautiful Maria Marten; and moreover, that it was now produced to grin a ghastly smile upon her faithless lover, and murderer? Had these dry bones been able to have performed their former functions in the power of articulation, they might have sung,
> "In youth, when I did love, did love,
>   Methought it was very sweet;"
> and then in frantic yells have exclaimed, "Vengeance, retribution. Lord avenge me of my adversary."

Not surprisingly, Corder's execution is also presented as a piece of theatre, with the backdrop drawn for us thus:

> the prospect from the place on which he stood is of the most beautiful description. The fore-ground consists of softly swelling hills, bounded in the distance by extensive plantations, which form a sort of amphitheatre around the prison (DM, 29).

This description is then followed by what could easily have been read as a very detailed set of stage directions:

> The executioner then drew the cap over his face ... Within a minute afterwards, the deadly bolt was withdrawn ... The hangman, after the corpse had fallen, performed his disgusting but necessary task of suspending his own weight

around the body of the prisoner, to accelerate his death. At the same moment, the prisoner, who appeared to be in the last agonies, clasped his hands tighter together, as if he was forming his last prayer for the mercy and forgiveness of offended Heaven. Immediately afterwards his arms, which were raised a little, fell – the muscles appeared to relax – and his hands soon sunk down as low as their pinioned condition permitted (DM, 29–30).

The moral polarity we would expect from the coverage of such a crime at this point in the century is everywhere apparent in the portrayal of both Corder and his victim. Maria is 'the unhappy sufferer' (Foster, 3), the 'wretched victim' (KL, 1), and 'the slaughtered victim of his cupidity' (Curtis, 215). The details of Maria's physical appearance and moral demeanour remain reasonably consistent across the various publications; she is

young and beautiful, and in the very "bloom of existence", with a frailty born of the constant importunity, and the unremitting solicitations which a rustic beauty, and the "flower of the village," expects and demands (KL, 7).

The George Foster version stands alone in offering the detail that Maria had 'a large excrescence or wen' (22) on the middle of her neck, and was missing two of her front teeth. The omitting of these details in all other physical descriptions (and portraits) of Maria shows a determination on the writers' part to exaggerate the heinous nature of Corder's crime; to kill a beautiful woman was somehow worse than killing a plain one. The emphasis on Maria's attractiveness also casts her more firmly as a type of melodramatic heroine – the village beauty. This distortion of Maria's appearance is also reflected in the illustrations that accompanied these accounts of the murder. There is no means of knowing what Maria looked like, but she was often portrayed as pretty, demure and innocent.

This contrast between Maria and Corder is also present in the written descriptions of Corder who is, variously, a 'ruthless monster' (Foster, 3), a 'tiger-hearted assassin', the 'vile murderer' (KL, 1), 'her dastardly but sanguinary murderer' (Curtis, 82), a 'cold-blooded and deliberate assassin' (Curtis, 22), and one whose conduct was 'incompatible with human nature' (*Times*, 1 May 1828, 3). Corder's statement to the court, his one chance to obtain a degree of humanity, is given in full in Curtis's version, but is footnoted throughout with Curtis's response to, and moral condemnation of Corder's words. These endless footnotes undercut the potential power of Corder's statement, as if someone were leaning over the reader's shoulder the whole time.

Such explicit moral condemnation of Corder was necessary also because, physically, he failed to conform to the public's idea of a murderer. What was exceptional about Corder was his ordinariness: he was of 'middle height, of a fair and healthy complexion, large mouth, turn-up nose, large eyes' (Foster, 9). The Knight and Lacey version, although quick to spot a 'cat-like ferocity about the eyes, and a somewhat sinister expression of countenance' was obliged to confess that his appearance did not suggest 'so cold-blooded a murderer' (KL, 7).

Press coverage of domestic murder at this time, as discussed in the previous chapter, drew heavily on the conventions of melodrama, and adopted the motif that evil was written 'on the body'; given the lack of any obvious depravity in Corder's façade, it became essential to highlight anything about his appearance or demeanour which betrayed his immorality.

For this reason all accounts of the trial gave full details of Corder's fashionable clothes to highlight both his social status (thus casting him more firmly in the role of the melodramatic villain, who was conventionally of a higher social status than his intended victim) and his cold-bloodedness, that he could take such care over his dress when facing a charge of murder (Foster, 9; DM, 12; *Times*, 24 April 1828, 7 and 8 August 1828, 21; KL, 7; Curtis, 110). The Knight and Lacey version offered the description of Corder 'dressed in a gentlemanly suit of black, over which was thrown a military Spanish roquelaure … he leant negligently, and in an indifferent and lounging manner, on the front rail of the dock' (6). The echoes here of the melodramatic villain are obvious.

Such composure was, however, eventually rattled. By the end of the first day of the trial we are told that he was visited by occasional convulsions, 'betraying, with a character not to be mistaken, the emotion under which he laboured during the delivery of particular passages in the evidence' (Foster, 46). The involuntary nature of Corder's convulsions supported the notion, current at the time, that guilt would eventually manifest itself, despite efforts to conceal it. Corder's outward manifestations of unease were also firmly in the tradition of melodramatic acting, with exaggerated gestures to indicate mental state.

By the second day of the trial, although still looking around him 'with seeming cheerfulness', Corder was not

> so entirely at ease as he appeared to be early on the previous day; his head was not so erect, and he repeatedly heaved deep sighs. Immediately on being put to the bar, he put on his spectacles, folded his arms, and displayed an oscillating and swinging motion of his body, while he leaned his back against the pillar of the dock. He hung down his head frequently during the examination of the witnesses (Foster, 47).

And, during the Lord Chief Baron's summing up, Corder was no longer able to disguise his agitation:

> the countenance of the prisoner repeatedly changed colour, from a deep flush to a pallid hue; he betrayed a very feverish anxiety, as to the result of the trial; he manifested great uneasiness, and appeared to be suffering considerable mental torture. Occasionally there was an apparent convulsive motion of the lower part of his face; his lips were parched, and he sighed deeply. Towards the conclusion of the trial, he rested his head against a pillar in the felons' dock, and closed his eyes (DM, 25).

Given the obvious melodramatic details of the case, the extent to which the theatrical potential was highlighted in written accounts of the trial, and the huge public interest in the case, it is hardly surprising that the murder was transposed to the stage almost immediately. Maurice Disher highlights the appetite for such theatrical retellings of the tale:

> puppets, peep-shows and balladmongers recognized it at once as matter for entertainment. Writers of condemned-men's confessions and full reports of trials came next, with illustrated histories published in sixpenny parts. Novelists elaborated the dry facts into penny dreadfuls and so the vengeful gypsy came into the story. Hacks at out-of-the-way theatres made Corder into the public's favourite villain though no playwright of any repute would notice the subject (128).

Disher does not expand on why 'no playwright of any repute would notice the subject', but the potential constraints of censorship would seem to be the obvious answer; the theatrical portrayal of such a recent crime would never have been passed by the Lord Chamberlain. Theatrical versions of the case were performed throughout the nineteenth century in East End theatres and in the provinces, but not in the West End – again, presumably for reasons of censorship. As Jones-Evans argues:

> though spurned by the metropolis, the hinterland was replete with Red Barns of all shapes and sizes. Over the years it was played in every playable place. Touring repertory companies, changing the bill nightly, would have a special evening for *Maria Marten* as the opus was now more generally known (xi).

Only three printed versions are now extant: part of an 1828 production at the Pavilion Theatre, Mile End Road; one from 1840 at the Marylebone Theatre; and one speculatively performed in 1877.[17] There are problems with identifying the authenticity of any of these versions, as there are overlaps and similarities across all three. In particular, the 1828 and 1877 versions bear striking similarities.

The first stage version of the crime for which any printed material still exists was first performed at the Pavilion Theatre, Mile End Road, on 8 September 1828, exactly four weeks after Corder's execution. Entitled *The Red Barn: or The Mysterious Murder*, no script for this piece exists *per se*, but the work is referred to by Curtis at the close of his account of the murder and trial, and he includes extracts. There is some confusion over the author of this early work; Jones-Evans, writing in 1966, argues for a Mr. Vaughan, but Curtis himself cites the author as West Digges. The 1877 version features in Michael Kilgarriff's *The Golden Age of Melodrama*. Kilgarriff gives the text as *Maria Marten: or, the Murder in the Red Barn*. No author is listed, but Kilgarriff suggests that the author was the resident writer for the Star Theatre, Swansea. The date of first performance is lost, but the date of publication 'seems to have been as late as 1877' (205). Kilgarriff argues that

---

[17]   Jones-Evans mentions a later play also entitled *The Red Barn* and a further play, *Advertisement for Wives*, is mentioned by Curtis, but no copies of either play were uncovered during the research for this book.

this is the only stage version published in the nineteenth century. The problem with Kilgarriff's provenance is that the version he publishes bears striking similarities to the extracts published by Curtis at the end of his account of the trial, that is, the version performed in 1828 at the Pavilion Theatre. For this reason, the Kilgarriff version of 1877 will be treated as the same play as that performed in 1828, and the play will be referred to as *The Red Barn*. The second play, *Maria Marten; or, The Murder in the Red Barn*, was first performed on 6 April 1840 at the Marylebone Theatre and will be referred to as *Maria Marten*. Written by John Latimer, a writer for the Queen's Theatre, Battersea, the written text of this play is itself somewhat unreliable; edited by Montagu Slater in an edition published in 1928, Slater admits to having 'translated and to some extent expanded' on the stage directions (21).

The Red Barn, *Maria Marten* and their various other manifestations were performed throughout the century at theatres with largely working-class audiences. Located on Mile End Road, in the East End of London, the Pavilion catered for a largely working-class audience with a smaller middle-class contingent. Although the theatre's repertoire was a predictable mix of melodrama and nautical drama, with legitimate drama 'also well represented', the Pavilion's reputation rested on plays which expressed some criticism of British society:

> Douglas Jerrold's powerful indictments of naval and domestic abuses, *The Mutiny at the Nore* (1830) and *Martha Willis the Servant Girl* (1831), both first performed at the Pavilion, may have marked the theatre not only as a home of melodrama, but of plays that were critical of aspects of British society in those turbulent years leading up to the first Reform Bill of 1832 (Davis and Emaljanow, 55–6).

This might seem, then, a fitting venue for an enactment of Corder's crime, whose elevation into an aristocratic villain had already been partly effected during the trial itself, with details of his fashionable clothes, and the appearance of Founs the family retainer, who visited Corder in gaol after the verdict and allegedly lamented: 'Oh, Master William, I am sorry it is come to this'. Certainly, Corder is portrayed in both *The Red Barn* and *Maria Marten* as being of a higher social status than Maria, partly because the elevated social status of the villain was a melodramatic staple, but also presumably to satisfy the high proportion of working-class members in both the Pavilion and Marylebone audiences.

In *Maria Marten* Corder's first entrance has him leering at Maria and tapping his leggings with his riding whip in a 'sinister way'; shortly after this, Maria asks Corder: 'Oh Sir, what will people say to see Maria Marten the poor labourer's daughter in company with the son of the rich Mr. Corder?' (Act I, scene 3, p. 36). This emphasizes not only Corder's greater affluence, but casts him in an elevated social position by virtue of Maria's addressing him as 'Sir'. Whilst there was undoubtedly some financial disparity between Corder and Maria, in terms of education there was little to choose: Maria had formerly been in service with a vicar's family, and was educated alongside the vicar's children; Corder's address to the jury revealed he was 'not a man of particular education' (*Times*, 9 August 1828, 3).

The portrayal of Corder in both these plays is largely to be expected, and accords with the portrayal of the villain in other plays featuring domestic murder. What is more significant, particularly given the location of both the Pavilion and the Marylebone, is the absence of any theatrical rendition of the public disorder surrounding the trial. There were, of course, logistical issues at work, but I feel the absence of the crowd on stage effectively denied the public any agency within the confines of the theatre. In effect, although the two plays did go beyond the boundaries of censorship, particularly in their portrayal of the actual murder, they were still sanitizing and diluting the original crime.

Part of this sanitizing lies also in the problematization of Maria's sexual history. Conveniently omitted from all but one account of the trial, Maria had already had two children before her relationship with Corder, one of them with Corder's brother. In *The Red Barn* Corder briefly refers to the fact that Maria has had a child by someone called Mathews, and her other children are not mentioned at all in *Maria Marten*, but both plays make reference to the suffering attendant on sexual misconduct, suggesting a socially conservative purpose which contrasts with the initial disruption occasioned by the crime, and would have been particularly pertinent to the audience of both the Marylebone and the Pavilion theatres. In *The Red Barn* Maria's final pleas for mercy emphasize the misery that can arise from moral laxity, even if one is not subjected to the ultimate punishment of being murdered:

> What have I not sacrificed for thy love? Am I not a creature lost in shame, for men to point at and women to mock? Am I not a poor, forlorn, frail thing, whose heart is bruised and bleeding with excess of agony – whose form is bowed with suffering miseries (Act I, scene 5, p. 225).

In *Maria Marten* Corder recounts being visited by Maria's ghost in his dreams; significantly she has been transformed into a fiend-like creature with her eyes shooting fire and her hands changed to eagle's claws. She pulls Corder down to the 'horrid demons and loathsome serpents' of Hell, yelling 'Welcome, murderer, to thy future home!' (Act V, scene 3, p. 76). Although such a scene undoubtedly offered the potential for dramatic spectacle, it is significant that Hell is not preserved for Corder alone: he is joining Maria there, presumably on account of her sexual history. Maria's life thus served as a cautionary tale to any women in the audience.

The murder in both plays is conveyed with a surprising amount of physicality, given that Sikes's murder of Nancy in the Almar version of *Oliver Twist* (1838) takes place off stage, and the Oxenford version of *Oliver Twist* (1868) has Nancy merely swooning.[18] Murders, where they did occur, generally took place off stage, or with a minimum of physical contact, but in *The Red Barn* Corder

---

[18]   Richard P. Fulkerson, '"Oliver Twist" in the Victorian Theatre', *Dickensian* (1974): 83–95.

seizes her – throws her round, she falls on her knees … She shrieks as he attempts to stab her … He again attempts to stab her. She clings round his neck. He dashes her to the earth, and stabs her. She shrieks and falls. He stands motionless till the curtain falls (Act 1, scene 5, pp. 225–6).

The detail of Maria 'clinging' to Corder's neck reminds us of the intimate nature of their union, and forms part of a highly dramatic sequence, particularly given that Corder confessed to shooting Maria, but always denied the stabbing. One suspects a vicarious thrill on the part of the playwright, and by extension the audience, at the manhandling of a woman which a stabbing entails.

In *Maria Marten* such physicality is again in evidence; Corder digs the grave in advance of Maria's arrival, and 'drags' her to it. When Corder reveals his murderous intentions to the accompaniment of thunder and lightning, Maria kneels and begs for mercy in a classic melodramatic tableau. Maria resists, 'they struggle, he shoots her, she falls in his arms'; again, the intimacy of their former union is recalled by this final detail. Maria dies to 'soft music', 'blessing and forgiving' Corder, her mercy firmly positioning her as the heroine of the piece (Act V, scene 1, pp. 63–4).

These plays sit uncomfortably between two agendas. The factual basis of the work and apparent disregard for any issues of censorship enable the playwrights to show the murder with a high degree of physicality, and run the risk of fuelling class discontent. But such potentially disruptive material sits awkwardly with edicts on the dangers of sexual laxity. Although, on the face of it, these plays do seem more willing to portray a disrupted domestic sphere, ultimately the pressure of the domestic myth was too great.

The domestic ideology promulgated by the nascent middle classes in the first half of the nineteenth century effectively resulted in self-censorship on the part of playwrights. Despite obvious public interest in the sensational elements of domestic life, as evidenced by the huge appetite for the coverage of murder trials in newspapers and street literature, those in control of the Victorian stage continued to perpetuate a domestic myth well into the 1870s. Such an ideology came under more direct and effective attack in the 1860s, with the birth of the sensation novel.

Chapter 3
'Mixed Motives and Mixed Morality': The Newgate Novel Debate

> Take a small boy, charity, factory, carpenter's apprentice, or otherwise, as occasion may serve – stew him well down in vice – garnish largely with oaths and flash songs – boil him in a cauldron of crime and improbabilities. Season equally well with good and bad qualities – infuse petty larceny, affection, benevolence, and burglary, honour and housebreaking, amiability and arson – boil all gently. Stew down a mad mother – a gang of robbers – several pistols – a bloody knife. Serve up with a couple of murders – and season with a hanging match.
>
> N.B. Alter the ingredients – a beadle and a workhouse – the scenes will be the same, but the whole flavour of vice will be lost, and the boy will turn out a perfect pattern. – Strongly recommended for weak stomachs ('Literary Recipes', *Punch*, 7 August 1841, 39).

The popularity of Newgate fiction during the 1830s and 40s meant that this 'Literary Recipe' – which appeared in *Punch* in 1841 – would have been immediately recognizable to *Punch*'s readership. This chapter engages with the debate surrounding the Newgate novel controversy, and the attendant charge levied at the time, that this fictional mode glorified the villain. Newgate novels typically focused on the criminal more than on the crime, with the chief protagonists afforded an individuality (and sometimes an appeal) that foreshadowed sensation fiction of the 1860s–70s. This represents, I argue, the early stages in the development of an individualized psyche for the criminal mind.

I will first contextualize the Newgate controversy by a brief examination of the content and generic features of *The Newgate Calendar*, which provided source material for the Newgate novelists. Setting this alongside contemporary news and street literature coverage of murder, the chapter then gives an explanatory account of the controversy surrounding the Newgate novel, before examining Dickens's *Oliver Twist* (1838) and Thackeray's *Catherine* (1840). Both novels have, at their heart, domestic murders – Sikes's murder of Nancy in *Oliver Twist* and Catherine Hayes's murder of her husband John in *Catherine*, a crime for which Hayes was burnt alive in 1725 – and both novels were seen as contributing to the Newgate novel debate, albeit unintentionally in the case of Dickens. The two authors' treatment of the disruption of the domestic sphere, however, differs radically. Dickens allies himself firmly with contemporary ideology in regarding domestic murder as the ultimate crime, and one for which Sikes must be seen to suffer. However, although appearing to position Sikes firmly within the melodramatic mode, Dickens actually creates something of a transitional figure in him;

Sikes exhibits elements of the psychological realism which sees fuller development in the character of Bradley Headstone from *Our Mutual Friend*, examined in greater detail in Chapter 4. Thackeray, on the other hand, by making the motive for the murder more domestic and sexualized than its source in *The Newgate Calendar*, actually mitigates Catherine Hayes's offence, and engenders a degree of sympathy for her. In his ambivalent treatment of his heroine, Thackeray foreshadows the more engaging figure of the sensation fiction villainess. Contemporary criticism of the sensation novel expressed particular concern that popular literature was being absorbed by a more educated readership but I will argue that the market for such literature among the middle classes was already firmly established in Newgate fiction, well before the advent of sensation fiction.

The Newgate Calendar

The first collection of crime stories under the title *The Newgate Calendar* appeared in 1773. Published in five volumes, the quality of the engravings and the sheer scale of the publication suggest a more affluent intended readership than later editions came to attract, showing that there was clearly an appetite amongst these classes for such publications. The Preface to the 1773 work states that 'all ranks of people will receive benefit from the perusal of the present work', and footnotes throughout the five volumes provide explanations of the various criminal terms – manslaughter, assault, petty treason, etc. – suggesting at least a partial readership unfamiliar with such crimes.[1] The scale and quality of the publication alone suggests less that the wealthier literate classes appropriated such material, and more that it was aimed specifically at them from the outset. This certainly seems to be the case with the newspaper coverage of crime in 'establishment' publications such as the *Times* and the *Daily Telegraph* (as discussed in Chapter 1); such early evidence of a cross-class appetite for crime would seem to undermine the concerns surrounding the advent of sensation fiction.

With the success of the 1773 volume, a host of similar publications followed, including *The New and Complete Newgate Calendar*, *The Chronicles of Crime*, and *The Newgate Calendar and Divorce Court Chronicle*.[2] *The Newgate Calendar* in its various manifestations continued to be sold in multi-volume format until Andrew Knapp and William Baldwin's 1824 single-volume edition; 1845 saw the publication of a slender pocket version, putting the work more firmly within the reach of the less affluent classes, and also suggesting a level of familiarity with the

---

[1]   *The Newgate Calendar or Malefactors' Bloody Register*, 5 vols. (London, 1773), i, v. Hereafter referred to in the text as NC 1773.

[2]   William Jackson, *The New and Complete Newgate Calendar*, 6 vols. (London: Alexander Hogg, 1795). Hereafter referred to in the text as NC 1795. Camden Pelham, *The Chronicles of Crime; or, The New Newgate Calendar*, 2 vols. (London: Thomas Tegg, 1841). Hereafter referred to in the text as NC 1841. *The Newgate Calendar and the Divorce Court Chronicle* (London: F. Farrah, 1872). Hereafter referred to in the text as NC 1872.

contents of previous editions. By 1863, the publication was sufficiently popular to be issued in a weekly periodical format, at the price of 1d per issue.

The basic format for the contents of *The Newgate Calendar* in all its incarnations remained largely the same, with coverage of cases from 1700 up to the recent past. The accounts generally opened with brief details of the protagonists' background, and pertinent details of their childhoods. By the 1841 edition there was a contents page with the criminals listed alphabetically and their crime next to them; this suggests a degree of familiarity on the part of the readership, and also the opportunity for selective reading, thereby perhaps eliding the moral edification to be gained from reading the work as a whole. The pocket edition of 1845 dispensed with naming the crimes, and simply listed the criminals; again, suggesting that these names would be familiar to the public, either through reading earlier editions of *The Newgate Calendar*, or through press coverage of the more recent crimes.

Much of what we come to expect from nineteenth-century newspaper coverage of crimes is there in the pages of *The Newgate Calendar*: an emphasis on the moral polarity of the criminal and victim; the uniting of the community against the murderer, as in the case of John Chappel from the 1773 edition, when 'the clamors of the people as is common in such cases, was very great against him'; and the inevitability of detection, with the assurance that 'of all crimes Murder is the only one that seldom passes undiscovered' (NC 1773, 1:332, 21).

All editions of the work were at pains to stress the moral content. Earlier, eighteenth-century versions carried a final paragraph or two at the close of each 'story', summarizing the moral lessons to be learned; in the case of Catherine Hayes, who murdered and decapitated her husband (and whose crime formed the basis of Thackeray's novel *Catherine*, examined later in this chapter), one of these lessons is 'the necessity of keeping a constant guard on our passions' (NC 1795, 2:128). By 1824 these closing didactic paragraphs had disappeared, but there remained a strong moral vein in the work: the 1841 Preface argued that 'the representation of guilt with its painful and degrading consequences, has been universally considered to be the best means of warning youth against the danger of temptation' (NC 1841, 1:v). However, given the content of the illustrations, and the tone of the writing (both of which are examined in detail below), the editions of the 1820s onwards were merely paying lip service to the concept of morality as a means of justifying their increasingly sensationalist content.

Lest the potential readership be put off by too high a moral tone, the various incarnations of the *Calendar* were at pains to stress that the work aimed to unite 'entertainment and instruction', a process whereby the reader 'will naturally become wiser and better' (NC 1773, 1:iv). As early as the 1795 edition there is a sense of shaping the material for the purposes of entertainment, with the Preface arguing that

> in all the Works of this nature that we have seen the materials are so jumbled together, without order or method, that the readers are disgusted, rather than entertained or instructed. Instead, therefore, of repeating the dull formal

repetitions used in trials, we have thrown the whole into a form of narrative; and
at the end of each life, deduced such practical inferences, as cannot fail to make
a lasting impression on the mind of our readers (NC 1795, 1:6–7).

It is noteworthy in this Preface that the two aims of entertainment and instruction
are given equal weight. As part of the means of entertaining the public, the 1795
and later editions tended to include more dialogue; this not only fictionalized
events but also drew the reader into a more intimate relationship with the key
players.

With each successive incarnation the number of illustrations declined, as well
as their quality; by 1824 the illustrations were more sensationalist, and sometimes
more humorous in content. This is easily demonstrated by a consideration of the
illustrations which accompanied the case of Catherine Hayes. Burnt alive in 1726
for the murder of her husband, John Hayes, Catherine Hayes featured consistently
in all editions of *The Newgate Calendar*, from 1773 until 1886 (the most recent
edition examined for this chapter).

One particular moment in the case invited the illustrator's attention, for
obvious reasons: the severing of John Hayes's head. This event was illustrated
in both the 1773 and 1824 editions of the *Calendar*. Both illustrations show the
event taking place by candlelight in the Hayes's bedroom (thus emphasizing the
domestic nature of the murder) with bedclothes dishevelled and an axe lying
nearby. Although the presence of an axe in a bedroom might not be as incongruous
as it first appears (it might be needed to chop wood into smaller pieces for the fire),
it is given sufficient prominence in these illustrations to warrant attention. Both
illustrations also feature the three individuals involved in the murder: Catherine
Hayes, Thomas Wood and Thomas Billings (Catherine's son). The 1773 edition
is a more restrained rendition of the event, with the actual slitting of the throat
masked by Wood or Billings's arm and with Hayes's face also partially hidden.
The 1824 edition is a more bloodthirsty affair: Hayes is now facing upwards,
and the slitting of the throat with accompanying blood sprays is more central to
the image. This later illustration is also more noticeably theatrical, with the bed
curtains framing the 'action'.

The captions also reveal a significant shift in emphasis. The 1773 edition is
captioned 'Catherine Hayes assisting Wood and Billings, in cutting off the head of
her husband John Hayes'. Catherine here is simply 'assisting' Wood and Billings,
whereas the 1824 illustration is captioned 'Catherine Hayes and her accomplices
cutting off her husband's head', placing Catherine much more at the centre of
the action. This shift in blame to pinpoint Catherine as the chief protagonist by
1824 might foreshadow the prominence of the villainess in sensation fiction of the
1850s to 70s, but it almost undoubtedly reflects contemporary thinking with regard
to women and their relation to the domestic space. Under Victorian thinking the
'home' was a female space; and the idea of a woman violating such a space by
the act of murder was particularly repellant. Placing a woman at the centre of this
crime created an even more sensationalist narrative.

To examine the changing narrative style of *The Newgate Calendar* in its various manifestations, it is useful to look again at the case of Catherine Hayes. It was quite common for copy to be lifted from earlier versions of the *Calendar*, and then reappear in later editions, but there are still sufficient changes in the material to warrant attention. The early editions of *The Newgate Calendar* devoted considerable space to the Hayes case. Much of what we would expect to find in nineteenth-century newspaper and broadside coverage is already present. Catherine and John Hayes are presented at opposite ends of the moral spectrum: John is 'of a very peaceable disposition, honest in his dealings and very quiet among his neighbours'; Catherine is 'of a temper and disposition directly opposite, often setting her neighbours at variance and fomenting quarrels wherever she went'. The inevitable mental torment attendant on committing murder is also present, with the writer's exhortation to 'those who shudder at the thoughts of committing murder, to judge what sort of sleep these men could enjoy, or what dreams they might be tormented with'. Coupled with this is the belief that detection is inevitable; the ultimately futile pains taken by Catherine's accomplices to hide the body are 'but so many strong proofs how difficult it is to conceal the crime of murder' (NC 1773, 2:187, 194, 128).

The murder itself is reported in quite a pragmatic fashion, again foreshadowing newspaper reports of the following century. For the most gruesome details of the case the style is factual and non-judgmental: 'Billings supported the head, while Wood cut it off with his pocket knife, and Catherine held the pail to receive it lest any of the blood should be spilt on the floor' (NC 1773, 2:192). By the 1795 edition, there is more authorial intervention. In the incident just mentioned where John Hayes's head is cut off, Hayes is now the 'poor man' and Catherine the 'infamous woman' who holds the pail to receive the blood (NC 1795, 2:106). By 1824, she has become a 'she-devil'.[3] This demonization of Catherine Hayes is clearly a gendered criticism; even as early as 1824, it was seen as a woman's 'job' to preserve the domestic space and offer a sanctuary for her husband from the stress of the working world. The desecration of the domestic sphere by a woman was viewed with particular alarm.

Another case which shows the increasingly 'shaped' narrative, but which does not appear until the 1830s and 40s, for obvious reasons, is that of William Corder, hanged in 1828 for the murder of Maria Marten (discussed in greater detail in Chapter 2). Set against the 'cold-blooded atrocity' of Corder's actions, we are offered Maria Marten, who is 'artless and inexperienced' (NC 1841, 2:146). The inevitability of detection is again forced home, with the suggestion that 'the circumstances, which eventually led to the discovery of this most atrocious crime, are so extraordinary and romantic a nature, as almost to manifest an especial

---

[3]   Andrew Knapp and William Baldwin, *The Newgate Calendar*, 4 vols. (London: J. Robins, 1824), 1:260. Hereafter referred to in footnotes as NC 1824.

interposition of Providence in marking out the offender' (NC 1841, 2:147).[4] Whether it be the murderer's own conscience, their suspicious behaviour attracting attention, or the intervention of providence, domestic murder will always out.

What is particularly striking when examining consecutive editions of the *Newgate Calendar* is how one crime is increasingly described in relation to another. Catherine Hayes's crime is compared with that of Greenacre's murder of his fiancée Hannah Brown, in 1837 (NC 1841, 1:65), and Corder's murder of Maria Marten is compared to John Thurtell's murder of William Weare in 1823, with the assumption that the readership will be fully conversant with both Greenacre and Thurtell's crimes. By connecting these murders with one another, not only is the horror of each case reinforced, it is almost as if we are witnessing the birth of a genre which gathers strength with every reiteration and interconnection with earlier cases.

It is easy to understand why fiction inspired by *The Newgate Calendar* was viewed with a degree of alarm. What originated in 1773 as an ostensibly respectable publication became ever more sensationalist in both tone and illustration, and the cost and quality of the publication clearly shows a change in the intended audience by the 1830s and 40s, the point at which the *Calendar* became embroiled in the Newgate novel debate. But the content of the novels alone does not explain the furore that greeted their publication; street literature offered similar material, and had been widely available for much longer than the Newgate novel. It is the issue of audience, rather than the content of the novels themselves, that lies at the heart of the Newgate debate.

The Newgate Controversy

Keith Hollingsworth, Juliet John, Lyn Pykett and Gary Kelly have all analysed the underlying spurs to the Newgate debate, a debate out of all proportion to the general cast of the fictional material in dispute, and marked by 'extreme moral, aesthetic and ideological confusion' (John, *Cult Criminals*, v). Hollingsworth, John and Kelly argue that the controversy was as much an issue of timing as the result of any inherent immorality within the novels themselves. For these critics, the historical event which holds the key to the debate is the 1832 Reform Bill:

> the widening of the political franchise, along with the radical social changes wrought by industrialization and urbanization, meant a complete change in the power structure of British society. Anxieties about the distribution of power were at their most intense in the 1830s and 1840s; the aggressively working-class Chartist movement (1837–48) triggered panic among some of the middle and upper classes about whether democracy had gone too far too soon (John, *Cult Criminals*, ix).

---

[4]   The 'extraordinary and romantic' circumstances refer to the fact that the victim's stepmother dreamt that Maria had been murdered and buried in the Red Barn, thus leading to the discovery of the body.

John's argument certainly seems to be supported by contemporary criticism of Newgate fiction. The *Athenaeum* review of William Harrison Ainsworth's *Jack Sheppard* (a 'bad book') argued that 'the demand for books having descended to the masses', inferior literature was now 'not merely tolerable, but acceptable' (26 October 1839, 804). The *Spectator*'s review of *Oliver Twist*, whilst not suggesting that 'all that is vulgar and low' should be banished from fiction, argued that 'such materials should never be made the staple of a long story; because our sympathies can only occasionally be excited for the actors, and therefore, though the higher will always yield moral instruction to the lower, the lower will more rarely yield it to the higher' (24 November 1838, 1115).

Concerns that, on the face of it, seem to be about the morally ambiguous content of the works, and their perceived glamorization of crime, are really about class and power and an increasingly literate population. A review of Bulwer Lytton's *Lucretia* (1847) in the *Morning Herald* lamented that

> the great body of the people are too apt to sympathise with criminals ... Those readers of 'Paul Clifford' and 'Jack Sheppard,' who carried off the bricks of the wall at Belsize Park last year, as mementos, are too numerous a class to teach by such inadequate examples of punishment as are given in this book, and far too likely to admire what the author desires to make odious (1 January 1847, 6).

The emergence of Newgate fiction also concurred with reforms of the criminal system, most notably a sharp reduction in the number of crimes warranting the death penalty. As a consequence of these reforms, the criminal came to be seen less as an aberration to be removed from human society and more as an individual needing to be accommodated within that society, albeit at one remove. Such a shift in understanding foreshadows later developments in psychology, most notably Henry Maudsley's concept of the 'borderlands', discussed in Chapter 5. Newgate fiction 'found interest in the criminal himself', focusing in particular on the relation between the criminal and their social environment (Hollingsworth, 15). In this sense, the fiction was ahead of contemporary newspapers and street literature, which was still working very much within a morally polarized universe where the criminal was instantly identifiable as 'bad', and where an interest in (and understanding of) the criminal *per se* did not really surface with any consistency of approach until the 1870s, with the burgeoning discipline of psychology.

By taking the criminal as the focus of attention, and endowing him or her with more human qualities than might be found in contemporary newspaper coverage of such crimes, the Newgate novelists were deemed guilty at the time of what Pykett has termed 'mixed motives and mixed morality' ('The Newgate Novel', 30). Critics of such work, according to Pykett, preferred the security of a more morally polarized universe where good and evil were instantly recognizable: in short, the universe of melodrama. This concurs with newspaper and street literature coverage of criminal activity, which was at pains to stress moral certainty and polarization, and also with the ideology of melodrama, a dominant cultural mode at the time of the Newgate debate. But the huge popularity of Newgate fiction would seem to suggest a public receptive to a greater ambiguity in representations of crime, a shift in popular thinking in advance of that being propagated on the stage and through the press. The ambiguity that characterizes the Newgate novel also characterizes sensation fiction. These shared preoccupations and approaches might help to explain the controversy surrounding sensation fiction. Rather than something new, the sensation novel may have been viewed as a continuation and perhaps disturbing refinement of what had gone before.

In addition to regarding the Newgate debate as the product of a very particular set of social and historical conditions, John and Pykett also suggest that the debate is about the nature of the novel itself, what the novel can or cannot represent, and attendant issues of readership and class. Pykett argues that

> the Newgate debate was also a debate about hierarchies, both social and literary. It was about keeping the different classes of society separate both in fiction and as readers of fiction. One of the objections to the Newgate novel was that it imported the literature of the streets (popular ballads and broadsheet gallows confessions) to the drawing room, and it is worth noting that the intensification of the Newgate controversy in the 1840s coincided with the extraordinary success of cheap publications such as G. W. M. Reynolds's long-running novel series *The Mysteries of London*, which combined romanticized criminals and a carnivalized low life with contemporary political debates and radical sentiment ('The Newgate Novel', 32).

Pykett's analysis pinpoints an incongruity between perception and material reality. The middle-class audience of the 1840s chose to believe that the Newgate novel was importing street literature into their homes, and yet the extent of the *Times* coverage clearly shows a middle-class audience for crime, even if the style is more restrained. What the Newgate debate did was make a middle-class audience's appetite for such material more visible, but the appetite had clearly existed for some time. Juliet John questions whether this absorption of street literature was

> a pattern of appropriation whereby oral narratives are eventually incorporated – via 'street literature' and *The Newgate Calendar* – into the bourgeois Victorian novel, or a process by which street culture forces itself, radically and subversively, into the Victorian drawing-room (*Dickens's Villains*, 128).

The pervasiveness of crime coverage in the 'respectable' press would seem to point towards a 'pattern of appropriation', and one which made it inevitable that there would be a middle-class audience for such fiction and, by extension, the sensation novel.

Concerns regarding the 'importing' of street literature into the drawing room are also linked to who the key players were in the Newgate debate. Bulwer Lytton, Dickens and Thackeray all had 'literary clout' (Pykett, 'The Newgate Novel', 20); even though Dickens and Thackeray sought to distance their own work from the accusations levelled at the Newgate novel, their involvement in the debate gave it a degree of respectability and seriousness that occasioned much alarm.

Dickens and the Newgate School

Dickens never intended for *Oliver Twist* to be apprehended by its readers as a Newgate novel, and it was Thackeray who first drew explicit parallels between the novel and the Newgate school, in his articles 'Horae Catnachianae' and 'Going to See a Man Hanged'. The first of these articles, 'Horae Catnachianae', is ostensibly an examination of street ballads purchased from James Catnach of Seven Dials (the most successful and notorious producer and retailer of street ballads), but the analysis is prefaced by a lengthy and explicit attack on the Newgate novel. Thackeray's main criticism of such works lies in their lack of realism when depicting the seediness and inhumanity of the criminal life: 'Bulwer's ingenious inconsistencies, and Dickens's startling, pleasing, unnatural caricatures … are perfectly absurd and unreal' (407). In the famous piece the following year 'Going to See a Man Hanged', Thackeray returns to this issue of realism. Describing a girl in the crowd who 'might have been taken as a study for Nancy', he confesses himself curious to look at her and her friend

> having, in late fashionable novels, read many accounts of such personages. Bah! what figments these novelists tell us! Boz, who knows life well, knows that his Miss Nancy is the most unreal fantastical personage possible; no more like a thief's mistress, than one of Gessner's shepherdesses resembles a real country wench. He dare not tell the truth concerning such young ladies. They have, no doubt, virtues like other human creatures; nay, their position engenders virtues that are called into exercise among other women. But on these an honest painter of human natures has no right to dwell; not being able to paint the whole portrait, he has no right to present one or two favourable points as characterising the whole; and therefore, in fact, had better leave the picture alone altogether (154–5).

Thackeray's attack on the realism of *Oliver Twist* was not shared by other contemporary reviewers, and may partly be explained by his rivalry with Dickens. With the exception of the *Spectator* review examined below, reviews of Sikes's murder of Nancy and its aftermath were unanimously positive, and both the *Quarterly Review* and the *Examiner* praised the novel for its veracity. The *Quarterly Review* commented that

> though dealing with the dregs of society, he is never indelicate, indecent, nor irreligious; he never approves nor countenances the gross, the immoral, or offensive: he but holds these vices up in a pillory, as a warning of the disgrace of criminal excess (June 1839, 90).

The *National Magazine and Monthly Critic* felt that 'although he takes us into scenes of the lowest description … there is not a single coarse word, or one allusion that could call a blush into the cheek of the most fastidious' (1837, 447–8). The *Athenaeum* found that 'in tracing what is most loathsome and repulsive, he contrives to enlist the best feelings of our nature in his cause, and to engage his readers in a consideration of what lies below the surface' (26 October 1839, 804). The *Era* felt that Dickens did demand the reader's sympathy for the crime but thereby charged 'the purest among us as a *particeps criminis*, and a partaker in the original sin of humanity' (18 November 1838, 92). The *Examiner*, in a lengthy review of the closing scenes of the third volume, questioned whether any advantage could be gained from

> scenes which represent humanity in its most debased and disgusting forms? The question has often been asked, and will always be repeated by those who confound the subjects of vulgar life with the treatment of the vulgar artist; but he who seeks an unanswerable refutation to what it implies will find it in *Oliver Twist* ... Few writers have achieved a nobler moral than that which is embodied here – not simply the scorn of vice but the 'pity of it' too – and none with so little of distortion in the means, or of compromise at the end. Vice loses nothing of its grossness, and virtue nothing of her triumph ... Everything in short is as we see it in life, and the retribution or repentance – the one too late, the other perhaps even too terrible – what we see there also (18 November 1838, 723).

Amongst the complimentary reviews *Oliver Twist* inspired, the *Spectator* was alone in feeling the novel lacked 'a general moral lesson': although 'all the guilty die' (and the reviewer included Nancy as one of the 'guilty' in contrast to the *Quarterly Review*, which regarded her as a 'heroine') they die not as the direct consequence of their crime, but because they are caught up in the fortunes of Oliver and Monks (24 November 1838, 1114).

Whatever Dickens's intentions, it is hardly surprising that the novel was treated as part of the Newgate school: both *Oliver Twist* and Ainsworth's *Jack Sheppard* (a notorious Newgate novel based on the life of the eighteenth-century criminal of the same name) were published in *Bentley's Miscellany* and for four months both novels appeared in the same volume, thus becoming linked in the minds of at least one set of readers. In addition, both novels were illustrated by George Cruikshank, and both novels featured boys associating with criminals. As Keith Hollingsworth observes, 'the connections were superficial, but the timing accentuated them' (131).

So widespread was this misrepresentation, in Dickens's eyes, of his original intention, that he sought to make his aims explicit in the Preface to the third edition, published in 1841. He argues that none of these Newgate fictions present 'the miserable reality' of criminals, and that, to show such associates in crime 'in all their deformity, in all their wretchedness, in all the squalid poverty of their lives ... would be to attempt a something which was greatly needed, and which would be a service to society'. Very much as Bulwer Lytton was to do five years later with *Lucretia*, Dickens argues that the 'very dregs of life' can serve a moral purpose, provided that the 'unattractive and repulsive truth' of their criminal existence is made clear (xxxvii–xxxix).[5] The content of contemporary reviews,

---

5   Edward Bulwer Lytton's *Lucretia: or, The Children of the Night* was first published in 1846. Partly conforming to the trend of Newgate fiction, Bulwer draws one of his characters

with the exception of the *Spectator*, would suggest that Dickens succeeded in his aim, certainly as far as the character of Sikes was concerned.

'A ferocious, consummate villain': Sikes and the Disruption of the Domestic Sphere

Dickens's intention in *Oliver Twist* was to show the hideous reality of criminal life, made manifest largely through the characters of Fagin and Sikes. What is striking about Dickens's portrayal of Sikes is that he is more inhuman before the murder than after it. Initially mirroring the portrayal of murderers in contemporary newspapers and street literature, there is little effort on Dickens's part to endow Sikes with any redeeming qualities until he actually commits the murder. It is as if Sikes is condemned in advance of the crime, and is portrayed as a 'monster' even before he kills Nancy; paradoxically, once he has committed the deed that would render him inhuman in the eyes of contemporary society and within the world of the novel, he becomes more humanized.

Up until the murder, Sikes is presented to us as 'utterly and irredeemably bad' (xl), more of an animal than a man. His speech is most frequently a growl, he moves and speaks swiftly with no apparent thought, and physical violence is the natural and frequent outlet for his anger. His actions seem beyond his own control, particularly just before the murder, where Fagin 'winds him up' and sends him off to commit the crime. As if to dehumanize him further, Dickens frequently refers to Sikes simply as the perpetrator of his crimes – 'the robber', 'the housebreaker', and later 'the murderer' – as if he were merely the sum of his wrongdoings. After the murder, as Toby, Kags and Chitling discuss the recent events, 'none of them called the murderer by his old name' (369), simply referring to him as 'he'. Dickens's reference to it as his 'old name' suggests Sikes has forfeited any right to it by his crime. Contemporary reviews shared this view of Sikes, with the *Quarterly Review* regarding him as 'a ferocious, consummate villain' (June 1839, 97). Prior to the murder, his behaviour and demeanour concord entirely with what a contemporary readership would expect of a murderer.

Provoked by Fagin's skilful manipulation of him, Sikes hurries home with his mind fixed on one purpose, much as he has operated for the earlier part of the novel. He darts 'wildly and furiously' (346), although he exhibits sufficient presence of mind to open the door 'softly', to stride 'lightly' up the stairs, and to double-lock the door (347); similarly, he is circumspect enough at the point of the murder to realize he will get caught immediately if he fires his pistol. It is only after the murder that his single-mindedness collapses into a plurality and confusion of purpose. The descriptions of Sikes just prior to the murder are bestial:

---

from the pages of the *Newgate Calendar*: Gabriel Varney is based on Thomas Griffiths Wainewright, a notorious forger and poisoner. Juliet John, in her introduction to *Cult Criminals*, suggests that Lucretia Clavering may have been a composite of Wainewright's wife and Lucrezia Borgia.

he progresses 'with savage resolution: his teeth so tightly compressed that the strained jaw seemed starting through his skin'. He sits and regards Nancy for a few seconds 'with dilated nostrils and heaving breast' (347); there is an emphasis on his involuntary physical responses which further dehumanizes him. This dehumanizing of Sikes at various points is perhaps one means whereby Dickens attempted to make this murder bearable, much as contemporary news coverage would emphasize any apparently demonic aspect of the accused, and highlight the supposedly unique nature of the crime. It is the details of this scene that make it so memorable; not so much the melodramatic gesture of Nancy raising Rose Maylie's white handkerchief up to Heaven and praying for mercy (an action which places her firmly, and finally, as the heroine of this piece), but more that she raises herself 'with difficulty, on her knees' (348).

Such details echo the coverage of similar crimes in *The Newgate Calendar*. The case of John Chappel, executed in 1731 for the murder of his pregnant lover Sarah Mann, in some ways foreshadows Sikes's murder of Nancy not merely in the attention to what seem almost inconsequential details, but also in the pathetic depiction of Mann, as she pleads for her life:

> At last his resentment became so great that he knocked her down with a large oaken stick he had in his hand, and continued to beat her in a most cruel and barbarous manner. She endeavoured, although to no purpose, to make some defence, but when she found he was too strong for her, she cried O! John, John, have mercy; O! John, John, have mercy, save my life. But he resolved to make an end of her, and therefore kept beating her till she was almost dead. When he was tired of beating her he threw down the stick, and pulled out a pen-knife, and one of those used for opening oysters, with both of which he stabbed her in several places, and left one of them sticking in her skull (NC 1773, ii, 332).

Mann's cry of 'O! John, John, have mercy' is theatrical and melodramatic in tone, but the domestic particularity of the knife being used for opening oysters, and the fact that Chappel pauses in his crime to select a less physically taxing weapon, brings home the full horror of the murder.

A review in the *Quarterly Review* commented on just such levels of detail in Dickens's work:

> The nearer we approach to the corpse, the more appalling is death. The circumstantiality of the murder of Nancy is more harrowing than the bulletin of 50,000 men killed at Borodino. Bloodshed in midday comes home to our peaceful threshold, it shocks the order of things; it occurs amid life (June 1839, 91).[6]

---

[6]   The Battle of Borodino was fought on 7 September 1812, during the Napoleonic wars. The journalist for the *Quarterly Review* underestimates the numbers killed in the conflict; there were at least 70,000 casualties.

It is the domestic nature of this murder that so appalls both the reviewer and the reader, the fact that it 'comes home to our peaceful threshold' is what causes such distress. The argument that this 'home' is the centre of existence ('amid life') and has come to represent some sort of natural order, and the attendant implication that Borodino is both physically and culturally at a distance, emphasizes the centrality of the domestic space to Victorian ideas of nationhood. Tens of thousands of casualties in Russia matter less than the murder of one woman living on our 'threshold'.

Lest we forget the nature of this particular crime, Nancy is placed firmly within the domestic setting, lying 'half dressed' on the bed when Sikes enters the room. The intimate recognition of her cry '"It *is* you, Bill!" ... with an expression of pleasure at his return' (347) reminds us again of the nature of their union, as does the intimacy of Nancy's face almost touching Sikes's, a detail which forms a gruesome counterpoint to the violence that he rains down on her, and the physicality of his actions.

Hollingsworth argues that the murder of Nancy is 'forced. Nancy has been portrayed as deeply attached and Sikes as violent by nature, but there has been nothing to show that his feeling for her could be attended by murderous passion at a supposed betrayal' (124). I disagree; Nancy has provided the only thing resembling a domestic setting for Sikes and she is the only one who genuinely cares for him. Her perceived betrayal is a betrayal of this domestic relationship. Sikes's decision to kill her shows that, even for such a hardened villain as he is, the supremacy of the domestic still holds true, and Nancy's violation of it means she has to die. This explains why it is Nancy's eyes that haunt Sikes after the murder because, as Juliet John argues, 'the eyes of Nancy, for Sikes, are both a reminder of his destruction of a human life, and a reminder that Nancy was the only human being who cherished any humane feelings towards him' (John, *Dickens's Villains*, 116).

Viewing this as a domestic murder, rather than simply the betrayal of one criminal by another, explains the revulsion of Sikes's criminal cohort as well as their rejection of him; it likewise explains his own torment in the aftermath of the murder. Dickens firmly embraces the dominant cultural mores that regarded domestic murder as the ultimate crime. Lest we be unsure of this, the narrator reminds us on numerous occasions. In an explicitly moralistic opening to the chapter 'The Flight of Sikes', he tells us that 'of all bad deeds that, under cover of the darkness, had been committed within wide London's bounds since night hung over it, that was the worst' (348). There are echoes here of contemporary newspapers and broadsides, but Dickens is making the point that this is 'the worst' of 'bad deeds' precisely because of its domestic nature.

After the murder has been committed, Dickens twice echoes the aftermath of the murder of Duncan in *Macbeth*, to emphasize again the particularly heinous nature of this crime ('such flesh, and so much blood'; 'there were spots that would not be removed' [349]). Just as the regicide committed in *Macbeth* is of sufficient gravity to upset the natural order of the universe, so does the murder of one's lover upset the natural order of the criminal universe that Sikes inhabits. Such a view dominates the newspaper and street literature coverage of domestic murder: in the case of Sarah Westwood (found guilty of poisoning her husband in 1843), the judge's belief that he could 'scarcely conceive a crime of greater enormity or one of a deeper dye' was by no means unique (*Times*, 30 December 1843, 7). Whilst the judge's horror in the Westwood case may have been partly triggered by the fact that Westwood was a woman, Dickens is making the point that domestic murder is an abhorrent crime, regardless of the sex of the perpetrator.

Within Sikes's world, the murder weakens him to the extent that Charley Bates addresses him directly as a 'monster' (371). Bates's moral judgement of Sikes accords with contemporary views of the domestic murderer as inhuman or even demonic: William Corder's murder of Maria Marten in 1827, and John Connor's murder of Ann Tape in 1845, led to them being described as, respectively, a 'monster' in the *Times* (1 May 1828, 3) and a 'foul monster' in one broadside ('Full particulars').

Bates's judgement also demonstrates that Sikes has lost his power over the boys. Prior to the murder, they would none of them have dared address him thus. Nancy's murder has united this disparate community, if only so far as to eject Sikes:

> The terrible events of the last two days had made a deep impression on all three, increased by the danger and uncertainty of their own position. They drew their chairs closer together, starting at every sound (369).

Not merely physically, by the act of drawing their chairs together, but also psychologically, in their ability to stand up to Sikes, the boys have created a community. John Bayley, in his article 'Oliver Twist: "Things as they really are"', sees the murder as 'a great uniter' (59), and this is very much how stories from *The Newgate Calendar* operated, with individuals uniting to expel the miscreant from their community. In the case of John Chappel mentioned earlier in this chapter, we are informed that 'the clamors of the people as is common in such cases, was very great against him' (NC 1773, 2:332). Sikes is sufficiently aware of this to try to propitiate Charley, attempting to shake hands with him, uttering the supplication: 'Charley … don't you – don't you know me?' (371), and being the first to look away when he and Charley attempt to stare each other out. Sikes's act has provided a kind of negatively defined moral standard for the boys: they may be criminals, but domestic murder is a depth to which they will not sink.

Whilst Sikes is attempting to win the boys over, the crowd which gathers on Jacob's Island becomes increasingly demonic as it strives impatiently to secure the murderer. The extremity of the crowd's response is crucial here. At one point Dickens informs us that 'it seemed as though the whole city had poured its population out to curse him' (373). The entire community, and beyond, is united in its condemnation of Sikes, again emphasizing the threat posed to such a community, to any community, by domestic murder.

Nancy's Murder and the Influence of Street Literature

For the description of the murder and its aftermath Dickens deploys a range of textual modes: journalism, melodrama and psychological realism, much as Thackeray attempts in *Catherine*. However, where Thackeray deliberately draws attention to these rhetorical strategies, Dickens weaves them together seamlessly, selecting pertinent details to further his aesthetic and moral aims.

For the details of the murder Dickens adopts the conventions of newspapers and street literature. The reader is offered what seem at first surprisingly visceral details, such as 'the pool of gore', the fact that Sikes 'struck and struck again', the hair on the end of the club, and the detail that 'the very feet of the dog were bloody' (349). Dickens stresses the visceral nature of murder as part of his desire to show the reality of crime in all its horror, but he is clearly working here within the contemporary journalistic mode, which was surprisingly detailed and matter of fact in its delivery of the physically gruesome elements of murder cases (see Chapter 1, p. 21 for details). Dickens's lack of euphemism and ambivalence is not so surprising within this context, and a contemporary readership would be well used to such details from their exposure to both newspaper and street literature coverage of murders.

By the same token, Dickens's direct moralizing and his insistence that Sikes will suffer for his crime echo the ideology of newspapers and street literature which was at pains to stress that murder would always be detected, and the murderer would always suffer: 'Let no man talk of murderers escaping justice, and hint that Providence must sleep. There were twenty score of violent deaths in one long minute of that agony of fear' (353).

After the murder Nancy takes on the role of Gothic avenger, a 'ghastly figure following at his heels', 'its garments rustling in the leaves, and every breath of wind came laden with that last low cry' (353). Dickens is here employing a gothic melodramatic trope – the ghost of the wronged one often haunts the wrongdoer – but he is also drawing on the imagery of murder and execution broadsides. The murder of Anne Barnham by Robert Cooper affords striking similarities. Although Barnham's murder took place in 1862, given the formulaic nature of broadside verses, it is more than likely that earlier cases would have featured similar text. Cooper killed Barnham for her infidelity (which could also be said of Sikes and Nancy), and the following is one of seven verses allegedly written by Cooper:

> When I had killed my own dear Annie,
> From the fatal spot I stayed away,
> And her innocent spirit haunted me
> From that time by night and day;
> I was both wretched and distracted,
> I wander'd through the world forlorn
> Justice closely did pursue me,
> And I must die a death of scorn (Untitled Broadside dated 17 November 1862).

The haunting by Barnham's 'innocent spirit' forms sufficiently strong echoes with Nancy's to suggest that Dickens may have drawn inspiration from such publications.

Whilst this connection is difficult to prove, there is a far greater degree of certainty that Dickens had read, and must surely have been influenced by William Hone's 1815 publication *The Power of Conscience Exemplified in the Genuine and Extraordinary Confession of Thomas Bedworth*. This slender volume recounts the story of Thomas Bedworth, who murdered his partner Elizabeth Beesmore in 1815. After the murder, Bedworth flees the house, first to Spa-fields, from whence he returns to London, and then on to St. Albans. He starts to hear Beesmore's voice saying, among other things 'Oh Bedworth! Bedworth! what have you done?' (10). She then appears to him on several occasions, as he roams in and out of London:

> *She walked with him, side by side*, until they reached the other side of the hill, and then *taking the hand of the miserable man, placed it upon her severed throat*, and groaned and mourned deeply! – Driven to despair, he fled into a *field*, where he threw himself down upon his face on some hay, hoping to elude at least the sight of his ghostly pursuer. Such, however, was the consequence of guilt, that *he felt her lying by his side* and crouching against him! (11).

Tormented by his guilt, Bedworth eventually gives himself up. The parallels between this text and the aftermath of Nancy's murder are sufficiently striking to suggest that Dickens must have had this text in mind (albeit perhaps unconsciously) when writing these scenes.

Sikes, Nancy and Melodrama

Elizabeth Beesmore and Nancy are both cast as Gothic avengers after their deaths, a familiar figure to a Victorian audience conversant with the conventions of melodrama. The influence of melodrama is apparent everywhere throughout the final section of *Oliver Twist*, to the extent that the details of the action even read like a set of stage directions on occasion, with the exaggerated gestures redolent of the melodramatic villain:

> The robber sat regarding her, for a few seconds, with dilated nostrils and heaving breast; and then, grasping her by the head and throat, dragged her into the middle of the room, and looking once towards the door, placed his heavy hand upon her mouth (347).

Where contemporary reviews mentioned Nancy at all, they were generally convinced by her portrayal. The *Examiner* praised the novel as a whole for its veracity, and singled out the portrayal of Nancy for special mention:

> That startling, nobly wrought, and impassioned picture of Sikes's mistress – of whose mixture of actual and great virtue with her vice we are more certain than we feel we could predicate of the more dispassionate considerateness of soft Rose Maylie under the like circumstances (18 November 1838, 740).

Fraser's was alone in finding the transformation of Nancy a little difficult to take:

> She talks the common slang of London, in its ordinary dialect, in the beginning
> of the novel; at the end no heroine that ever went mad in white satin talked
> more picked and perfumed sentences of sentimentality ('Charles Dickens and
> His Works', 395).

Assuming this review to have been written by Thackeray, or at least endorsed
by him as editor of *Fraser's*, and bearing in mind his rivalry with Dickens, this
criticism of Nancy is carried through to 'Going to See a Man Hanged' where
Thackeray disparages Dickens for creating a 'most unreal fantastical personage'
(154).

Undoubtedly, Nancy's vocabulary and manner of speaking undergo a startling
transformation in the course of the novel. As she pleads for her life, her diction
resembles Rose Maylie's:

> Let me see them again, and beg them, on my knees, to show the same mercy
> and goodness to you; and let us both leave this dreadful place, and far apart lead
> better lives, and forget how we have lived, except in prayers, and never see each
> other more. It is never too late to repent. They told me so – I feel it now – but we
> must have time – a little, little time! (348)

Not only does Nancy's speech here call Rose Maylie to mind, she also specifically
refers to those members of the middle class who have occasioned Sikes's
downfall. The reference to 'they told me so' may provide the final trigger for
Sikes, as he sees Nancy's betrayal not just of himself, but also of his whole class.
His striking her with a 'heavy club' (348) emphasizes the primitive and brutal
nature of the crime, in contrast to the refined rhetoric of Nancy's final words, and
the final melodramatic tableau of her raising Rose Maylie's white handkerchief
up to Heaven and praying for mercy. Nancy's more educated manner of speech is
perhaps the means whereby Dickens is able to distance her more clearly from Sikes
(in speech now, as well as in behaviour), and thereby form a clearer dichotomy
between murderer and victim. But there is something more interesting at work
here. It is almost as if Dickens is suggesting that the domestic heroine/victim and,
by extension, the idealized domestic space must of necessity be middle-class; and
the working-class 'animal' that is Sikes is the violator of such a space.

There was certainly no need for Dickens to elevate Nancy closer to the middle
classes to make her a more instantly recognizable 'heroine'. There were sufficient
numbers of working-class melodramatic heroines on the Victorian stage, and
contemporary murder and execution broadsides offered examples of the murder of
prostitutes where, simply by virtue of the crime, the victim became transformed
into the heroine of the piece. The account of the murder of Ann Tape by John
Connor, in a broadside from 1845, although published seven years after the
publication of *Oliver Twist*, is representative of such publications, which were
extremely formulaic in their content and moral tone. The broadside detailing the

apprehension of Connor for the murder refers to the victim as 'poor Ann Tape', and Connor as a 'monster' and later as 'some dreadful fiend' ('Apprehension of John Connor'). With such material clearly influencing Dickens, one wonders why he felt the need to change Nancy to such an extent. Perhaps his transformation of her into a more uncomplicated, but more middle-class melodramatic heroine can be best explained by his equating the idealized domestic space with the middle classes, and the attendant desire to appeal in particular to this readership. The punishment of Sikes could then be read in the light of the middle classes asserting the supremacy of the domestic space in the face of any perceived threat posed by the working class.

While Nancy may evolve into the heroine of melodrama, Sikes is something considerably more than simply the villain – we need only look at how his character is handled by a lesser novelist to see exactly what Dickens is doing. *Oliver Twiss*, a blatant piece of plagiarism published in 1839 under the pseudonym 'Bos' transforms Sikes and Nancy into Jem Blount and Poll Smiggins.[7] Blount is cast firmly in the mould of a stage villain, whose exaggerated gestures could be lifted straight from an actor's manual: he stamps his foot, gnashes his teeth, his heart is 'filled with fiendish thoughts', and his 'assassin's eyes' glare with 'demoniac fury' as he laughs 'a wild laugh of hellish triumph' (451, 574). His vocabulary is similarly theatrical; when Lilian (Rose Maylie's counterpart) implores him not to harm Oliver, Blunt responds: 'Psha! I know not such a feeling as pity … my life has been given up to crime, and with a heart hardened as mine is, pity is an utter stranger' (572–3). 'Bos' also has Blount articulate his feelings much more clearly, but strangely enough this fails to humanize Blount, perhaps because 'Bos' is working solely within a melodramatic mode. When explaining his feelings, and how they led up to the murder, Blount tells Lilian and Oliver:

> I watched her narrowly and found that to save him she would sacrifice the life of the man she professed to regard; this roused my fiercest anger – a demon seemed to rage within my soul – and then I resolved to visit her with the heaviest punishment man can inflict upon his fellow. I was mad! – thoughts of blood constantly rose to my mind (572).

Whilst there are clearly elements of the melodramatic villain in Sikes, not least his unmitigated villainy, he is not fully embedded in the conventions of melodrama. Dickens rarely offers us direct access to Sikes's thoughts, and Sikes rarely articulates his villainy in the way we would expect of a melodramatic villain. By the same token, Sikes doesn't actually propel the action after the murder and, even leading up to the event, it could easily be argued that he is simply Fagin's tool.

---

[7]   Bos, *The Life and Adventures of Oliver Twiss, the Workhouse Boy* (London: E. Lloyd for J. Graves, 1839). The British Library catalogue entry suggests the work may have been written by Thomas Peckett Prest. An earlier version of *Oliver Twiss*, of which the British Library only holds the first four numbers, is edited by the pseudonymous 'Poz', suggested by the British Library to be Gilbert Abbott à Beckett.

The aftermath of the murder shows an immediate and striking change in Sikes, a change which is occasioned by the domestic nature of the crime; the violation of the domestic space cannot leave the perpetrator untouched or untroubled. Sikes, a creature of impulse and action, has not moved since the murder, too afraid to stir. This is the first time he has ever exhibited fear or any capacity for imagination; his ability to visualize Nancy's eyes moving under the rug is a new development for him. Literary critic Juliet John in her work *Dickens's Villains* argues that, for Dickens, the concept of psychology was synonymous with deviance because it privileged the individual over society. If Dickens was working within the melodramatic mode (as John suggests), whose ideology stresses the importance of transparency, then any character possessing an 'inner life' is a villain, because they are hiding their real face from the world. Such an argument could be extended beyond the world of melodrama. With a healthy domestic sphere being seen as a vital constituent of the nation's health and success, anyone who used this space to conceal their real self was of particular concern. Certainly, as the century progressed, the potential for the home to conceal deviant behaviour, and the consequent calls for some surveillance of the home, gained ground.

After the murder, we are offered what feels like some form of access to Sikes's psyche, because, following John's argument, he is now firmly cast in the role of villain and can therefore, to an extent, possess on 'inner life'. Under the conventions of the realist novel, 'getting under the skin' of a character almost invariably renders them more sympathetic; but this is not the case with Sikes because, at this point in the century, we cannot be afforded the potential to sympathize with a domestic murderer.

Sikes regains some of his old resolve when he leaves the house, walking away 'rapidly' and striding up the hill at Highgate, but then he becomes 'unsteady of purpose, and uncertain where to go' (349). Having destroyed his domestic space, Sikes now lacks a refuge and his crime has effectively expelled him from all community. He wanders aimlessly for some time, then resolves to go to Hendon for food and drink. When he gets to Hendon, he discovers he has developed both a conscience, and an awareness of himself as a separate being: 'all the people he met – the very children at the doors – seemed to view him with suspicion' (350). He can now see himself as separate because the murder of Nancy has placed him outside of any human community.

Vincent Newey argues that this 'meandering' pattern after the murder is a manifestation of Dickens's struggle to 'find a way forward in the troubled aftermath of wrongdoing.' For Newey, Dickens's crime 'has been to indulge a genius of low writing, dealing out the gross stimulants of a populist genre' (96). Newey's analysis suggests a lack of control and intention on Dickens's part, but one need only compare Dickens's handling of the murder with similar examples in fiction and journalism to understand that he readily transcends the 'gross stimulants of a populist genre', and merits Chesterton's comment on 'this strange, sublime, vulgar melodrama, which is melodrama and yet is painfully real' ('Oliver Twist', 1911, qtd. in John, *Charles Dickens's Oliver Twist*, 64).

What is important about Sikes at this stage in the novel is to ask if his suffering accords with his earlier amoral character, and to question why he has to suffer to this extent. His sensitivity to the spectre of Nancy suggests a level of interiority and imagination he shows no evidence of possessing before the murder, and which we suspect he would not possess if the victim had been anyone other than Nancy, and that is, of course, the whole point. It is the domestic nature of this crime that renders Sikes's suffering both credible and essential. If he were to kill Nancy, and remain relatively untroubled by the act, then the domestic sphere could be deemed as lacking in power; for the ultimate violation that the act of murder constitutes, Sikes must be seen to suffer.

Much has been made of the 'humanizing' of Sikes after the murder, and there is undoubtedly some transformation of his character; Dickens shows us that Sikes has a conscience and some inner existence, which are distinguishing marks of humanity. But some critics, such as Newey and Rodensky, have gone so far as to suggest that this makes Sikes a likeable or sympathetic character. Rodensky suggests that 'the lynching complicates our attitude toward Sikes, who suddenly at the moment of punishment appears more victim than villain' (36) and Newey argues that 'we are glad the dog escapes … But Sikes too is a hunted creature. A part of us doesn't want him to be caught either' (98). The change in Sikes after the murder does undoubtedly complicate our response to him, as twenty-first-century readers. If Dickens's intention is to show the full horrific consequences of murder, he can only do this by showing Sikes's inner distress, what Humphry House declared his 'confused and pitiable humanity' ('The Macabre Dickens', 1847, qtd. in John, *Charles Dickens's Oliver Twist*, 66). A modern reader, well versed in a psychological reading of fiction, will almost inevitably argue that this leads to greater empathy with the character. But a reader of 1838 would have been less likely to experience such ambivalence. Sikes's suffering, for a contemporary readership, would simply have accorded with the melodramatic mode, where all emotion must be made manifest, and with the tropes of street literature, where the suffering of the murderer is always articulated and made much of. By the same token, returning to Juliet John's argument, the manifestation of some form of individual psyche might also have been treated by a contemporary audience as evidence of Sikes's villainy; it is not until the closing decades of the nineteenth century that such an approach would be more likely to engender sympathy in the readership. We are struck by Sikes's behaviour after the murder because it seems so out of character, and we are also afforded an intimacy with one individual, which we have not been offered elsewhere in the novel, but it is going too far to suggest that a Victorian readership would, at this point, have found Sikes likeable or sympathetic. He has committed a violent and unprovoked domestic murder, and Dickens is in no way inviting us to 'understand' Sikes.

In his portrayal of Sikes's remorse Dickens is working firmly within the mode of street literature, showing the consequence of a crime of this gravity by outwardly manifesting the agonies of guilt. But this psychology of terror and remorse is more marked in Dickens than in contemporary broadsides or editions of *The Newgate Calendar*. The remorse expressed in these publications is, to a degree, formulaic. Stock phrases occur repeatedly within a conventional patter of crime and repentance: for example, Billings (accomplice to the murder of John Hayes in 1726) declares that 'had he a thousand lives, he would have laid them all down, as no punishment could be too great for such a wretch' (NC 1773, 2:207). What Dickens offers us (and, of course, has the luxury of offering us within the more generous framework of a novel) in the character of Sikes is a transitional figure. Prior to the murder Dickens is working with the conventions of the melodramatic villain, after it he is working with the conventions of street literature, but he is also making tentative steps towards the more fully psychologized characters he creates in Bradley Headstone (*Our Mutual Friend*) and John Jasper (*The Mystery of Edwin Drood*), both of whom are discussed in Chapter 4. A contemporary audience would have been resistant to the concept of a fully psychologized Sikes with the attendant possibility of sympathizing with the man (it is debatable that a contemporary audience would even have grasped the concept of a 'fully psychologized' Sikes at this point). This, after all, was the charge levelled at the Newgate novel, a charge Dickens was at pains to refute for his own work of fiction. By 1870 (the date of publication of *The Mystery of Edwin Drood*) murder trials were increasingly employing psychological state as a means of defence, so the greater interiority afforded to the likes of Bradley Headstone and John Jasper would have sat more easily with Dickens's readership. These later decades of the nineteenth century also witnessed a decline in the idealization of the domestic sphere. Whilst it would be difficult to conceive of a late-Victorian readership finding anything particularly 'likeable' in Sikes as he is presented in *Oliver Twist*, there is certainly the potential to consider how his crime might have been presented had Dickens written the novel nearer the end of his life, where the 'home' was increasingly viewed as the site of potentially aberrant behaviour, and the source of discontent and restraint for both men and women. It is because Sikes commits a *domestic* murder that he is painted in such villainous colours for the readership of 1838.

Thackeray's *Catherine*: the Domestic Murderer 'as (s)he really is'

Thackeray's *Catherine: A Story* was serialized in *Fraser's Magazine* from May 1839 to February 1840, but was not published in novel form until 1869, in the posthumous collected works. At the time of serial publication, it invited brief, rather lukewarm comment in the *Morning Post*, the *Observer*, the *Court Journal*, the *Sunday Times*, the *Spectator* and the *Sun*.[8] The *Morning Post* commented on the 'strain of graphic and sarcastic drollery', and 'unabated spirit'; the *Observer* found it 'a very interesting and well-told tale'; for the *Sun* it was a 'clever tale, of the quizzical order', with 'easy and natural' dialogue, but too long and 'wanting in general interest'. The *Sunday Times* found the conclusion of the novel 'low, as usual'.

---

[8]   The reviews of *Catherine* which follow are listed in the edition of the novel edited by Sheldon F. Goldfarb, 253–4.

The novel was written as a clear and direct attack on the Newgate school, Thackeray's criticism of which had been made explicit in the pages of *Fraser's* for some time, and which is discussed earlier in this chapter. Thackeray's main criticism of the Newgate school was the lack of realism in depicting the criminal underworld; for him, artistic veracity demanded either the whole picture or nothing at all, no matter how unpleasant that might be in the telling. Having declared himself 'almost sick' (30) of his characters as early as chapter 3 of *Catherine*, Thackeray justifies his actions with the following direct address to the reader:

> The public will hear of nothing but rogues; and the only way which poor authors, who must live, can act honestly by the public and themselves, is to paint such thieves as they are; not dandy, poetical, rose-water thieves, but real downright scoundrels, leading scoundrelly lives, drunken, profligate, dissolute, low, as scoundrels will be (30).

He criticizes Edward Bulwer Lytton's *Eugene Aram* (1832) and *Oliver Twist* for, respectively, creating a scholarly villain and 'white-washed saints, like poor Biss Dadsy' (30), and says that the purpose of the novelist is to make the reader loathe and detest such creations:

> No, my dear madam, you and your daughters have no right to admire and sympathize with any such persons, fictitious or real: you ought to be made cordially to detest, scorn, loathe, abhor, and abominate all people of this kidney (30).

In an earlier article for *Fraser's* of March 1834, Thackeray argues that, to achieve a moral purpose through the depiction of the criminal life, the criminal must be portrayed

> as he really is in action and in principle; recount if you can his education and first associates, his first temptations, and all that may palliate or aggravate his first yielding to the tempter; exclude poetic adornment and speculative reverie ('Hints for a History of Highwaymen', 286–7).[9]

Such an aim would seem to be in direct contradiction with the more melodramatic, or romantic depiction of the criminal, and would seem to carry within it the inherent danger of understanding the criminal, perhaps even sympathizing with him/her, an action which newspaper coverage of domestic murder at this time would suggest was not yet deemed possible. Again, this might suggest that the fiction of the period was in advance of the press coverage, in that there are at least moves on Thackeray's part towards a more sympathetic portrayal of Catherine; in the end, what he offers us is a deeply ambivalent portrait of a notorious murderess.

---

[9]   There is some disagreement over whether Thackeray or John Hamilton Reynolds wrote this piece, but the sentiments expressed concur with Thackeray's other writings on the Newgate school.

Thackeray operates firmly within the conventions of the Newgate school by using an actual case from *The Newgate Calendar*, that of Catherine Hayes, who was burnt alive at Tyburn on 9 May 1726, for the murder of her husband John. The gruesome nature of the case and its aftermath presumably suited Thackeray's purpose of showing crime in all its ghastliness, but it is more significant that he chose a female protagonist from all the cases available to him in *The Newgate Calendar*. One could argue that Catherine was a forerunner of Becky Sharp in *Vanity Fair*, in which case it makes sense that the author chose a feisty, dishonourable female for this earlier novel. But there is more at work here. As discussed earlier in this chapter, the violation of the domestic space by a woman was seen as particularly abhorrent, and the portrayal of Catherine Hayes's case in *The Newgate Calendar* shifted the focus of blame from the three key protagonists to rest almost solely on Catherine's shoulders. By choosing a female murderer for his novel, it might be felt that Thackeray was attempting to show the full horror of domestic murder, but in reality Catherine's gender conflicts with Thackeray's stated purpose in the novel. Almost in spite of himself, we feel that he develops a grudging fondness for his heroine.

This ambivalent response to Catherine is partly effected by Thackeray's handling of his source material. He creates an entirely new character, Count Galgenstein, who is Catherine's lover and the father of her child, thus giving Catherine a motive for murder other than financial gain and a dislike of her husband. In effect, Thackeray makes the murder more domestic, more sexualized than the original source, but he works against contemporary mid-nineteenth-century thinking. For Thackeray the fact that this murder is motivated by sexual desire makes it more excusable than it would have been had it simply been motivated by financial gain.

Thackeray also makes John Hayes a far more unpleasant character than in *The Newgate Calendar*, where he is described in the 1773 edition as being 'of a very peaceable disposition, honest in his dealings and very quiet among his neighbours' (NC 1773, 2:187). In *Catherine*, Hayes is first introduced as a 'poor weak creature ... notoriously timid, selfish, and stingy' who loves Catherine 'with a desperate, greedy eagerness and desire of possession, which makes passions for women often so fierce and unreasonable among very cold and selfish men' (11). The marriage of Catherine and John is hardly desirable or worthy of preserving, and Thackeray paints a particularly repellent picture of the sleeping Hayes which, while not excusing Catherine's actions, goes some way to explaining her desire to rid herself of such a husband:

> Mr Hayes was snoring profoundly; by his bedside, on his ledger, stood a large, greasy tin candlestick, containing a lank tallow-candle, turned down in the shaft; and in the lower part his keys, purse, and tobacco-pipe; his feet were huddled up in his greasy, threadbare clothes; his head and half his sallow face muffled up in a red woollen nightcap; his beard was of several days' growth; his mouth was wide open, and he was snoring profoundly: on a more despicable little creature the sun never shone. And to this sordid wretch was Catherine united for ever (152).

Thackeray's Catherine is physically and emotionally abused by both Galgenstein and Hayes, the former attempting to marry her off to someone else when he tires of her, even though she is expecting his child. At one point she is referred to as a 'poor wench' (39), and at the end of the novel Thackeray draws a moving picture of her concern for her son, allowing her to demonstrate 'appropriate' female sentiments, and thus again undermining his stated purpose of creating a thoroughly unlikeable protagonist.

Catherine's accomplices, her son Thomas Billings and an acquaintance of Hayes, Thomas Wood (aka Captain Brock in the novel) are also transformed under Thackeray's pen. In *The Newgate Calendar* both Billings and Wood are at first reluctant to carry out the murder; Wood, in particular, is shown after the crime as being 'haunted with all the horrors of a guilty conscience, and in terror of every person whom he met' (NC 1773, 2:203), much as Sikes is in *Oliver Twist*. No such delicate sensibility is apparent with Thackeray's Wood. Also *The Newgate Calendar* offers the very strong suggestion that Catherine and Billings (her son) were lovers, a detail which Thackeray omits from the novel, along with the fact that Catherine was literally burnt alive. The omission of the suggestion of incest enables Thackeray to endow Catherine with a degree of maternal feeling, particularly when facing execution:

> She frequently expressed herself to be under no concern at her approaching death; she showed more concern for Billings than for herself; and when in the chapel, would sit with her hand in his, and lean her head upon his shoulder … one of her last expressions to the executioner, as she was going from the sledge to the stake, being an inquiry whether he had hanged her dear child (181).

Catherine's concern for her son is yet more evidence of the ambivalence Thackeray portrays towards his creation, as well as reflecting contemporary newspaper coverage of crimes, where the visit of the accused's children would often prompt an outpouring of emotion (see Chapter 1).

Throughout the novel Thackeray, or his narrator Ikey Solomons, is at pains to stress the truth of his tale. At one point he admits that part of his story is 'not very romantic or striking' but says he has had to include it because 'we are bound to stick closely, above all, by THE TRUTH – the truth, though it be not particularly pleasant to read of or to tell' (52). As Thackeray was obviously aware of the changes he had made to his source material, this is clearly an ironic attack on *The Newgate Calendar* and, by implication, the Newgate school, both of which justified inclusion of gruesome details on the grounds of veracity.

The problem with *Catherine* is that Thackeray's changes to the original story, his deviations from the 'truth', undermine his stated intention of attacking the Newgate school. In the character of Catherine, in particular, he provides a degree of justification for her actions and sympathy for her plight that make her more appealing than her original counterpart. Thackeray was well aware of the shortcomings of his novel, which presumably explains why it was not published as a whole until after his death. In a letter to his mother, the author confessed his dissatisfaction, and his belief that the work had failed in its moral purpose. For Thackeray, *Catherine*

> was a mistake all through – it was not made disgusting enough that is the fact, and the triumph of it would have been to make readers so horribly horrified as to cause them to give up or rather throw up the book and all of its kind (Ray, 1:433).

One wonders if Thackeray's belief that his readers should have been 'horribly horrified' rests partly on his selection of a female domestic murderer, and the consequent revulsion that this could, potentially, have aroused in his readership. However, his admission later in the same letter of a 'sneaking kindness' for his heroine, and the desire not to make her 'utterly worthless' belie his professed intention of making us loathe and detest his creation (Ray, 1:433).

In the novel, Thackeray makes a distinction between Catherine and Captain Brock, arguing that the latter is a more 'loveable rogue', and that novelists make a mistake in divesting their villains of all human qualities. This is symptomatic of his ambivalent treatment of villains: he professes a desire to portray them as thoroughly unlikeable, and yet he almost cannot resist investing them with some redeeming virtues. In this sense, he is very much in opposition to newspapers and street literature of the 1830s and 40s, which rarely presented the domestic murderer as possessing any human qualities at all, and quite regularly portrayed the murderer as a 'monster'. Cabot argues that

> Catherine's final, awful crime, upon which the Newgate Calendar focuses its full attention, is seen by Thackeray as one event (climactic, to be sure) in a whole series of events, with the result that it becomes understandable, if not excusable. This makes the criminal so much more than the agent of a criminal act: she becomes a character of psychological complexity (412–13).

Whilst I would agree with Cabot's suggestion that Catherine's crime becomes more understandable than in the *Newgate Calendar* version of the tale, I would disagree that she is a character of 'psychological complexity'. Much as Dickens does with Sikes, Thackeray uses Catherine's tale to play with the varying styles of melodrama, journalism, and realism, but the outcome falls short of Dickens's achievement. Hollingsworth pinpoints the

> curious quality of nearness with distance that permeates most of [Thackeray's] work. The figures are like those in a stereopticon; they move projected in depth from their correct surroundings, but one remembers always that they are contrived (153).

It is no accident that we remember 'always that they are contrived', because that is what Thackeray wishes us to feel. As soon as we draw closer to a character he intervenes, and highlights the artificiality of the tale. The novel is a *tour de force* of different literary styles, constantly calling attention to itself and the author's cleverness, and playing with the reader's response in, at times, a quite disconcerting way, and one which would seem to undermine Thackeray's literary and moral purpose. Whilst at times the full horror of the domestic murder is made manifest, at others Thackeray seems intent on diffusing such an effect. When Catherine attempts to murder her lover, Count Galgenstein, early on in the novel, she confesses to poisoning him in a scene of broad humour. After having her flee with barely a penny to her name, Thackeray deliberately refutes the suggestion that we feel pity for Catherine, by arguing that she is in league with the devil, but at the same time using bathos to undermine the dramatic potential of her being watched over by a 'dark angel'. At one point Thackeray suggests the events of the novel would make a suitable play, and provides us with two mock playbills to support his argument. Having made direct reference to the language of melodrama and romance, and how the characters in reality fail to deliver such rhetoric (a deliberate and repeated undercutting of the dramatic potential of the story), Thackeray then adopts a mock-heroic style, laden with irony, as events draw closer to the murder of Hayes.

The murder itself is subject to a variety of narrative modes. Initially it is not recounted at all, merely suggested by way of some chilling details, which are lifted straight from the *Newgate Calendar* version of events:

> Mrs Springatt, the lodger, came down to ask what the noise was. "'Tis only Tom Billings making merry with some friends from the country," answered Mrs Hayes; whereupon Springatt retired, and the house was quiet.
>
> …
>
> Some scuffling and stamping was heard about eleven o'clock.
>
> …
>
> After they had seen Mr Hayes to bed, Billings remembered that he had a parcel to carry to some person in the neighbourhood of the Strand; and as the night was remarkably fine, he and Mr Wood agreed to walk together, and set forth accordingly (170).

Thackeray then draws attention to his telling of the murder, and the merits of his writing, making a clear attack on Bulwer Lytton's more high-flown narrative style:

> In the first place, it is perfectly stilted and unnatural; the dialogue and the sentiments being artfully arranged, so as to be as strong and majestic as possible. Our dear Cat is but a poor, illiterate country wench, who has come from cutting her husband's throat; and yet, see! She talks and looks like a tragedy princess, who is suffering in the most virtuous blank verse. This is the proper end of fiction, and one of the greatest triumphs that a novelist can achieve; for to make people sympathize with virtue is a vulgar trick that any common fellow can do; but it is not everybody that can take a scoundrel, and cause us to weep and whimper over him as though he were a very saint (174–5).

Thackeray's reference here to Catherine as a 'tragedy princess, who is suffering in the most virtuous blank verse' may also have been a swipe at Dickens's transformation of Nancy into a more middle-class heroine. Having satirized the 'stilted and unnatural' style of the Newgate novel, Thackeray then gives a full and factual account of the murder and subsequent events, in the baldest and hence most gruesome style imaginable:

> Catherine held the pail, Wood supported the head, and Billings cut it off with his pocket-knife, – having first dragged the body over the side of the bed, that the blood might not stain the clothes ... Mrs Hayes then proposed, in order to prevent a discovery, that she would take the head and boil it in a pot, till only the skin remained, whereby it would be altogether impossible for anybody to distinguish to whom it belonged (177).

In adopting this style, Thackeray is echoing the gruesomely factual press reports of criminal trials, and the various versions of Catherine's crime published in *The Newgate Calendar*; in the 1773 edition we are told how 'Billings supported the head, while Wood cut it off with his pocket knife, and Catherine held the pail to receive it lest any of the blood should be spilt on the floor' (NC 1773, 2:192). Thackeray argues that this pragmatic style is more effective than the 'lengthened and poetical report' of the novelist (183).

Thackeray's desire to move across different discourses must surely be to further his literary purpose in writing the novel; the constant intervention of Thackeray/Solomons draws attention to the artificiality of the tale and prevents us fully identifying or empathizing with any of the characters. But Thackeray moves between these discourses in a much more self-conscious way than Dickens, as if he cannot trust his readership to 'get the joke' and so has to belabour the punchline. Ultimately, the novel fails both on moral and artistic grounds.

Cabot argues that Thackeray, at this stage in his career, is 'torn between ... two voices and postures': the 'witty, playful' eighteenth-century satirist, and the nineteenth-century critical reviewer 'who could on occasion employ scurrilous abuse as one of his weapons, and make use of parody and lampoon, which was to typify the writing of *Punch*.' Cabot suggests that Thackeray attempts to imitate Fielding's 'satiric pose and ironic voice, only to discover that rather than engaging his audience as he felt a satirist must, he alienated it instead' (405).[10] Part of this alienation may be caused by the uncomfortable marriage of style and content in this novel. The audience of the 1840s appears not to have been ready to view domestic murder with any degree of ironic detachment. Catherine's crime in itself would be abhorrent to a contemporary audience, never mind the particularly brutal means by which it is effected, or the bloody aftermath.

***

---

[10]   Colby also detects a similar disparity between Thackeray's aims and his effects. Commenting on the scene where Hayes's head is planted in Saint Margaret's Churchyard, Colby argues that the event is treated 'in so pseudo-genteel and pseudo-romantic a manner as to remove all gruesomeness from the episode' (387).

Significantly, both Dickens and Thackeray chose to place domestic murders at the heart of their novels. Dickens, even if resolved to have Sikes commit a murder, could easily have selected a different victim, and Thackeray had a host of cases from *The Newgate Calendar* as potential source material. So, why domestic murder? In the case of *Oliver Twist*, the murder of Nancy reflects contemporary thinking that domestic murder is the worst of all crimes, thus revealing Sikes as the worst of criminals, and subsequently the most wretched of individuals. By having Sikes commit this barbaric and unjustified act, Dickens succeeds in his aim of showing the wretchedness of criminal life, and emphasizes the centrality of the domestic sphere to his work. It is also significant that Dickens chooses to portray a working-class domestic murder; the suffering exhibited by Sikes and the wider criminal community shows the importance of the crime, regardless of the class of the protagonist. To this extent, Dickens is in conflict with the dominant press coverage at this crime, where a domestic murder was more likely to receive attention if it were committed by a member of the middle classes. For Dickens, any disruption of the domestic sphere is significant, regardless of class, but there is still an ambivalence at work in Dickens at this point, made manifest by Nancy's transformation into a more middle-class heroine.

Thackeray's choice of the Hayes murder also makes sense, in the light of his aims for the novel. The barbarity of the dismemberment and the fact that the crime was committed by a woman (the murder of a husband was of sufficient gravity to warrant the charge of petty treason) would lend themselves to Thackeray's aim of portraying the seediness and immorality of criminal life. The difficulty with *Catherine* is not the choice of material, but rather with Thackeray's handling of that material; most notably his 'sneaking kindness' for his heroine and desire to justify her crime, in part at least.

Both *Oliver Twist* and *Catherine* were part of the Newgate debate but tangential to it. The significance of the novels is less the part they play in the controversy and more the extent to which both authors foreshadow later developments in the novel. As a transitional figure, Sikes anticipates the more fully psychologized criminals of the 1870s onwards, as examined in Chapters 4 and 5; Catherine, with her feistiness and pragmatism, is a forerunner of the amoral 'heroines' of sensation fiction.

Chapter 4
'Monsters of Affection':
The Male Domestic Murderer
and Models of Masculinity

> Because it is in touch with the deepest, subconscious anxieties of its age, in
> spite of its reliance on outworn convention, the sensation novel becomes absurd
> in a more sinister and disturbing way. If it had not been disturbing, if it had
> not undermined the most cherished of values, it would not have provoked such
> visceral outrage (Hughes, 65).

The fiction of the middle decades of the nineteenth century, particularly sensation
fiction, both reflected and contributed to a growing problematization of the
domestic sphere; it also generated fierce debate in contemporary journals and
newspapers. Sensation novels, the most notorious of which were Wilkie Collins's
The Woman in White (1860), Ellen Wood's *East Lynne* (1861), and Mary Elizabeth
Braddon's *Lady Audley's Secret* (1862), provoked a violent negative reaction
from the press, constituted partly by what was seen as an invasion of working-
class reading matter into middle-class homes. The novels, with their fantastic plot
twists revolving around crimes and mysteries, and narrative strands of bigamy,
adultery, madness, poisoning, disguise and coincidence were viewed by many
literary critics with disdain, and charged with rendering the literary marketplace
into a form of 'manufactory', providing mass-produced works which focused
on suspense and action at the expense of psychological depth or philosophical
reflection (Mansel, 483).

One of the most pertinent features of sensation fiction, as regards this book,
was that its plots dealt with contemporary, recognizable middle-class concerns; as
Dean Mansel notably argued in his, by now very well-known, lengthy *Quarterly
Review* article:

> the sensation novel ... is usually a tale of our own times. Proximity is, indeed,
> one great element of sensation. It is necessary to be near a mine to be blown up
> by its explosion; and a tale which aims at electrifying the nerves of the reader is
> never thoroughly effective unless the scene be laid in our own days and among
> the people we are in the habit of meeting (488–9).

Not merely were such works 'laid in our own days and among the people we are
in the habit of meeting', they also focused on the hopes and fears of the Victorian
middle classes: the nature and status of the family, gender roles, the expectations of
marriage, legal matters, social class, property and financial security. This invasion
of the middle-class home was not, in itself, particularly disturbing; it was more

what such novels made of their material. E. S. Dallas, in his influential work *The Gay Science* (1866), argued that contemporary fiction was witnessing a rise in

> the little men and the private men and all the incidents of privacy ... We dwell far more than we used to on the private side of human life. We have learned to feel that there is as much greatness in the family as in the state (251).

However, unlike the domestic novel and the melodrama, both of which indeed saw 'greatness in the family', the sensation novel, while taking the family as its focus and thus elevating its status, often dwelt on the disorder and discontent inherent within the domestic space. The home was no longer a source of purity, and the means whereby virtue was restored; instead it was an environment dominated by secrecy, one just as likely to foster violence and unregulated desire as the restoration of social order.

Critical work on sensation fiction has tended to focus on the transgressive actions of the female characters within these novels, not very surprising given that the birth of the genre corresponded with an upsurge in the number of female authors, much sensation fiction featured female protagonists, and contemporary criticism of the works often focused on the portrayal of these female characters and their likely impact on a female audience. That the position of women should become the focus of sensation fiction is hardly coincidental; Lady Caroline Norton's campaign for maternal custody, which resulted in the Infant and Child Custody Bill of 1839, was the start of a heightened awareness of the anomalies in women's legal status, an awareness which reached new heights with the passing of the 1857 Matrimonial Causes Act, and the lurid newspaper reporting of divorce trials that followed in its wake. As Lyn Pykett has argued:

> the sensationalised divorce cases, the sensation novel and the wider sensation debate all turned on the question of women, and all put women in question. They were part of a mid-century explosion of discourse on woman – an explosion that ... 'made a spectacle' of woman ... in which women and the subject of woman were examined, scrutinised and looked at (*'Improper' Feminine*, 54).

However, the function of the male characters is no less significant. Whilst the female characters in works such as Wilkie Collins's *Armadale* (1866) and Mary Elizabeth Braddon's *Lady Audley's Secret* are undoubtedly disruptive of the domestic sphere, they are generally motivated by a financial imperative, as opposed to a discontent with the domestic sphere itself. In *Armadale* Lydia Gwilt's initial motive for murdering Allan Armadale is financial gain, and to redress the wrongs imposed on her by Allan's mother. When she falls in love with Ozias Midwinter, and acknowledges that love, her murderous impulse dissipates; it is only when she believes Ozias no longer loves her that the desire to murder Allan (and gain financially) returns. By the same token Lucy Graham's attempted murders in *Lady Audley's Secret* are motivated solely by her love of money and status; there is no suggestion that she is particularly unhappy in her second marriage.

When we come to examine the problematic relationship between men and the domestic sphere in the fiction of this period, the focus shifts. Rather than seeking to disrupt the domestic idyll for financial gain, the male characters in the novels examined later in this chapter have a problematic relationship with the domestic space *per se*, questioning their very existence within it. In addition, the male sexual impulse is also called into question in these works, a trend not detectable in the female protagonists of sensation fiction: Lady Audley, for example, seems almost asexual, as if the Victorian public could not accept a woman who was both criminally minded and sexualized. The 1857 trial of Madeleine Smith for the murder of her lover Emile L'Angelier is a perfect illustration of this discomfort with middle-class female sexuality; despite obvious evidence to the contrary in the shape of Madeleine's sexually explicit letters to L'Angelier, both defence and prosecution persisted in portraying her as a sexual innocent, led astray by her lover.

This chapter will argue that unstable and contested models of masculinity were refracted through trial transcripts and novels that concern themselves with domestic violence and murder during these middle decades of the century. To determine why this might be the case, the chapter will outline the conflicting models of Victorian masculinity examined in the work of John Tosh and others, demonstrating how some of the key issues surrounding ideas of masculinity and male behaviour were reflected in Dinah Craik's best-selling novel *John Halifax, Gentleman* (1856) and also three notorious murder trials: Frederick and Maria Manning's murder of Patrick O'Connor (1849), the Reverend Watson's murder of his wife (1871) and the Stauntons' murder of Harriet Staunton (1877). I will argue that the ideal of male conduct espoused in popular works such as Samuel Smiles's *Self-Help* (1859) and John Ruskin's *Sesame and Lilies* (1865) was a contested one.

The chapter will then assess how contemporary debates on models of male behaviour, and the problematic issue of male desire, are played out in five novels: Wilkie Collins's *Basil* (1852), Thomas Hardy's *Desperate Remedies* (1871) and *Far From the Madding Crowd* (1874), and Charles Dickens's *Our Mutual Friend* (1865) and *The Mystery of Edwin Drood* (1870). Although *Desperate Remedies* is the only one of these works consistently read as a work of sensation fiction, the other four works all exhibit the characteristics and concerns of the sensation novel. The male protagonists in these works all commit acts of domestic murder or violence with murderous intent: the eponymous protagonist of *Basil* disfigures his love rival, Mannion, by grinding his face into a freshly tarmacadammed road; Aeneas Manston in *Desperate Remedies* accidentally murders his wife, but then cold-bloodedly disposes of the body and later attempts to rape his second wife, Cytherea; Boldwood in *Far From the Madding Crowd* shoots Sergeant Troy, his rival for Bathsheba's affection; Bradley Headstone attempts to murder his love rival, Eugene Wrayburn, in *Our Mutual Friend*; and there is the very strong suggestion that John Jasper murders Edwin Drood in *The Mystery of Edwin Drood*. By causing their characters to commit violent acts upon their loved ones or love rivals, Dickens, Hardy and Collins are all questioning the gospel of male self-control so dominant within Victorian society at this point, and demonstrating that 'self-sacrifice and sexual postponement are manly virtues, but when pathologically obeyed create "monsters of affection," gentlemen whose moral rectitude limits their potential for sexual self-knowledge' (Federico, 59). While their relation to the domestic space is central to the actions of the male protagonists in all five of these novels, the relationship between desirable male behaviour and the domestic sphere is a problematic and contested one, and one which remains unresolved. The problems encountered by these male protagonists, and the multiple acts of murder and disfigurement with which they are associated in the novels, have their roots in an uneasy relationship to the domestic and to what it means to 'be a man'.

Models of Masculinity

> For most of the nineteenth century home was widely held to be a man's place, not only in the sense of being his possession or fiefdom, but also as the place where his deepest needs were met. Questions to do with domestic affections and domestic authority permeated the advice books read by men, as they did the novels of Charles Dickens. In an age when, in the estimation of the Victorians, economic and social advance reached unprecedented levels, the men credited with these achievements were expected to be dutiful husbands and attentive fathers, devotees of hearth and family (Tosh, 1).

Whilst the home has traditionally been regarded as the female sphere in Victorian life, the work of John Tosh and others on masculinity and domesticity has highlighted the oversimplification of such a division. Through his examination of advice books aimed at men Tosh has established that a man's self-respect came not just from his conduct in the public sphere, but also, very much, within his home life:

> the man's duty to *protect* the home was more than an expression of power over his dependants; it implied collective measures alongside other householders, and thus underpinned the association of masculinity with physical self-reliance and personal bravery (Tosh, 3).

Peter Stearns argues that middle-class male involvement in business and commerce was initially regarded very much in terms of the family:

> business and family were inextricably intertwined during the first decades of the industrial revolution, as merchants and manufacturers sought to solidify their companies as the basis for an enduring family fortune (118).

Lisa Surridge, in her study of marital violence and Victorian fiction, argues that Dickens's interest in masculinity and domestic assault was part of 'a growing tendency to scrutinize men's marital behaviour and to connect manhood with the cherished Victorian ideal of domesticity' (46). James Hammerton suggests that the 1857 Divorce Act, which revealed marital discord operating at all levels of society, opened up the debate on masculinity 'so that one result of the long marriage debate was a challenge to prevailing concepts of masculinity. The 'manliness' of husbands was tested increasingly by their marital conduct' (3).

The importance of male conduct at this time, and the public interest in appropriate male conduct, is borne out by the extraordinary success of Dinah Craik's novel *John Halifax, Gentleman*. Published in 1856, the novel achieved second place in the 1863 bestseller lists (sacrificing the number one spot to *Uncle Tom's Cabin*) and the work continued to enjoy popular success for a further 50 years. The novel charts the progress of the eponymous hero from working-class poverty to a position of middle-class stability, magistracy and the promise of a seat in Parliament. The novel is narrated by Phineas Fletcher, a childhood friend of John Halifax. The emphasis throughout is on the inherent 'gentlemanlike' quality of John Halifax, who is presented to the reader as 'the devoted husband, the loving father, the paternalist employer, the responsible public man, generous to all his dependants whether child, servant, or apprentice, kind to animals or misguided Luddites, pleading on behalf of oppressed slaves'; in short, 'English middle-class manhood personified' (Hall, 262–3). Most significant is John Halifax's attitude to marriage and the domestic sphere. After his marriage to Ursula,

> he lifted his eyes upwards; there was in them a new look, sweet and solemn, a look which expressed the satisfied content of a life now rounded and completed by that other dear life which it had received into and united with its own – making a full and perfect whole, which, however kindly and fondly it may look on friends and kindred outside, has no absolute need of any, but is complete in and sufficient to itself, as true marriage should be (Craik, 189).

Later in the novel, when John travels to France to sort out his son Guy's gambling debts, all at home miss him terribly, with Phineas declaring that 'the life and soul of the house seemed to have gone out of it from the hour the father went away' (369). The link between a 'true gentleman' and a happy and secure domestic life is clear.

Before examining what was deemed appropriate masculine behaviour within the domestic sphere, it is important to understand that these models of masculinity did not go uncontested, nor was there a single 'ideal' to be adopted. Sussman argues against the 'monolithic' view of nineteenth-century masculinity, suggesting instead the term 'masculinities' as a more accurate way of showing 'the plurality of formations of masculinity among the Victorians'. For Sussman, Victorian masculinity is 'an historical construction rather than an essentialist given' (8), a view shared by McLaren in his examination of the construction of masculinity later in the century. McLaren argues that doctors, sexologists, magistrates and sex reformers in the period 1870–1930

> exploited the stereotype of a virile, heterosexual, and aggressive masculinity. They did not so much "create" the stereotype; it would be more accurate to say that they selected and declared pre-eminent one particular model of masculinity from an existing range of male gender roles (2).

For McLaren, the fact that 'exertion and activity was required to "be a man" meant that the public accepted implicitly the notion that manliness was a constructed identity'; in effect, a man had to prove repeatedly that he was a 'man', whereas the same was not true for a woman (33–4).

As constructs, such models of masculinity were not necessarily adopted wholesale; there was a degree of conflict between the discourse of masculinity and the lived experience which is particularly evident in the novels that I focus on in this chapter. For Sussman, male identity was an 'unstable equilibrium, so that the governing terms of Victorian manhood become contradiction, conflict, anxiety' (15). Davidoff and Hall argue that writers such as William Cowper and Hannah More 'played a vital part in establishing the social codes which informed middle-class propriety for many generations. ... Their ideas were, however, contested. Discourses on manliness and femininity were not closed' (155).

Models of male behaviour had first been challenged earlier in the century, under the influence of Evangelicalism:

> an earlier notion of masculinity, which focused more on military and public power and private pursuits like hunting and drinking, made important concession to the softening features of domestic virtues. Tenderness, love and care, the protection of the weak, especially women, and the education and cultivation of dependents, became the new hallmarks of male virtue (Hammerton, 150).

Such a focus on 'tenderness, love and care' is foregrounded in Craik's *John Halifax, Gentleman*. From an early age John Halifax exhibits genuine compassion; assisting the young Phineas (the novel's narrator), he exhibits 'a quality different from kindliness, affectionateness, or benevolence; a quality which can exist only in strong, deep, and undemonstrative natures, and therefore in its perfection is oftenest found in men' (21). Later in the novel, John explains why his workforce will work harder for him after he has thrown them a party: 'Our people will work the better, because they will work from love. Not merely doing their duty, and obeying their master in a blind way, but feeling an interest in him and all that belongs to him; knowing that he feels the same in them' (250). Catherine Hall argues that the novel 'contributed to the discursive construction of a particular masculinity, one which emphasized that men were emotional beings, capable of love, of warmth, of tears' (261).

The 'hallmarks of male virtue' exhibited by the likes of John Halifax did not pass uncontested. Hammerton draws on Davidoff and Hall's influential work *Family Fortunes*, reiterating their argument that this model of masculinity was problematic from the start:

> since the model developed alongside that of separate spheres, which emphasized gender segregation and celebrated men's public virtues and women's domestic containment, it is hardly surprising that tensions developed rapidly. Critics were quick to equate manly emotion and tenderness with effeminacy and weakness, and the passionate outbursts associated with Romanticism gradually fell into disfavour, to be replaced by a more controlled and rational male demeanour (150–51).

Davidoff and Hall highlight the perils of men becoming too attached to the home, which could result in 'feebleness of character and dependence, characteristics that could never be associated with manliness' (113). Similarly, Tosh identifies a growing discontent with the identification of masculinity with domesticity as the century progressed. He suggests that from the 1860s onwards 'bourgeois men were increasingly disturbed by the identification of the home with the feminine, represented as the "tyranny of five-o'clock tea"' (7).

Dinah Craik would seem to be addressing these issues of 'effeminacy and weakness' and an over-dependence on the home in the character of Phineas in *John Halifax, Gentleman.* As the narrator of the story, Phineas importantly renders visible the domestic idyll of John and Ursula, but he also problematizes the idea of the domestic. While John is able to reconcile his tender nature with an active sense of industry, the same cannot be said of Phineas, whose non-specific illness renders him unfit for any work. His presence within the domestic space embodies the concern that the domestic could be essentially a feminizing zone, much as it is for the eponymous hero of Wilkie Collins's *Basil* (examined later in this chapter). If John Halifax represents the ideal of middle-class male behaviour, Phineas represents the potential danger of 'emotion and tenderness' ungoverned by any sterner principle. Whilst there is no overt criticism of Phineas in the novel, his position as the effeminate foil to John Halifax's rugged masculinity could hardly be one that a Victorian man would have aspired to. The perils of an excessive attachment to the domestic space are also evident in Frank Danby's much later novel *Doctor Phillips* (1887). Having married for money, the 'luxurious prostitution' of his marriage causes Doctor Phillips to fall into 'the half indolent ways of a man whose slippers are always warmed and whose meals are always ready' (78, 20) and abandon his scientific enquiry and aspirations.

The dangers of 'tenderness, love and care' equating to emasculation are also evident in the trial of Maria and Frederick Manning in 1849. Although taking place slightly earlier than the period under examination in this chapter, the trial is nonetheless a significant cultural barometer of appropriate masculine behaviour. There is also the fact that the 'character' of Maria Manning could be viewed as a forerunner of the deviant females of sensation fiction; certainly, Dickens modelled the murderous Hortense in *Bleak House* on Mrs. Manning. As Andrew Mangham observes:

> the Bermondsey murder did not combine murder and the home in a way that was horrifying and unexpected (as one might presume) but confirmed growing suspicions that every home and every woman could harbour the potential for extreme violence (9),

a sentiment that characterized much criticism of sensation fiction.

In November 1849 Maria and Frederick Manning were hanged for the murder of Patrick O'Connor, Maria's lover. The body of O'Connor, a gauger in the Customs at the London Docks, was discovered on 17 August 1849, buried in the kitchen of 3 Miniver Place, Bermondsey (the Mannings' home). The post-mortem revealed he had died on 9 August, having been shot twice in the head before suffering 'repeated blows of a hammer or crow-bar to the back of the skull' (*Times*, 21 August 1849, 8). Both Frederick and Maria Manning fled the scene of the crime, but were subsequently arrested: Maria in Edinburgh on 21 August, Frederick in Jersey eight days later. The trial took place over 26 and 27 October, and both were found guilty. They were executed on 13 November 1849 before a crowd variously estimated as somewhere between 10,000 and 30,000.

Although it was suggested that the murder had been effected for financial gain, coverage of the crime focused increasingly on the relationship between the Mannings, and the attendant issues of male submission and female dominance. The portrayal of both Maria and Frederick Manning changed as the case progressed, finally establishing Maria as the dominant partner, and Frederick as an emasculated weakling who merely responded to Maria's bidding, a kind of forerunner for the Lydia Gwilt/Bashwood relationship in Wilkie Collins's *Armadale* (1866). Early reports portrayed Frederick Manning as 'overbearing', 'rude', 'insolent' and 'swaggering', 'a repulsive looking individual', with a huge head and very thick neck (*Times*, 1 September 1849, 5). By contrast, Maria was initially described as 'fine-grown' and 'handsome' (*Times*, 20 August 1849, 6), but a mere five days later such description of her physical charms was already being modified: 'it would ... be a mistake to call her either handsome or beautiful ... Her features are neither regular nor feminine, yet the general impression of her face is rather pleasing than otherwise, and she has evidently been a comely woman' (*Times*, 25 August 1849, 5). By mid-September, the *Times* was commenting on the fact that Maria's figure was 'masculine' and that she had 'all the appearance of unusual strength for a woman' (17 September 1849, 8). By the time the court proceedings commenced Frederick had degenerated from an insolent and overbearing individual, to one more frequently described as nervous and restless, casting 'furtive glances' at Maria who, in turn, 'was never seen, throughout the day, to turn her eyes towards her husband' (*Times*, 26 October 1849, 4). Maria allegedly referred to Frederick as 'the unmanly wretch' and, after sentence was passed, steadfastly refused her husband's requests for one final meeting (*Times*, 29 October 1849, 5).

Maria's dominance was partly effected by her husband; when Frederick was arrested, he admitted guilt, but argued that Maria had instigated the crime, and it was she who shot O'Connor. This transparent effort on Frederick's part to pin the blame on Maria was willingly adopted by the press, with descriptions of her as Frederick's 'evil genius', alongside reports of violent quarrels between them, one of which resulted in Maria pursuing Frederick 'with a large dirk knife, with which she threatened to stab him' (*Times*, 27 August 1849, 5).

By the time sentence was passed the press was free to indulge in the full range of melodramatic rhetoric. Towards Frederick, the *Times* declared there could be only 'the one feeling of loathing and disgust'. Even if he had been the one to strike the first blow, the paper argued that he was merely 'the butcher who slaughters the ox without a feeling of the bloody work in which he is engaged.' Contrast Frederick's 'shrinking repentance' with the 'fixed determination' of Maria who was portrayed as 'his sterner partner', 'the wife who quenched his last scruples, and by her sarcasm and reproaches spirited him up to strike the fatal blow.' Maria was 'the protagonist, and her brutal partner but as the minister and executor of her will' (27 October 1849, 4).

Two weeks later the *Times* again embarked on an elaborate piece of rhetoric, comparing Maria to both Jezebel ('the daring foreigner, the profane unbeliever') and Lady Macbeth

> in her insatiable cupidity and ambition, in her atrocious conceptions, her undaunted soul and her unflinching nerve; in her dominion over a sottish and a cowardly husband, in her treachery to her guest, in the complacency with which she could behold her victim, in the vigour with which she could smite him "as 'an ox in the shambles,'" and perhaps also in the steadiness with which she could encounter her doom ... Such is Lady MACBETH on the Bermondsey stage.

By contrast, Frederick was referred to in the same editorial not just as 'sottish and cowardly', but as 'the thing who was her husband, but not a man' (14 November 1849, 4).

This polarization not only made for entertaining reading, but enabled a more straightforward 'reading' of the case than a detailed analysis of what must have been a highly complex marital relationship. Maria was, undoubtedly, a formidable woman; the day after her execution the *Times* carried a report that she had earlier tried to kill herself, having grown her nails long enough to pierce her own windpipe. Add to this the fact that she was of foreign extraction, born in Geneva, and therefore not operating within the accepted parameters of British female behaviour, and the press portrayal of her demeanour and behaviour starts to make more sense. In addition, the emasculation of Frederick may also be linked to ideas of nationhood; he is weak because he is not British.

But the press portrayal of Frederick is also part of the more general contemporary debate on male behaviour; he exhibits the extreme of the more feminized model, acquiescing in all things to his wife, and thus encapsulating some of the concerns that were increasingly being expressed regarding the emasculating role of the domestic. The vitriol which was reserved for Frederick must surely suggest a degree of discontent with this model of domesticated masculinity. He is held up for ridicule, in contrast with Maria, for whom more than one press report shows a grudging level of admiration. The *Times* of 17 September, 1849 admitted that 'amidst all the coarseness and sensuality of her expression, there is something almost approaching to good nature about her irregular features, which certainly makes her less unprepossessing than Manning' (8). A later *Times* editorial of 14 November commented that Maria exhibited

> an amount of courage and nerve which contrast[s] strangely with the terror-stricken aspect of her husband. There had been a diabolical energy of character displayed by her throughout, which has attracted to her conduct a still larger share of public attention than to that of Manning. Her handsome figure, foreign

origin, and various other considerations, contributed to this effect, and it is due to her to say that no man could have borne himself more firmly than she did in the terrible part which she had to perform (4–5).

Such comments are as much an indictment of Frederick's weakness as admiration for Maria's strength.

To the same extent that we should not view these models of masculinity as uncontested, it is equally important to stress that this focus on male behaviour was very much a middle-class concern. As Catherine Hall has identified, part of the shaping of the middle classes as a separate class rested on the ideology of separate spheres, and notions of ideal male and female behaviour, which separated the middle class 'from both the aristocracy and gentry above them and from the working class below them' (95). Stearns argues that

> middle-class manhood was conditioned, through much of the nineteenth century, by a vigorous desire not to fall into working-class patterns … Adding to the constraints on middle-class manhood, and particularly adolescent manhood when working-class culture offered particularly compelling allures, was the pressure to define, and to live up to, a certain respectability; this contributed a variety of kinds of self-control to the list of achievements defining a real man (109).

For Sussman, this concept of self-control 'validated the hegemony of the bourgeoisie by valorizing manliness as self-regulation over what was seen through middle-class eyes as the libertinism and idleness of the gentry and the irregularity and sexual license of the working class' (11). Turning again to Craik's *John Halifax* we see this battle to separate and define the middle classes at work in the central figure of John. Starting the novel as a penniless orphan he is elevated to the ranks of the middle classes through sheer hard work and industry. At various points in the novel he pits himself against the local aristocracy, asserting his right to the title of gentleman through his behaviour rather than by birth. Later in the novel, he rejects Lord Ravenal's proposal for his daughter's hand in marriage, stating that

> her mother and I would rather see our little Maud lying beside her sister Muriel than see her Countess of Luxmore … do you not see yourself that the distance between us and you is wide as the poles? Not in worldly things, but in things far deeper; – personal things, which strike at the root of love, home – nay, honour (378).

It is only after Lord Ravenal uses his inheritance to pay off his father's debtors and goes into partnership with John Halifax's son, Guy, that he is deemed a worthy partner for Maud.

The establishment of self-control as the foundation of 'acceptable' male behaviour, however, has its roots in something more than just an attempt to define a class. E. S. Dallas may have believed that the 1860s was an era where 'the home life is proclaimed on the housetops; and the secrets of the hearts are made an open show' (252), and the 1857 Divorce Act may have opened up the middle-class home to more public scrutiny, but the domestic space still offered a level of privacy that could conceal disturbing behaviour, particularly on the part of men. Martin Wiener, examining crime statistics from the 1860s to the 1880s, found fewer cases of homicide than in earlier decades, but more of them within the family, suggesting that the home was now 'the "last retreat" of men's violence' (*Men of Blood*, 146). If, indeed, the home were now perceived as the last bastion of male violence this might be seen as an unforeseen side-effect of the worship of the private sphere, as promulgated through the work of Ruskin and others. Ruskin's much-quoted words from *Sesame and Lilies* are worth another examination in the light of Wiener's findings:

> This is the true nature of home – it is the place of Peace; the shelter, not only from all injury, but from all terror, doubt, and division. In so far as it is not this, it is not home; so far as the anxieties of the outer life penetrate into it, and the inconsistently-minded, unknown, unloved, or hostile society of the outer world is allowed by either husband or wife to cross the threshold, it ceases to be home (88).

Ruskin's suggestion that 'the hostile society of the outer world' should not be permitted to cross the threshold affords the home a shield from the public gaze that could be used to hide all types of transgressive behaviour, including violence. The murder of Harriet Staunton illustrates this concern perfectly.

In September 1877 four individuals were found guilty of the murder of Harriet Staunton: Louis Staunton (Harriet's husband), Alice Rhodes (Louis's lover), Patrick Staunton (Louis's brother), and Elizabeth Staunton (Patrick's wife). A post mortem of Harriet's body revealed that she weighed just five stone at the time of death, and the cause of death was entered as starvation.

What is particularly interesting about the case is the 'exterior of seemliness' (*Times*, 27 September 1877, 9) which the Stauntons maintained for several months, reinforcing the notion that the Victorian home and attendant need for privacy could conceal all manner of aberrations, including the systematic starvation of a young woman by four family members. Having taken Alice Rhodes as his lover, Louis Staunton dispatched Harriet to live with his brother and sister-in-law in a remote part of Kent, and then lived openly with Alice as his 'wife'. After Harriet's mother complained to the magistrates that she had been denied access to her daughter, the police were told to watch the house but neither Frank Quested nor Alfred Hollands (police constable and inspecting constable, Kent County Constabulary) were aware that Harriet Staunton was even living at Woodlands; indeed, the *Times* remarked that 'it is practically impossible to hear or know what is going on in a lonely house … it appears that Mrs. Staunton was seen by no one' (11 July 1877, 11). Part of the Stauntons' defence rested precisely on this 'exterior of seemliness'; when questioned as to why they had not called out a doctor when Harriet first fell ill, the answer was simply that they did not wish it known that Alice was not Louis's wife, a fact which would have readily come to light if a doctor had visited Harriet.

During the course of the trial, and in the aftermath of the conviction, public opinion shifted the focus of the crime from starvation to adultery. By focusing on Louis Staunton's adultery the man's sexual desire became the focus of moral disapproval, and adultery was a crime which the public knew how to respond to. Far more troublesome was the idea of a number of related individuals imprisoning and systematically starving a young woman over a period of at least three months, while her husband conducted an adulterous relationship in the full glare of the public gaze. Everyone was hoodwinked, nothing was as it seemed, this truly was a case where 'fearful errors lurk in our nuptial couches; fiends sit down with us at table', a comment made in a *Temple Bar* article on sensation fiction ('Our Novels: The Sensational School', 422) – but this was no fiction.

As the Stauntons' case illustrates, the potential for aberrant behaviour within what Collins famously termed 'the secret theatre of home' was clearly not unrecognised by the Victorians and many male conduct manuals stressed the need for personal restraint and self-control, with the implication that men's conjugal behaviour was a problem that required some form of regulation. Samuel Smiles's *Self-Help* (1859), one of the most influential works of the second half of the century, emphasized the importance of individual conduct for the health of the nation as a whole:

> National progress is the sum of individual industry, energy, and uprightness, as national decay is of individual idleness, selfishness, and vice. What we are accustomed to decry as great social evils, will, for the most part, be found to be but the outgrowth of man's own perverted life; and though we may endeavour to cut them down and extirpate them by means of Law, they will only spring up again with fresh luxuriance in some other form, unless the conditions of personal life and character are radically improved. If this view be correct, then it follows that the highest patriotism and philanthropy consist, not so much in altering laws and modifying institutions, as in helping and stimulating men to elevate and improve themselves by their own free and independent individual action (18).

Sussman, Dowling and Stearns all stress the supremacy of self-control as part of appropriate male conduct. For Sussman, nineteenth-century manhood was viewed as 'an unstable equilibrium of barely controlled energy that may collapse back into the inchoate flood or fire that limns the innate energy of maleness' (13). Dowling argues that Victorian masculinity was 'an ideal structured around a controlling metaphor of discipline' (13) and for Stearns 'self-control, through careful formation of character, was the key resolution urged to reconcile the intense passions attributed to male nature and the disciplined focus necessary for success' (128).

This focus on control and the domination of passion was, if not always openly expressed, clearly linked to the prevailing concerns regarding masturbation and spermatorrhoea, a persistent concern in much mid-century scientific and psychological writing on the male gender. Influential writers such as William Acton and Robert Ritchie stressed the dangers inherent in giving way to physical impulses; unhealthy indulgence could ultimately lead to insanity or death. Ritchie suggested that middle-class men were twice as likely to suffer masturbatory-induced insanity as working- or upper-class men, such insanity generally endangered by disgust at their own conduct. What was also significant about the practice of masturbation was that it was a solitary 'vice', causing Ritchie to lament 'that the finest qualities of our nature may frequently but cloak the hidden evil, and ... the apparently well conducted, studious youth may be but too certainly preparing a manhood of misery and uselessness.' The only safeguard against such an enervating condition was persistent self-control and denial: 'the *want* will be an irresistible tyrant only to those who have lent it strength by yielding' (in Taylor and Shuttleworth, 216, 212).

This dominant motif of control suggests that the Victorians believed there was something inherent in men that needed to be controlled, a 'chaotic, uncontrolled energy [which] was the 'natural' element of men' (Dowling, 22). But this imposition of control, and the differing levels of it, was clearly a contested issue during the middle decades of the nineteenth century, as is evident when we look more closely at the fiction of the period.

The male protagonists of all five novels under examination struggle to position themselves comfortably within a traditional domestic setting. In *The Mystery of Edwin Drood* John Jasper is first revealed to us within a gruesome and degraded parody of the domestic setting. He is in 'the meanest and closest of small rooms', lying dressed 'across a large unseemly bed' alongside 'a Chinaman, a Lascar, and a haggard woman' (7). The overtones of sexual misconduct and the cultural mix of the protagonists only serve to reinforce this violation of the domestic space, a fact further emphasized by the Luke Fildes illustration to accompany this opening scene, which shows the 'Chinaman, Lascar and ... haggard woman' in a state of physical abandon. What is important, and striking as an introduction to the character of Jasper, is that he is at home within this setting. The illustration shows him drawing back the curtain to survey the scene and the text informs us of his leisurely contemplation and interactions with the semi-conscious characters. A few short paragraphs later he is within the body of the cathedral, attending a religious service.

In a significant early exchange with his nephew Edwin, Jasper complains of the 'daily drudging round' of his existence, marked by 'no whirl and uproar around me, no distracting commerce or calculation, no risk, no change of place, myself devoted to the art I pursue, my business my pleasure ... . The cramped monotony of my existence grinds me away by the grain'. For Jasper the merging of the public and private spheres offers no 'change of place' between work and home, a source of deep frustration for him. He is 'troubled with some sort of ambition, aspiration, restlessness, dissatisfaction' (19–20). Interestingly, though, what drives him to commit the murder of Edwin is not the desire to enter the public sphere but to gain precisely the quiet domestic life with Rosa that Edwin rejects. Jasper's appropriation of this particular domestic idyll is unseemly, though, because his relationship with Rosa should be avuncular, not sexual.

The eponymous hero of Wilkie Collins's *Basil* suffers the greatest difficulties with the domestic space, and is not at ease within any home until the close of the novel. When he visits his father and his sister Clara on their country estate, not having yet informed them of his marriage to Margaret Sherwin, he feels that 'home seemed home no longer' (118). But Margaret's home offers no solace either. North Villa is situated in Hollyoake Square, a suburb of new houses 'intermingled with wretched patches of waste land, half built over'; the 'newness and desolateness of appearance' of this suburb revolt Basil, bringing into sharp relief the social gulf between him and Margaret (30–31). Everything within the Sherwins' home is 'oppressively new', garish and uncomfortable (53). It is hardly surprising that Basil is uneasy within both these domestic spaces, given that he is deceiving his family, and being duped by the Sherwins; but clearly there are also class issues at work. By a union with Margaret, Basil is in grave danger of being pulled down the social ladder, a direction that no Victorian man could possibly contemplate with ease.

Having agreed not to consummate his marriage to Margaret for a year, Basil discovers the night before the year is up that Margaret has been conducting a sexual relationship with Mannion, her father's clerk. In a murderous rage of sexual jealousy, he confronts Mannion and grinds his face into a newly surfaced road, thereby disfiguring Mannion.

Significantly Basil's cuckolding is revealed within the pseudo-domestic space of a hotel; a domestic space which Mannion has control of, and which Basil is an uncomfortable visitor in. The flimsy structure of the hotel, with walls so thin that Basil can overhear everything that passes between Margaret and Mannion on the other side, is redolent of North Villa, again suggesting the perils of downward social mobility. After the maiming of Mannion, Basil is forced to wander from place to place; Mannion's actions or, rather, Basil's action of disfiguring Mannion, mean that nowhere is 'home'.

Conversely, Mannion appears to be at home in any domestic situation. On first meeting Mannion, Basil observes that he is master of North Villa, 'master in his own quiet, unobtrusive way', but Mannion's adoption of another man's home as his own is clearly intended as an indicator of his duplicitous personality (92). Later in the novel Basil and Mannion take shelter in Mannion's home. Basil notes that the house is tastefully furnished, suggesting an interest in the domestic space on Mannion's part; but, more significantly, he observes that

> almost all men, when they stand on their own hearths, in their own homes, instinctively alter more or less from their out-of-door manner: the stiffest people expand, the coldest thaw a little, by their own firesides. It was not so with Mr. Mannion. He was exactly the same man at his own house that he was at Mr. Sherwin's (99).

If we agree with Tosh's argument that, for the Victorians, 'only at home could a man be truly and authentically himself' (33), Mannion's inability or unwillingness to drop the mask within his own home is suggestive of a degree of self-control which might have been disturbing to a contemporary audience. But it is also significant that Basil himself is never at ease within any domestic space until the close of the novel when he is living with his sister Clara in Lanreath Cottage, Clara's own home inherited from her mother. His comfort within this older, inherited home, as opposed to North Villa, suggests he is now positioned in the correct social sphere. He is, though, a recluse, confessing that 'I am still resolved to live on in obscurity, in retirement, in peace. ... The mountain-path of Action is no longer a path for *me*; my future hope pauses with my present happiness in the shadowed valley of Repose'. He has rejected his brother Ralph's call to action and public life, choosing instead to adopt a more traditionally feminine mode of occupation, 'to serve the cause of the poor and the ignorant, in the little sphere which now surrounds me ... to live more and more worthy, with every day, of the sisterly love which, never tiring, never changing, watches over me in this last retreat, this dearest home'. Basil insists that his current life of retirement is not a failure, maintaining that the suffering he has endured 'has shown me uses to which I may put my existence, that have their sanction from other voices than the voices of fame', but his reference to the 'little sphere' he now operates within highlights the problems of his reclusive state. Basil's inability to embrace the physical side of his nature leaves him only half a man. He embraces the domestic sphere at the close of the novel, but he is unable to marry this with any engagement with the public sphere (271, 272). He is also involved in no occupation, another indictment of his masculinity; as Hall makes clear, 'failure in the public world could mean a loss of male identity' (257–8).

Basil was not widely reviewed, and many of the reviews that were written were scathing of what was deemed the unsavoury content of the material. *Bentley's Miscellany* was alone in offering a positive review of the novel, commenting particularly on the

> startling antagonism between the intensity of the passion, the violent spasmodic action of the piece, and its smooth, common-place environments. The scenery, the *dramatis personae*, the costumery, are all of the most familiar every-day type, belonging to an advanced stage of civilization; but there is something rude and barbarous, almost titanic, about the incidents; they belong to a different state of society (Page, 46–7).

It would seem that this conjunction of the commonplace with the barbarous is no accident on Collins's part. By allowing his characters to exhibit such 'barbarous ... titanic' actions and emotions within recognizable domestic settings, he is surely offering a criticism of the credo of ideal male behaviour.

In Hardy's *Desperate Remedies* Aeneas Manston does create a home for himself, but the closing stages of the novel witness his attempted rape of Cytherea, his wife. In a grim parody of domestication, Manston seeks entry to the house Cytherea is sharing with her brother Owen, calling 'let me come in: I am your husband'. Denied legitimate access to the house, he forces his way in, chases Cytherea round the table like a 'panting and maddened demon' and is on the verge of assaulting her when Edward Springrove intervenes (358–9).

Manston's desire for Cytherea is not, in itself, problematic; indeed, it is initially presented as not unpleasurable. When they first meet Cytherea finds herself interested in Manston's 'marvellous beauty, as she might have been in some fascinating panther or leopard' (139), but is later repelled by his overt interest in her. After he asks her to marry him she shrinks from

> the hot voluptuous nature of his passion for her, which, disguise it as he might under a quiet and polished exterior, at times radiated forth with a scorching white heat. She perceived how animal was the love which bargained (213).

Animal imagery of this nature dominates the novel, with Cytherea repeatedly referred to as a helpless bird, Manston as some sort of beast or, ultimately, 'a panting and maddened demon' (359). Manston's desire is problematic because it is misplaced; he is already married at the start of the novel, and later conceals his wife's murder in order to marry Cytherea. What is disturbing about Manston is the intensity of his sexual desire and the sense in which it brings him closer to an animal than a man; being at the mercy of his sexuality lowers him to the level of an animal and his desire cannot ultimately be controlled, despite his best endeavours at adopting a mask of merely polite interest in Cytherea.

Manston's behaviour at this point in the novel clearly points to the dangers of unlicensed male sexual desire. In the actions of Manston, of Troy in *Far From the Madding Crowd* (and of Alec in *Tess of the D'Urbervilles*), Hardy is clearly condemning such uncontrolled desire. Collins and Dickens express similar condemnation in the characters of Mannion, who can happily and knowingly violate Margaret's marital vows and who is accordingly punished for his actions by the removal of all physical appeal, and John Jasper, whose desire for Rosa makes him give little regard to the obvious discomfort and fear he is causing her. But I would argue that these three novelists are even more condemnatory of the unnatural suppression of male sexual desire urged upon Victorian men. The violent actions that govern *Far From the Madding Crowd, Desperate Remedies, Our Mutual Friend, The Mystery of Edwin Drood* and *Basil* are all the result of sexual suppression and unhealthy levels of self-control. Annette Federico, in her examination of masculine identity in Hardy and Gissing, argues that Boldwood exhibits 'the potential power of subdued sexual consciousness when it is disturbed into awareness' (63) and I believe that this applies to all of the novels examined in this chapter.

The eponymous hero of *Basil* exhibits almost unnatural levels of restraint in agreeing not to consummate his marriage for a year. On learning that his wife is sexually involved with another man, Basil's restraint gives way, and he maims his rival in an act of particular violence. In the same novel, the 'villain' Mannion exhibits preternatural levels of willpower, to the extent that he is impossible to 'read'. In Hardy's *Desperate Remedies* Aeneas Manston controls himself to an unnatural degree, until his 'true' nature emerges and he commits murder and attempts to rape his wife. Similarly, Bradley Headstone in *Our Mutual Friend* and Boldwood in *Far From the Madding Crowd* exhibit unhealthy levels of restraint which ultimately erupt into psychotic and deranged behaviour. Given the importance placed on self-control in self-help and advice manuals, it is interesting to note how often the concept is portrayed as a problematic one by the novelists of the day. Although these same novels all exhibit the dangers of unregulated passion (Basil's attack on Mannion, Manston's attack on Cytherea, Headstone's attempted murder of Eugene Wrayburn, Boldwood's descent into psychosis), they are also preaching the dangers of excessive control. As Sussman argues

> while psychic discipline defines what the Victorians term manliness, if such discipline becomes too rigorous the extreme constraint of male desire will distort the male psyche and deform the very energy that powers and empowers men. Setting the intensity of discipline, then, becomes the crucial issue within practice of the self (3).

The case of the Reverend Watson illustrates the inherent dangers of 'too rigorous [a] constraint of male desire'. Found guilty in January 1872 of the murder of his wife the previous year, the Reverend Watson was a 67-year-old clergyman and former headmaster of Stockwell Grammar School. Dismissed from his job after 25 years Watson subsequently became subject to depression and, in a fit of rage, beat his wife to death. After murdering his wife, Watson left a suicide note, reports of which varied significantly from the first mention in the *Times* on 12 October 1871, to the second mention on 11 January 1872. Initially, Watson is alleged to have written: 'in a fit of fury I have killed my wife. Often and often have I endeavoured to restrain myself, but my rage overcame me, and I struck her down' (*Times*, 12 October 1871, 5). This initial version of the letter would suggest the perilous consequences of excessive and prolonged self-control, which could erupt forth in such a violent attack. However, when the letter was read out in court, the wording had changed to: 'I have killed my wife in a fit of rage to which she provoked me. Often, often, has she provoked me before, but I never lost restraint over myself with her till the present occasions, when I allowed fury to carry me away' (*Times*, 12 October 1871, 5). Significantly, Watson confessed to being unable to restrain himself, to exercise self-control, any longer; but, by the time of the trial, his wife's culpability had come to the fore. She had 'provoked' Watson before, and this time he was unable to control himself. A letter to the *Times* from the Rector of Avington, a friend of Watson's, reiterated the argument that Anne Watson was somehow culpable in her own murder, stating that

> I have good reason to feel certain that, in his depressed, melancholy state, he received from his wife some outrageous provocation which deprived him of his habitual self-mastery, and made him for the time quite irresponsible. She was always fretful, and often violent in temper (*Times*, 17 January 1872, 11).

Much of the press coverage centred on the incongruity of the 'master of a grammar-school 25 years, who was a learned and accomplished scholar, and had a high literary reputation' (*Times*, 21 November 1871, 9) committing an act of such ferocity and violence. Hardly surprisingly, many wished Watson to be found insane, in order to 'understand' his crime (in the next chapter, I will show how this kind of justification came to the fore in the closing decades of the century). An editorial in the *Times* argued that

> the power of self-control increases by exercise, while the passions are chastened and subdued by age; and it is not likely that an elderly clergyman, long habituated to external decorum, should have cast its bonds aside under the influence of anything short of madness (19 January 1872, 8).

This desire on the part of the paper to view Watson's crime as an act of madness, rather than the almost inevitable result of exhibiting unnatural self-control for much of his life, demonstrates perhaps a complicity on the part of the press with the hegemonic model of male behaviour that is not so evident in the five novels under examination in this chapter. Collins, Hardy and Dickens all place this concept of self-control at the heart of their works, and all three novelists seem to question its validity as part of appropriate male conduct.

John Jasper (*The Mystery of Edwin Drood*), Mannion (*Basil*), and Aeneas Manston (*Desperate Remedies*) all exhibit superhuman self-control at various points in the novels, but their control is consciously adopted by them to conceal their true intentions or past actions. Whilst adopting this 'exterior of seemliness' they are able to thrive within society, but their masks conceal darker intentions and/or actions. In *The Mystery of Edwin Drood*, as Jasper professes love to Rosa in the garden overlooked on all sides by Rosa's school, there is a marked contrast 'between the violence of his looks and delivery, and the composure of his assumed attitude' – he knows they may be watched, and so feigns an attitude he does not feel. This contrast between appearance and reality is as 'hideous' to Rosa as it is to the narrator, who declares that 'his preservation of his easy attitude [rendered] his working features and his convulsive hands absolutely diabolical' (214–15).

The Luke Fildes illustration which accompanies this scene shows Rosa flinching from Jasper, a detail borne out by repeated references in the text. Rosa's fear of Jasper and his ability to pursue her wherever she goes are reminiscent of Little Nell and Quilp in *The Old Curiosity Shop* (1840–41), again a relationship with disturbing sexual undertones. When Rosa discusses her feelings with Helena Landless she states that Jasper

> has forced me to understand him, without his saying a word; and he has forced me to keep silence, without his uttering a threat. When I play, he never moves his eyes from my hands. When I sing, he never moves his eyes from my lips. When he corrects me, and strikes a note, or a chord, or plays a passage, he himself is in the sounds, whispering that he pursues me as a lover, and commanding me to keep his secret. I avoid his eyes, but he forces me to see them without looking at them … to-night when he watched my lips so closely, as I was singing, besides feeling terrified I felt ashamed and passionately hurt. It was as if he kissed me, and I couldn't bear it, but cried out (70–71).

Through her repeated references to Jasper 'forcing' and 'commanding' her and the sense in which he seems to be devouring her every movement, Dickens leaves us in no doubt that Jasper's attentions towards Rosa are bordering on physical violation; later she declares that his declaration of love has 'soiled' her, leaving her stained with 'impurity' (222). Jasper's interest is misplaced and that is why it is problematic; although young enough to figure as a suitable suitor for Rosa, as Edwin's uncle his response to her is inappropriate.

The *Saturday Review* took exception to the style of Jasper's confession of love, arguing that

> in this precious oration we recognise the worst style of Mr. Dickens, "ticking off" each point ... by the burden of "I loved you madly." But do we recognise anything like the language of a passionate and black hearted villain trying to bully a timid girl? It is the sort of oration which a silly boy, nourished on bad novels, might prepare for such an occasion; but it is stiff and artificial and jerky to a degree which excludes any belief in real passion ... it has an air of affectation and mock-heroics which is palpably inappropriate to the place. It is really curious that so keen an observer should diverge into such poor and stilted bombast whenever he tries the note of intense emotion (17 September 1870, 369).

What the reviewer identifies as 'poor and stilted bombast' is not an error on Dickens's part; Jasper's desire for Rosa is not natural, and therefore the 'stiff and artificial and jerky' nature of his protestation is entirely appropriate.

In *Basil*, when Mannion gets the letter informing him of Margaret's marriage, he notes that 'other people were in the room with me when I read that letter; but my manner betrayed nothing to them. My hand never trembled when I folded the sheet of paper again'. He reads it again later, alone 'with no necessity now for self-control, because no human being was near to look at me' (193). When Basil first meets Mannion he notes that Mannion's expression is

> an utter void ... No mask could have been made expressionless enough to resemble it; and yet it looked like a mask. It told you nothing of his thoughts, when he spoke: nothing of his disposition, when he was silent. His cold grey eyes gave you no help in trying to study him.

His voice 'was as void of expression as his face: it was rather low in tone, but singularly distinct in utterance. He spoke deliberately, but with no emphasis on particular words, and without hesitation in choosing his terms' (90–92). Effectively, Mannion is presented here as some sort of automaton, but what we do not know at the time is that Mannion is exhibiting almost preternatural control at this point in the novel, disguising his loathing of Basil and bitter disappointment at having lost Margaret.

In *Desperate Remedies* Manston constantly hides his true feelings for Cytherea, and there are frequent references to the discrepancy between his outward appearance and true feelings. He remains guarded not only in public 'but even more markedly in secluded places, on occasions when gallantry would have been safe from all discovery ... all the strength of a consuming passion burning in his eyes the while' (140).

Jasper, Mannion and Manston are all ultimately revealed as the 'villains' of these novels, and their self-control is seen as unhealthy from the outset (I am working here on the premise that Jasper murders Edwin Drood). When we examine the ostensibly more sympathetic male characters, however, the novelists' indictment of the gospel of self-control becomes even more telling. The eponymous Basil, Boldwood in *Far From the Madding Crowd*, and Bradley Headstone in *Our Mutual Friend*, would seem in some ways to offer ideals of male behaviour, and yet they are all suppressing their true natures; this unhealthy suppression inevitably leads to eruptions of violent and unnatural acts.

In *Basil*, Mr. Sherwin's bizarre proposal that Basil and Margaret marry, but wait a year before consummating the union, is readily accepted by Basil although, with hindsight, he admits that 'some men more experienced in the world, less mastered by love than I was, would, in my position, have recognized in this proposal an unfair trial of self-restraint – perhaps, something like an unfair humiliation as well' (70). Certainly, Margaret is unimpressed by his self-restraint. As she lies dying of typhus, she raves 'A nice wife I've been to him, and a nice husband he has been to me – a husband who waits a year! Ha! Ha! He calls himself a man, doesn't he? A husband who waits a year!' (233).

Basil's self-control is all the more significant, because he is clearly attracted by Margaret's overt sexuality. The first detail of her appearance that registers with Basil is that she is dark; indeed 'her hair, eyes, and complexion were darker than usual in English women', perhaps hinting at a 'reason' for her moral laxity with Mannion. Her eyes are large and dark, with 'the voluptuous languor of dark eyes', and her lips might be viewed by some as '*too* full' (29). The sensuality of this description is obvious. After Basil's first sight of Margaret he finds his mind 'in utter confusion'; a second viewing leaves him

> insensible for the time to all boding reflections, careless of exercising the smallest self-restraint. I gave myself up to the charm that was at work on me. Prudence, duty, memories and prejudices of home, were all absorbed and forgotten in love – love that I encouraged, that I dwelt over in the first reckless luxury of a new sensation (31, 35–6).

Later, when Mrs. Sherwin's cat kills Margaret's canary, Basil witnesses Margaret's fury, finding her more beautiful in 'the fury of passion' than at any other time. The description of Margaret as she vows to kill the cat is, again, highly sexualized: 'the blood was glowing crimson in her cheeks – her lips were parted as she gasped for breath' (109). Just prior to this incident, having had his one-week engagement to Margaret finalized, Basil rides his horse in a masterpiece of sublimated desire:

> All my wearing and pressing emotions of the morning, had now merged into a wild excitement of body and mind ... The dashing through the rain that still fell;

the feel of the long, powerful, regular stride of the horse under me; the thrill of that physical sympathy which establishes itself between the man and the steed (81).

Despite her obvious physical appeal, Basil is at pains to make clear that he never once thinks of simply seducing Margaret and not marrying her: 'Had such a thought as this, in the faintest, the most shadowy form, crossed my mind, I should have shrunk from it, have shrunk from myself, with horror' (40). He repeatedly expresses his feelings for Margaret in terms of love, not lust. He is 'sickened and shocked' when a shop boy refers to Margaret as 'a very fine young lady, Sir!' with a (presumably lecherous) grin (33).

It is hardly surprising that Basil erupts in an orgy of violence on learning of Margaret's adulterous liaison with Mannion; having hurled Mannion 'with the whole impetus of the raging strength that was let loose in me' face down onto a road laid with new granite, Basil is only prevented from his desire 'to lift him again, and beat out of him, on the granite, not life only, but the semblance of humanity as well' by the sound of someone opening the hotel door nearby (132).

At first glance it might seem as though our sympathies are intended to lie with Basil as the wronged party. Wiener's research shows that killing your wife's lover in the Victorian era was viewed with 'some indulgence' (*Men of Blood*, 202), provided the man was legally married to the woman, and the adultery was accepted as true, both of which provisos are fulfilled in the novel. But there is no evidence of such a straightforward dichotomy between Basil and Mannion; indeed, Collins is exhibiting a great deal of ambivalence in his portrayal of both individuals, and is thereby problematizing the prevailing concepts of masculinity.

Basil and Mannion are clearly intended to be two sides of the same coin, prefiguring the 'doubling' motif that occurs more frequently in fin-de-siècle fiction (see Chapter 5). Dorothy Goldman, in the introduction to the Oxford World's Classics edition of the novel, posits the idea that they are

the same person, forming a single protagonist, incapable of dealing with what then become the conflicting demands of romantic and sexual love. Mannion is the sexually aware and sexually active element, Basil the sentimental and passive element who responds to sexuality with repugnance and guilt (viii–ix).

More than this, Basil is able to control his lust, and not his anger – Mannion the reverse. To labour the comparison even further there are repeated echoes of *Frankenstein* throughout the novel, with the suggestion that the disfigured Mannion is somehow Basil's 'creation' or a part of him. Basil views Mannion as 'an enemy who combined the ferocious vigilance of a savage with the far-sighted iniquity of a civilised man' much as Frankenstein's creature combines the looks of a 'savage' with the educated reasoning of a 'civilised man' (210).

Collins is addressing two extreme models of male sexuality in this novel – abnegation and abandon – and neither is offered as suitable. Mannion must be punished for his cold-blooded seduction of Margaret and cuckolding of Basil, but Basil too must suffer for his reluctance to embrace the physical side of his nature. His final picture of himself, living in Clara's home, willfully retired from the world, is not offered by Collins as a successful blueprint for male behaviour. Basil's fate is surely offered as a criticism of the overly feminized model of male conduct.

To a certain extent, the same is true of Aeneas Manston in Hardy's *Desperate Remedies*. There is a considerable degree of ambivalence in Hardy's portrayal of Manston: partly cast in the mould of a Gothic villain, dark and mysterious, an 'extremely handsome man, well-formed, and well-dressed' with a 'clear, masculine voice' (127, 126) there is also a strangely feminine quality to his looks, contributing to what Mary Rimmer has identified as the 'pervasive instability of gender' in the novel as a whole, where '"womanly" and "manly" attributes keep turning up in people of the wrong gender' (xxv, xxvi). His complexion is wonderfully clear and his lips are 'full and luscious to a surprising degree, possessing a woman-like softness of curve, and a ruby redness so intense, as to testify strongly to much susceptibility of heart where feminine beauty was concerned' (128). Later in the novel, the woman masquerading as Manston's wife goads him about his anxiety, declaring that 'anybody would think that you were the woman and I the man' (325). Perversely, Manston is unable to control his male sexual drive precisely because of this feminine quality to his looks; his woman-like lips are indicative of weakness and susceptibility. Richard Nemesvari argues that Manston is 'not masculine in the right way'; because his masculinity 'cannot be safely integrated into the constraints of Victorian society, he becomes a disruptive force which must be contained' (85–6).

Boldwood, in Hardy's *Far From the Madding Crowd*, is a man in constant control of his feelings, unable ever to express what he truly feels until he murders Troy:

> The quiet mean to which we originally found him adhering, and in which with few exceptions he had continually moved, was that of neutralization: it was not structural at all. That stillness which struck casual observers more than anything else in his character and habit, and seemed so precisely like the rest of inanition, was the perfect balance of enormous antagonistic forces – positives and negatives in fine adjustment. His equilibrium disturbed, he was in extremity at once.
>
> Boldwood was thus either hot or cold. If an emotion possessed him at all, it ruled him: a feeling not mastering him was entirely latent (105).

Boldwood is here exhibiting precisely the level of self-control that was expected of the Victorian male, holding in balance 'enormous antagonistic forces', and Hardy is exploring the cost that exacts upon the male psyche. Once his attention rests on Bathsheba, initially almost as an experimental attempt to understand the allure she holds for other men, Boldwood is undone:

> When Bathsheba's figure shone upon the farmer's eyes it lighted him up as a little moon lights up a great tower. A man's body is the shell or the tablet of his

soul as he is reserved or ingenuous, overflowing or self-contained. There was a change in Boldwood's exterior from its former impassableness: his face showed that he was now living outside his defences for the first time, and with a fearful sense of exposure. It is the usual experience of strong natures when they love (106–7).

As Bathsheba comments, 'How was I to know that what is a pastime to all other men was death to you', and even Gabriel Oak remarks that 'his life is a total blank whenever he isn't hoping for you' (176, 311). Boldwood is so undone by his love for Bathsheba that Oak perceives that 'this constant passion … had left him not the man he once had been' (320). Indeed, he is not 'the man he once had been' because that man was a social construct, a creature fighting its natural impulses. Having exhibited such masterful self-control and almost monastic seclusion from the life of the passions for 40 years, Boldwood is unable to control the impulse that arises within him. Through the character of Boldwood Hardy is both questioning the 'rules' governing male behaviour and also criticizing a nature which has formerly sought to remove itself from all contact with the domestic sphere. His ignorance of women (to the extent that he views them as 'remote phenomena … comets of … uncertain aspect' [102]), and his lack of realization that flirtation is a 'pastime', are his undoing. After he has murdered Troy, a locked closet is discovered in Boldwood's room. Within the closet are several lady's dresses all in Bathsheba's favourite colours, two muffs and jewellery 'all carefully packed in paper, and each package was labelled "Bathsheba Boldwood", a date being subjoined six years in advance in every instance' (337–8). Here we have the necessary adjuncts of domesticity, but locked away and representing a perverted response to the domestic sphere – Bathsheba is not yet his wife. Hardy appears, then, to be calling into question the male gospel of self-control, but also suggesting that men should, indeed, embrace the domestic sphere and marital relations.

The character of Boldwood is prefigured by Dickens's Bradley Headstone in *Our Mutual Friend*. The two men both exhibit an unhealthy removal from the normal affairs of mankind, and are both totally undone when exposed to the power of passionate affection. The consequences of such unnatural restraint are manifested as extreme violence in both men.

Bradley Headstone is perpetually ill at ease. He sits 'in a constrained manner' (395); his mouth is so dry he has difficulty articulating (399); frequent reference is made to his 'grinding out' (401) his speech, at one point 'separating his words over-carefully, and speaking as if he were repeating them from a book' (446); he sweats a lot; he has 'a curious tight-screwing movement of his right hand in the clenching palm of his left, like the action of one who was being physically hurt, and was unwilling to cry out' (400). In the closing stages of the novel, his lack of ease within his own skin and emotional torment reduce him to simply a 'haggard head' (610). His efforts at suppressing his true nature result in spontaneous nose bleeds, which he explains to Rogue Riderhood thus: 'I can't keep it back. It has happened twice – three times – four times – I don't know how many times – since last night. I taste it, smell it, see it, it chokes me, and then it breaks out like this' (704). Rarely has a character been created who is so entirely ill at ease with himself and the world.

In a lengthy early description of Bradley, Dickens dwells on the discomfort he exhibits in his 'uniform' of

> decent black coat and waistcoat, and decent white shirt, and decent formal black tie, and decent pantaloons of pepper and salt, with his decent silver watch in his pocket and its decent hair-guard round his neck ... He was never seen in any other dress, and yet there was a certain stiffness in his manner of wearing this, as if there were a want of adaptation between him and it, recalling some mechanics in their holiday clothes (266).

It is only when he adopts the disguise of Rogue Riderhood that he looks at ease: 'whereas, in his own schoolmaster clothes, he usually looked as if they were the clothes of some other man, he now looked, in the clothes of some other man or men, as if they were his own' (697).

Dickens's criticism of Bradley seems a little puzzling at first. In some senses, one feels that Bradley should be the hero of this novel, a self-made man who has acquired a respectable position in society through hard work and fortitude, an exemplary model of male conduct. It is only when we come to examine the cultural context of Bradley's profession that it becomes apparent why he is cast in such an unattractive light. Lauren Goodlad has examined the notion of the pauper-schoolmaster (Bradley's position), and Dickens's resistance to such a concept. Although a vociferous exponent of public education, Dickens was opposed to the pupil/teacher scheme, believing that 'the wrong kind of education would dehumanize the working classes' and that moral fibre was improved 'through the curbing of social mobility, and the affirmation of a stable hierarchy in which individuals are, like the Boffins, content to develop within the bounds of their native rank' (Goodlad, 162, 163–4).

The pupil/teacher scheme originated by Sir James Kay-Shuttleworth enabled pauper children to have a five-year pupil-teacher apprenticeship (just as we see in Bradley and Charlie Hexam) and then compete for a place at a training college. Inevitably, in order to instill sufficient knowledge in these working-class men to enable them to impart it to others, there was an element of hot-housing about their training, evident in Bradley's 'mechanical' acquisition of knowledge which masks the 'kind of settled trouble' in a face 'belonging to a naturally slow or inattentive intellect that had toiled hard to get what it had won, and that had to hold it now that it was gotten' (266).

The scheme was not without its opponents, Dickens included, and caused particular concern for the fact that working-class men would be promoted into the middle classes; in order to mitigate these fears, teachers were ostensibly raised above their working-class charges (and their own working-class origins), but kept subordinate to the local ruling classes, by means of clergymen and prominent families being placed in a supervisory role over the schools. Pauper-teachers were thus placed in a societal no man's land, positioned above their charges, but subject to the scrutiny of a class they could never belong to; hence Eugene's view of Bradley 'as a creature of no worth' and his addressing Bradley for much of the novel as simply 'Schoolmaster ... a most respectable title' (341). This goes some way to explaining the permanent discomfort Bradley suffers from:

> suppression of so much to make room for so much, had given him a constrained manner, over and above. Yet there was enough of what was animal, and of what was fiery (though smouldering), still visible in him, to suggest that if young Bradley Headstone, when a pauper lad, had chanced to be told off for the sea, he would not have been the last man in a ship's crew. Regarding that origin of his, he was proud, moody, and sullen, desiring it to be forgotten. And few people knew of it (266–7).

Bradley labours under a double set of unnatural constraints; not simply as a pupil/teacher operating in a societal no man's land, but also as a man subject to 'animal ... fiery ... smouldering' passions which he is forced to sublimate. Because he has been placed in an invidious position, he remains permanently ill at ease within his own body and his dis-ease becomes 'the expression of Dickens's antipathy toward social engineering' (Goodlad, 176). As Juliet John argues, 'the privileging of the mind above emotion underpins, for Dickens, the misguided intellectual elitism which, far from improving the lot of the workers, compounds their cultural alienation' (Dickens's Villains, 3).

When Rogue Riderhood visits Bradley in his schoolroom, there is something horrific about this 'slouching man of forbidding appearance' appearing in the context of Bradley's professional life. But it is precisely because Bradley does not truly 'belong' in this setting that Riderhood is able to invade his professional space with such ease. Throughout the exchange Riderhood refers to 'Totherest' (his name for Bradley) in the third person, as if they were referring to someone else, which in a sense they are; 'Totherest' is the true Bradley, the schoolmaster is an act. In a final affirmation of identity Riderhood asks Bradley to write his own name on the board, and the children chant it out; when Riderhood reveals that he knows all that Bradley has been up to, Bradley 'turned his face to the black board and slowly wiped his name out', effectively erasing the veneer of respectability he has acquired for himself (864, 867).

In the light of Goodlad's thesis, the positioning of Bradley becomes far more understandable, but it is important also to consider whether Bradley's unease is indicative of some deeper-rooted malaise, and the means whereby Dickens may be questioning at a more profound level the relationship between masculinity and the domestic sphere.

Throughout the novel Bradley resists the attentions of Miss Peecher, a fellow teacher at his school who is in love with him. Significantly Miss Peecher is always shown in a domestic setting, frequently 'watering the flowers in the little dusty bit of garden attached to her small official residence'. Miss Peecher's charms are considerable: 'small, shiny, neat, methodical and buxom ... cherry-cheeked and tuneful of voice', and she seems the living embodiment of the domestic sphere:

'a little pincushion, a little housewife, a little book, a little workbox, a little set of tables and weights and measures, and a little woman, all in one' (268). Yet Bradley resists this entirely suitable companion, choosing to torture himself with his love for Lizzie, an affection which in itself brings him no pleasure, only physical and mental distress.

Eve Kosofsky Sedgwick, in her seminal analysis of *Our Mutual Friend*, argues that Bradley's 'initial, hating terror of Lizzie was a terror of … being "drawn" from himself, having his accumulated value sucked from him down the void of her illiteracy and powerlessness' (169). Sedgwick goes on to argue that this sense of being 'drawn' from himself is as much about sublimated feelings of homosexuality as it is about illiteracy and powerlessness. If Bradley is indeed subliminally attracted to Eugene Wrayburn, this would explain the compulsive and tortured nature of his obsession with the man (and, of course, Eugene's corresponding fascination with Bradley, albeit masked under a veneer of indifference); but I would argue that Dickens is using this potentially homoerotic material to explore wider issues of male discontent with the domestic. Both men resist the domestic sphere, and exhibit a degree of discomfort with the traditional role afforded them. When Eugene finally succumbs to marriage with Lizzie, she is cast as much as a carer as a wife and, conversely, the most functional domestic relationship in the novel is that between Eugene Wrayburn and Mortimer Lightwood. Just as the presence of Phineas in *John Halifax, Gentleman* shows the problem of how the domestic can be a feminizing, potentially emasculating zone, so Bradley and Eugene's resistance to a traditional domestic set-up reveals this as a place where their masculinity can come unstuck.

Dickens is using both Bradley and Eugene to problematize models of male behaviour. Bradley should be the hard-working hero, Eugene the indolent villain, and yet a simple reversal of this dichotomy is far too clumsy for someone of Dickens's capabilities. Dickens is questioning the validity of either of these models of masculinity, and finds both wanting. Hence the fact that many readers have found the pairing of Eugene and Lizzie an unsatisfactory conclusion to the novel, because Eugene does not feel like the 'hero' of the work.

Dickens uses Bradley to explore the perilous effects of social engineering and unnatural self-restraint; but he is equally critical of the indolent and effete 'born' gentleman, encapsulated in the character of Eugene. The torturous battles between the two men can thus be viewed as both a criticism of and perhaps an attempted working out of these conflicting class-based models of masculinity. It is particularly useful to examine Eugene in the context of the 'gospel of work' (Donahay, 23), another model of masculinity which dominated mid-Victorian thinking.

Alongside the importance of rigorous self-control, a true man was seen as industrious and working hard for the preservation and elevation of his family, a credo which runs throughout the most influential writings of the period. Examining Samuel Smiles's *Self-Help*, Donahay argues that 'if you do not work you cannot be called a man … so that "work" is the basic building block of masculine identity' (30). For Ruskin, the Victorian male was 'active, progressive' and 'eminently the doer' (82). As Donahay argues, 'if you are not working you are not masculine' (27). Davidoff and Hall argue that the concept of work became a central tenet of manliness: 'work was not to be despised, rather it was to be seen as doing God's duty in the world. Work was dignified, serious and a properly masculine pursuit' (111).

What is again important to stress is that this linking of industry with manliness was central to a *middle-class* view of masculinity. Donahay's reading of Smiles, that 'if you do not work you cannot be called a man', carries within it an implied criticism of the upper classes, who were not necessarily compelled to work. Davidoff and Hall emphasize the importance of industry to the middle classes 'whose livelihood so often derived from the despised activities of commerce' to the extent that middle-class men in the mid-nineteenth century saw their 'masculine self' as 'more deeply implicated in what they did rather than in who they were in terms of kinship or religious loyalties' (112, 230). Hall identifies the middle-class critique of the aristocracy as resting on the latter's perceived

> softness, sensuousness, indolence, luxuriousness, foppishness, and lack of a proper sense of purpose and direction. Central to their new and alternative set of values was the concept of the dignity of work ... A man's individuality, his male identity, was closely tied to independence. That independence, however, was no longer predicated on having the wherewithal not to have to work but rather on the dignity of work itself (257).

Hence, in Braddon's *Lady Audley's Secret* Robert Audley is transformed from an indolent reader of French novels into a man with a purpose; as a result, he becomes a 'real' man who is worthy of the love of Clara Talboys. The eponymous hero of *John Halifax, Gentleman* becomes a 'gentlemen' partly through his hard work and industry.

At the start of *Our Mutual Friend* Eugene Wrayburn is cast in the role of the aristocratic gentleman who lacks an occupation, marked exactly by that 'indolence, luxuriousness, foppishness, and lack of a proper sense of purpose and direction' that Hall identifies as being associated with the aristocracy. This indolence is stressed throughout the early part of the novel, and again in the penultimate chapter with Mortimer commenting that he believes his small private income 'has been an effective Something, in the way of preventing me from turning to at Anything. And I think yours has been much the same' (885). In direct contrast to Bradley, ill at ease on all occasions, Eugene moves with consummate ease,

> coolly sauntering ... with a cigar in his mouth, his coat thrown back, and his hands behind him. Something in the careless manner of this person, and in a certain lazily arrogant air with which he approached, holding possession of twice as much pavement as another would have claimed, instantly caught the boy's [Charley's] attention (279).

The prevailing term used to describe Eugene's movements is 'lounged', a pejorative suggesting lassitude as much as physical ease.

It is his growing interest in Lizzie which prompts the first changes in Eugene, which are exhibited through a burgeoning sense of industry, or at least focus. Mortimer notices the first change in Eugene 'best expressed perhaps as an intensification of all that was wildest and most negligent and reckless in his friend' (213). When Eugene visits Lizzie in the house she shares with Jenny Wren 'it might have been rather more perceptible that his attention was concentrated upon her for certain moments, than its concentration upon any subject for any short time ever was, elsewhere' (285).

After the attack by Bradley Eugene becomes dehumanized, his body referred to repeatedly as 'it', as Lizzie struggles to pull him into the boat. Once Lizzie confirms that the body is Eugene, the body becomes 'him' and 'he', but with a repetition of the word 'disfigured' (four times on p. 769), and the fact that Eugene is now a 'wreck' (824). In a sense, Eugene has to die before he can prove himself worthy of Lizzie's love; for him to become morally better he has to be physically destroyed, to lose the physical ease which characterizes his class. Immediately after the attack, he has to subject himself to repeated effort simply to stay conscious: 'Keep me here for only a single minute. I am going away again. Don't let me go. Hear me speak first. Stop me – stop me!' (810). Effectively, Eugene has to work at simply being a man, and once he has worked hard enough he is deemed worthy of Lizzie's love. From being the 'gentleman' who, by virtue of the moniker, is suspected by all of simply intending to seduce and abandon Lizzie, he becomes a true gentleman; as Twemlow declares of the marriage, it is 'a question of the feelings of a gentleman … gratitude, of respect, of admiration, and affection' (891).

Conclusion

These novels mark a significant shift from earlier portrayals of domestic murderers; the male protagonists are no longer simply 'evil', or working as a tool of the devil, they are men struggling to position themselves within a society which imposes unnatural constraints. Their actions of murder, rape or mutilation are all, to an extent, presented as a response to the unhealthy demands society imposes on them and, as a result, we feel a degree of sympathy for them. Even a character such as Manston in *Desperate Remedies* is afforded a certain level of understanding, and Headstone's tortured psyche, while not making us *like* him, certainly makes us feel for him. That is not to say, of course, that their actions are deemed acceptable or forgivable; Basil, Manston, Boldwood and Headstone all suffer visible torment and remorse; and, whilst it is impossible to know how *The Mystery of Edwin Drood* would have developed, John Jasper, even in the early stages of the novel, could in no way be described as happy or content.

Using the actions of the male protagonists to critique societal models of masculinity, these novels are effecting a transition between two views of transgressive behaviour. Earlier in the century, the actions of Manston or Jasper would have been viewed as the work of the devil; later in the century, an author might have examined the biological or environmental factors that determined the character's actions. Positioned in the middle decades of the century, a man's propensity to good or evil was increasingly seen as subject to the exercise of his own will and the actions of these characters would be seen as a result of their lack of self-government; yet it is precisely this over-reliance on self-control that all three novelists are critiquing, and which places the reader in a sometimes uncomfortable relationship with the male protagonist. With psychology in its infancy, none of the novelists can draw on the full lexicon of psychological analysis to explore fully the psyche of their characters, so we are offered a degree of access to their minds, and yet we are pulled back by a moral imperative to condemn their actions. It is not until the closing decades of the century, with an upsurge in writing about the psyche and an increased emphasis on biological and environmental factors, that authors are in a position to present a transgressive character without the need to condemn their actions.

Chapter 5
'Changed, indeed, but not transformed': The Fin de Siècle and the Female Domestic Murderer

During the interval of two or three weeks that usually elapses between the condemnation and the execution of some distinguished – one might almost be tempted to say "fashionable" – murder, in this country, the public are, as a rule, treated, through the medium of the press, to a series of details respecting the convict which, to all decent and well-regulated minds, must be nothing less than nauseating. We are told from day to day how he slept over night, and sometimes what he dreamed about; what he ate and drank for breakfast, and dinner, and supper; what he thought of the judge and jury that tried him, and the counsel that prosecuted and defended him; we are regaled with all the mendacious stories he has concocted in the desperate hope of securing a reprieve; we are invited to peruse his farewell letters to his parents, if he has any, or to some wretched woman whom he has deceived; and, worst of all, we are dosed with copious draughts of sickening cant, the almost blasphemous utterances of the condemned wretch – utterances so unctuous in their hypocritical pretence of piety that the perusal of them causes an ordinarily sober-minded man to feel as though he were quite an inferior being, spiritually speaking, beside the seraphic creature who is about to leave a world not half good enough for him.

This account of the figure of the murderer and his (or her) last days, taken from the article 'Murder Madness' in *Sala's Journal*, 5 November 1892, could have been lifted straight from a broadsheet much earlier in the century, or even from the century before. Details such as those listed could certainly have come from the trial of William Corder in 1828, the first case examined in this book. If we pursue the argument further, though, a shift in thinking becomes apparent. The piece goes on to argue thus:

If the murderer is very bad indeed – and there are degrees of heinousness in murder, though the law, in its wisdom, declines to recognize any distinctions – an endeavour is made by a knot of busybodies to show that he is mad, and therefore irresponsible, and therefore ought not to be punished. If the fantastic antics of the cunning culprit do not seem sufficiently irrational to prove him crazy, the history of his father and mother, his sisters, his cousins, and his aunts, is diligently traced in order to ascertain whether one or more of his family did not show, at some time or other, more or less pronounced symptoms of dementia, and so set up a plea of hereditary insanity.

With its focus on the murderer's mental state and ancestry, this second paragraph gestures towards a more 'psychological' reading of the accused and shows a significant change in the treatment of and public attitudes towards those committing murder.

The two viewpoints expressed in this article, one harking back to at least one hundred years previously, another perhaps gesturing towards the new century (for the historian at least, if not for contemporaries), encapsulate the cultural ambivalence exhibited during the fin de siècle. This is not to say that the fin de siècle was subject to any more instability than earlier decades of the nineteenth century, but what is significant is that this ambivalence generated by differing and conflicting discourses was directly reflected in the portrayal of the domestic murderer.

These closing decades of the nineteenth century reveal a society caught between two epochs: harking back to the Victorian era and gesturing forwards towards Modernism. As Sally Ledger and Roger Luckhurst identify:

> the Victorian fin de siècle was an epoch of endings and beginnings. The collision between the old and the new that characterized the turn of the century marks it as an excitingly volatile and transitional period; a time when British cultural politics were caught between two ages, the Victorian and the Modern; a time fraught with anxiety and with an exhilarating sense of possibility.

This combination of 'anxiety' and the 'exhilarating sense of possibility' touched on almost all areas of life, with a 'constellation of new formations: the new woman, the new imperialism, the new realism, the new drama, and the new journalism, all arriving alongside "new" human sciences like psychology, psychical research, sexology, and eugenics' (Ledger and Luckhurst, xiii).

A period of enormous social, literary and technological advancement, it was also a time of genuine concern about the direction society was heading in. The security of the domestic sphere was challenged to a certain extent by the burgeoning feminist movement, by questions surrounding sexual orientation (as manifested most visibly in the 1895 trials of Oscar Wilde), by early attempts at a more psychological reading of actions, by growing anxiety that the privacy afforded by the home could conceal transgressive actions, and by concerns regarding the enervation of the city and the subsequent perceived degeneration in the health of the nation.[1] Gail Cunningham encapsulates it as

> a period in which everything could be challenged, a time of enthusiastic extremism and gleeful revolt ... But it was also a period of deeply serious inquiry, of impassioned debate over central questions of moral and social behaviour

---

[1]   Marie-Christine Leps has argued that the 'management problems' of nineteenth-century cities such as London and Paris were 'perceived as symptoms of a physical and moral deterioration of society' and 'the notion of crime was thus included in a web of concepts where pathology, sociology and morality interconnected' (23).

which created acute anxiety in those who felt themselves to be witnessing the breakdown of the rules traditionally thought to hold society together (1).

For Lyn Pykett,

> the fin de siècle was a time of great cultural ferment ... the rending of social, moral and aesthetic traditions, the growth of mass society, the spread of urbanism, the development of a consumer culture, and the physical and mental deterioration of 'civilised' man; in short, it was a crisis in civilization (*Reading Fin de Siècle Fictions*, 2).

This chapter argues that the portrayal of the female domestic murderer at the fin de siècle was subject to the same shifting configurations exhibited elsewhere at this time; I have focused on the *female* murderer because the changing role of women was of particular interest at this time, with the emergence of the so-called New Woman, discussed later in this chapter. In both trial coverage and in fiction, an uneasy alliance of melodrama and a more modern moral outlook results in an uneven representation of the protagonist, often affording her a greater degree of sympathy, but ultimately still punishing her for her transgressions. Such ambivalence was a manifestation of three key areas of change: the perceived changing relationship between women and the domestic space, a process of change that was both a cause and an effect of the burgeoning feminist movement; developments in criminology and the treatment of the criminal; and the emergence of psychology as a scientific discipline. Individually, and also together, these areas of 'cultural ferment' account for the shifting portrayal of female domestic murderers in particular. The shifts in representation occur not only in the trial proceedings, but also in the fiction of the period; the clear dichotomy of good and evil and the certainty of evil being punished from the earlier decades giving way to what Weiner has identified as

> a diffusion of evil and to more incomplete resolutions. If a certain crudity and violence of feeling were in retreat, so too was an assurance of the complete defeat of evil. Villainy was appearing in more unexpected social locales and in more complex and unpredictable forms that were less clearly distinguishable from good (*Reconstructing the Criminal*, 246).

In what follows I will, firstly, establish a context for these shifting portrayals, in parallel with an account of three notorious court cases of the period: Adelaide Bartlett's trial for the murder of her husband in 1886; Florence Maybrick's trial for the murder of her husband in 1889; and Eleanor Pearcey's trial for the murder of her lover's wife and child in 1890. Thereafter I will move on to an examination of female domestic murderers in two fictional works, Mona Caird's *The Wing of Azrael* (1889) and Thomas Hardy's *Tess of the D'Urbervilles* (1891). In determining the shifts in portrayal of the key protagonists in each case, the chapter will examine the interplay that took place at this time between the discourses of psychology, criminology, criminal trials and works of fiction, arguing ultimately that the portrayal of the female domestic murderer at the fin de siècle gestures towards a revision of domestic ideology as a whole.

Firstly, then, briefly to contextualize the changing relations between women and the domestic sphere, which were manifold. On an institutionalized level, the legal position of women within marriage was significantly improved by the Married Woman's Property Act of 1882, which gave property rights to married woman, and an Act of 1891, following the *Regina v. Jackson* case, which denied men the right to detain and imprison their wives. Alongside these changes to the legal status of married women, an increasing number of women were remaining single. A census of 1891 revealed just under 2.5 million unmarried women within a total population of approximately 900,000 more women than men. One solution to this perceived problem of 'surplus' women was to send them to the colonies, but campaigners for women's rights resisted such moves, calling instead for proper education and employment for these women to enable them to support themselves. Such moves were partly supported by changes to the education of women in the closing decades of the century. The 1870s to 90s saw the establishment of many new secondary schools for girls, and by 1898 80,000 girls over the age of 12 were attending secondary school. Alongside this establishment of secondary education, there was significant expansion of higher education for women. By 1897, there were nine women's colleges in Oxford, London and Cambridge, with a total of 748 students.[2] It was, of course, largely women of the middle and upper classes who benefited from such educational reform.[3]

Together with these changes to married women's legal status and women's education, there was a general movement of women away from the sanctity of the home and into the wider world:

> changes in the economy increased the demand for female employees in schools, hospitals and offices. As a result the numbers of women teachers, nurses, secretaries and clerks grew substantially, while women made smaller but highly visible inroads into professions like journalism and the factory inspectorate. By 1891 some 240,000 women were reckoned to be in 'professional occupations' ... The working girl had become a familiar feature of offices and shops in all the big cities (Tosh, 152).

These changes to women's position in society brought with them enormous cultural anxiety. To understand this level of anxiety, it is important to reiterate the persistent belief within the Victorian establishment that, without a marital system that saw the wife safely ensconced at home and providing a retreat for her husband from the cares of commerce or business, the social fabric would simply crumble,

---

[2]   See Ledger, *The New Woman*, chapter 1, for a fuller exploration of the changes in women's education.

[3]   For an examination of working-class moves towards greater emancipation, see Judith R. Walkowitz's discussion of the Hallelujah Lasses of the Salvation Army, and the match-girl strike of 1888, in Judith R. Walkowitz, *City of Dreadful Delight*, 73–80.

and Britain's supremacy on the world stage would be undermined. Education was deemed to be masculinizing women, leading to fears of degeneration, with the belief that such women would give birth to weaker stock.[4] More than this, the new breed of burgeoning feminists, collectively entitled the New Women, were perceived as endorsing 'free love' and rejecting motherhood, thus undermining the institution of marriage as a whole.

The New Woman is one of the most resonant figures of these closing decades, but it is worth noting that, much as the models of masculinity examined in the previous chapter were simply that – models, or constructs – so was the New Woman. She was, according to Lyn Pykett, a 'representation ... a construct ... a beacon of progress or beast of repression, depending on who was doing the naming' (*The 'Improper' Feminine*, 137, 139). Consequently she could be portrayed in any number of ways:

> a mannish, chain-smoking and aggressive virago; a physically and morally strong, caring and altruistic, rationally dressed, above all sophisticated woman, whose steadfast refusal to shut her eyes to injustice and oppression had made her into an impassioned advocate of her sex; or a bicycle-riding and latchkey-wielding, athletic and yet fashionable young lady, whose knowledge and experience had widened her horizons without deflecting her from her wish to have a husband and family (Heilmann, *The Late-Victorian Marriage Question*, i, x).

As a result, she was subject to what Heilmann has identified as 'semantic instability', resulting in part from the 'multiplicity of agents who had an ideological stake in constructing her' (Heilmann, *New Woman Fiction*, 2). Although the individual concerns of New Woman writers varied widely over issues such as marriage and motherhood, there was a common thread concerning the idea of domestic entrapment; all the New Woman writers sought greater emancipation within the domestic sphere. As a result, the New Woman

> unequivocally represented a challenge to patriarchy. She sought to lead an independent life not so much from necessity as from choice ... Most important of all, the New Woman's determination to live away from the parental home challenged traditional notions of domestic order (Tosh, 153).

When we come to examine the portrayal of women charged with domestic murder at this time, and also the fictional portrayals of female murderers, a similar instability occurs to that identified by Heilmann, with Hartman suggesting that female murderers

> were almost never presented as the women they were. They assumed multiple identities fashioned both by themselves and by others. In legal proceedings the

---

[4]   For a fuller discussion of the issues surrounding degeneration, see Daniel Pick, *Faces of Degeneration: A European Disorder c. 1848–c. 1918* (Cambridge: CUP, 1989).

masks they wore proved useful to them in some cases and detrimental in others, but in all they served to shield contemporaries from the disturbing countenances of real women (255).

Despite what Hartman identifies as the masking of the true countenances of 'real women', there were some positive shifts in the representation of domestic murderers, with the accused not always subject to straightforward moral opprobrium. In particular, there was an increasing ability and willingness to separate out the two issues of adultery and murder. Earlier in the century, proof of adultery or sexual misconduct was tantamount to proof of murder: during the 1857 trial of Madeleine Smith for the murder of her lover, Emile L'Angelier, Smith's defence team was at pains to play down the specific sexual content of her letters to her lover, believing that an open expression of her desire for him would prejudice her in the eyes of the court. However, the later case of Florence Maybrick reveals no attempt to hide her adultery. An American by birth, Florence Maybrick married her husband, James, in 1880 at the age of 18; he was 23 years her senior. Found guilty in August 1889 of the murder of her husband, Maybrick's death sentence was commuted to life imprisonment after conflicting medical evidence over the cause of death roused huge public support in her favour (it was alleged that Maybrick had extracted the arsenic from fly-papers by soaking them in water, and then administered the poison to her husband, James). Letters were sent to the Queen, the Prince and Princess of Wales, and nearly all the government ministers, and one petition alone carried 50,000 signatures (*Times*, 15 August 1889, 5) with the total number of signatures across all petitions numbering almost half a million.

Leaving aside the moral issues surrounding the death sentence and the distaste the public felt for the hanging of a woman (particularly a middle-class woman, as Maybrick was), what is particularly significant about the case is that Maybrick was openly conducting an affair with a Mr. Alfred Brierley, and that the allegations of infidelity were never denied during the trial. They did attract much interest on the part of the press, but not sufficient to alienate Maybrick from the public's sympathy. Unlike trials earlier in the century, where openly professed adultery would be seen, at the very least, as evidence of a possible inclination to commit murder, much was made in Maybrick's trial of the need to distinguish clearly between the act of adultery, and the act of murder. Sir Charles Russell, in his summing up of the defence, argued that

> there was a great chasm between such an offence against morality, grave as it was, and the felonious killing of her husband. Moral faults in a man were too often regarded as venial; but in the case of the woman it was the unforgivable sin. She was regarded as a leper and deprived of all sympathy and comfort. Were the jury, because she had sinned once, to misjudge her always? When woman fell, if all was known, some palliation might frequently be found, though no excuse.

Mr. Addison, summing up for the prosecution, argued that Maybrick's letters to Brierley 'showed that the prisoner was capable of duplicity, deceit, and falsehood' but was forced to concede that adultery was not evidence of murderous instinct (*Times*, 6 August 1889, 9). An editorial in the previous day's *Times* argued similarly that Maybrick's passion for Brierley should not be assumed as 'so intense as to lead her to commit murder in order to be free to marry him.' A letter to the newspaper from 'a barrister of six years' standing' argued that Mr. Justice Stephen, in his summing up, had dwelt too much on 'the heinousness of Mrs. Maybrick's admitted immorality' (10 August 1889, 4). There is clearly a shift in public, or perhaps even official thinking at work here (the letter is, after all, from a barrister). Whilst still regarding an adulterous wife as guilty of a heinous crime, there is a very clear distinction made between adultery and murder. It is difficult to determine whether this results in a clarity of approach, in the sense that one crime is not blurred into another, or in confusion, in that the public might condemn the adulterer and yet be forced to defend them against the charge of murder. Mary S. Hartman has argued that 'it was proof of adultery, not proof of murder, that convicted Florence Maybrick' (218), suggesting that the distinction between the two crimes may not have been so effective a defence as it first appears.

Although perhaps suggestive of a more liberal attitude to infidelity, there is still evidence within Maybrick's trial of the centrality of the domestic sphere to a woman's existence, or perhaps the desire to perceive it as such. When questioned by Michael, James Maybrick's brother, as to why she had not called in nurses sooner to look after James, Florence said 'she had nursed him herself and no one had a better right to do so'. A *Times* editorial took umbrage with 'the hysterical agitation which has made of Mrs. Maybrick a species of heroine', arguing that, even if not guilty of murder, her infidelity meant she had exhibited 'treachery as a wife' which ought to 'exclude her from the category of ladies who deserve sentimental admiration and bouquets of flowers' (reported in the *York Herald*, 12 August 1889, 5). What certainly comes through in the various witness testimonies is the stifling lack of privacy within a middle-class household, with Maybrick rarely left alone with her husband, and under the constant surveillance of servants, doctors, and her brother-in-law. The claustrophobic quality of her life resonates with one of the central concerns of the fin-de-siècle feminist movement, that of domestic entrapment.

The Adelaide Bartlett trial, three years prior to Florence Maybrick's, offers another insight into the domestic position of women in these closing decades of the century. In April 1886, Adelaide Bartlett was tried for the murder of her husband, Edwin. It was alleged that Adelaide and her lover, the Reverend George Dyson, had poisoned Edwin with chloroform. Adelaide was initially charged alongside Dyson, a Wesleyan minister, but charges against Dyson were dismissed at the start of the trial, and Adelaide was tried alone, and acquitted to great public support: 'the sympathy for the thirty-year-old accused was near universal. Her lawyer was mobbed by enthusiastic crowds when he emerged from the Old Bailey' (Hartman, 179). The case generated enormous public interest not simply because Bartlett was a woman, but also because of the peculiar circumstances of her marriage. Adelaide and Edwin had been married for nearly 12 years at the time of Edwin's death on

New Year's Day, 1886. In conversation with Alfred Leach, the Bartletts' doctor, Adelaide revealed the peculiar nature of her married life:

> being married young, she had been induced to enter into a marriage contract, scarcely understanding the meaning of it. The marital relations, in deference to the view of her husband, were to be strictly platonic. That compact was adhered to between them for a time. After her confinement the platonic relations were resumed. Her husband was affectionate, and they strove in every way to fulfil each other's wishes, and succeeded in living on most amicable terms ... No female acquaintances were invited but he liked to surround her with male friends; he thought her clever, and the more admiration she obtained the more he was pleased, and their attentions to her seemed to give him pleasure ... They became acquainted with Mr. Dyson, her husband threw them together and asked them in his presence to kiss, and seemed to like it. He had given her, she said, to Mr. Dyson in a platonic sense (*Times*, 15 April 1886, 3).

Despite her protestations of conjugal bliss on the day before Edwin's death, Adelaide subsequently confessed to Dr. Leach that

> her relations with her husband had not been pleasant, that there had been no intercourse between them for a very considerable time; that the deceased had, in conversation, spoken to her as if he were contemplating his own death, and in that case making her over to Mr. Dyson; that when, after his illness, and when he was in returning health, he seemed to have manifested some desire to renew intercourse with her that she did not desire it, as she considered that she had been made over in the future to Mr. Dyson; and that, as her husband was manifesting this desire to renew intercourse, she wished to have chloroform for the purpose of waving it before his face and lulling him into a kind of stupor, and so preventing him from giving effect to his passion (*Times*, 13 April 1886, 11).

Dyson denied any illicit relationship with Adelaide, although he did confess to having kissed her in her husband's presence. However, if the evidence of Alice Foulcher, servant to the Bartletts, is to be believed, there certainly was a considerable degree of intimacy between Adelaide and Dyson:

> on one occasion, while Mr Dyson and Mrs Bartlett were together, she went into the room. The curtains were pinned together. She saw Mrs Bartlett sitting on the floor with her head on Mr Dyson's knee. She went into the room in the ordinary way, and she never found the door locked (*Times*, 14 April 1886, 6).

Due to the inconclusive nature of the medical evidence on chloroform poisoning, the jury returned a verdict of Not Guilty, despite their conviction that 'circumstances of grave suspicion' attached to Adelaide. The verdict was received with great 'popular enthusiasm' (*Times*, 19 April 1886, 4). Adelaide had clearly aroused the public's sympathy, perhaps because she was portrayed as so passive a female victim, in contrast to some of the more atavistic images of feminine behaviour in the press; as Hartman argues 'the defense worked because everyone, or practically everyone, wanted very much to believe it' (189). Conflicting details emphasize her comparative youth, with early reports suggesting that she was only 16 when she married. The *Times* later revised this to 20, but the *Illustrated Police News* persisted in reporting her as 16 at the time of the marriage. Sympathy for Adelaide may also have increased in the light of Dyson's ungentlemanly self-defence, confessing that Adelaide had persuaded him to buy a large quantity of liquid chloroform just a few days before Bartlett's death.

Whatever the nature of Adelaide's relation with Dyson, she certainly seemed to be treated as a possession by both men. In his evidence during the trial, Dyson said of Edwin:

> He had made a statement which left no doubt on my mind that he contemplated Mrs. Bartlett and myself being ultimately married. He had been finding fault with or correcting Mrs. Bartlett – not angrily – and I said, "If ever she comes under my care I shall have to teach her differently." He smiled and said something to the effect that he had no doubt I would take good care of her (*Times*, 14 April 1886, 6).

Whilst Adelaide's marriage with Edwin might not be regarded as a particularly happy one, there is the suggestion in Dyson's argument that he would 'teach her differently' that she might not have fared much better with him.

Whilst some of the details of the case gesture towards an idealized domestic situation – a pair of slippers were kept at the Bartletts' home for the Reverend Dyson's visits, and Edwin Bartlett was unable to sleep unless Adelaide 'sat at the end of the bed and held his toe' (*Times*, 15 April 1886, 3) – such details are positioned within a unhealthy alliance, and a marriage contract which saw Adelaide Bartlett treated as a possession to be passed readily from one man to the other. Although Edwin Bartlett's views on marriage were unconventional, the issues of domestic entrapment and female entitlement which the trial raised were highly topical, and may go some way to explaining the level of public support Adelaide Bartlett received.

Given the importance of the domestic space to Victorian ideology, there was understandable concern about this increasing sense of domestic entrapment and female discontent. Efforts to 'explain' this malaise often drew on the lexicon of psychology, with the discontent of women being justified by reference to 'nerves' or 'hysteria', much as, earlier in the century, female criminality was 'explained' as madness.[5] In Ibsen's *A Doll's House* (1879), Nora's decision to leave her husband Helmer and their children, in order to 'find out the truth about myself and about life' prompts a number of responses in Helmer.[6] He declares her 'unreasonable and ungrateful', and suggests that she exaggerates and romanticizes. Failing in his

---

[5]   Mary Elizabeth Braddon's *Lady Audley's Secret* is the most obvious example of this phenomenon.

[6]   Ibsen was not, of course, an English playwright, but the sentiments expressed by Helmer concur with contemporary British writing.

attempts to change her mind, Helmer then infantilizes her (much as he has done throughout their marriage), telling her she talks 'like a stupid child', and then attempts to find some biological or psychological explanation for her conduct: 'You're out of your mind! ... What kind of madness is this? ... You're ill. You're feverish. I almost believe you're out of your mind' (99, 98, 102, 99, 101). It is far easier for Helmer to believe that his wife is insane, than to accept her discontent with the married lot.

The particular psychological phenomenon that Helmer is implying Nora may suffer from is hysteria, viewed largely as a female malady throughout the nineteenth century. For his entry on hysteria in *A Dictionary of Psychological Medicine* (1892), H. B. Donkin posited that hysteria was brought on by the 'obstacles' that women met during their development, an argument which might have lent itself to moves towards female education and occupation. Donkin argued that 'the surroundings and general training of most girls' provided 'few channels of outlet for her new activities' and that 'all kinds of other barriers to the free play of her powers are set up by ordinary social and ethical customs. "Thou shall not" meets a girl at almost every turn'. However, Donkin's view that 'regular work and definite pursuits' would alleviate the symptoms of hysteria was not supported by all psychiatrists (619–20). Henry Maudsley, one of the foremost thinkers in the development of nineteenth-century psychology, contended that women had a finite amount of energy, and that energy needed to be devoted to reproduction and motherhood: 'whether they care to be mothers or not, they cannot dispense with those physiological functions of their nature that have reference to that aim ... and they cannot disregard them in the labour of life without injury to their health' ('Sex in Mind and in Education', 468).

This increased tendency to view discontent or unhappiness in relation to the psyche was embedded in the developing discipline of psychology during the latter decades of the nineteenth century. Coupled with concurrent developments in criminology, a changing view of the accused started to emerge, one which lent itself to a greater degree of sympathy, although not empathy. It is important to note that much early criminological thinking focused on the need to identify a criminal 'type', an habitual offender; the domestic murderer (with a few notable exceptions) was a one-off offender, but the changing representation of domestic murderers in the closing decades of the nineteenth century does clearly reflect developments in criminology. Whilst it was impossible to 'identify' the domestic murderer as a 'type', it was feasible to 'understand' them, with a tendency to view criminals as less threatening, and more as 'social wreckage and stepchildren of nature, rather than willful enemies of society' (Wiener, *Reconstructing the Criminal*, 12). What is noticeable, and will be demonstrated in this chapter, is that the representation of the domestic murderer sits between two modes of discourse, with traces of an earlier melodramatic rhetoric contending with a more scientific approach. Newspaper reports of domestic murder trials right up to the end of the century still dwelt at considerable length on the demeanour and appearance of the accused, with the result that the pseudo-science of physiognomy often sat, sometimes uncomfortably, alongside the more academically respectable discourse of psychology.[7] This may partly be due to the nature of the crimes; often coupled with some form of adulterous conduct, they cannot escape the more sensationalist and moralistic reporting of the earlier decades, but the conflicting discourse is also reflective of the disciplines of criminology and psychology themselves, which were in their infancy and often drew on earlier modes of expression.

***

Psychology had its roots in the changes in the treatment of the insane which had first occurred in the mid-nineteenth century with the passing of two Lunatic Acts in 1845, and the establishment of public asylums. With the passing of these Acts, and the M'Naghten Rules of 1843 which argued that the accused could be found 'not guilty by reason of insanity', or 'guilty but insane', the insane started to be distinguished from the criminal, and the treatment of insanity carried within it the possibility of recovery. This treatment took on a greater urgency in the closing decades of the nineteenth century; as part of the ongoing debates concerning degeneration and the enervating effect of industrial society, insanity was perceived to be escalating, and was certainly increasingly used as a defence in domestic murder trials.[8]

Although, by the close of the century, the discipline of psychology was enjoying greater respectability and professionalism, such attributes had been some time in coming, and the discipline was still very much in its infancy. Rick Rylance identifies four components of nineteenth-century psychological discourse – the soul, philosophy, physiology and medicine – and argues that these were 'four distinct *ways of looking* at the human mind. ... All of these psychological discourses ... were available, and all were used, sometimes in deep contention. The intellectual environment was essentially febrile and disorderly' (242). Woodward and Ash suggest that the nineteenth century saw the emergence of 'the possibility of psychology as a science', but argue that 'this possibility was not realized; psychology did not fully emerge as an autonomous discipline until the twentieth century' (7), a view supported by Rylance, who argues:

> until the very close of the century, nineteenth-century psychology was largely an eclectic, generalist field, the nature and role of which was hotly debated. It lacked an established disciplinary identity, career structure, and specialist outlets for publication. New theorists, often drawn from non-traditional intellectual and social backgrounds, argued with those of established standing and disciplinary identity. Scientists competed with theologians; philosophers were divided

---

[7]   As late as 1895, the Wilde trials appeared to offer the opportunity 'to read identity and character directly from the body' (Cook, *Culture of Homosexuality*, 62).

[8]   The first case of those examined for this book that uses mental state as a defence was that of Christiana Edmunds in 1871.

among themselves; doctors, economists, social policy-makers, imaginative writers, educationalists, all had their say (239).

Although undoubtedly 'eclectic' and 'generalist', this burgeoning discipline of psychology did start to position itself as offering a solution to the treatment of transgressive behaviour:

> throughout the second half of the century, physiological psychologists and alienists were staking out new claims for both understanding and treating social problems ... In professional journals after midcentury, arguments were increasingly being put forth that more and more forms of deviant behaviour could be regarded as physically rooted and analogous to insanity, and therefore within their province (Wiener, *Reconstructing the Criminal*, 231).

Much of this early psychological approach to crime held within it the potential for a greater understanding of the criminal. Maudsley suggested that the lunatic and the criminal alike were 'as much manufactured articles as are steam-engines and calico-printing machines'. Arguing against the earlier view that lunatics were simply mad, much as criminals were viewed as simply wicked, Maudsley questioned the origins of insanity and criminality:

> They are neither accidents nor anomalies in the universe, but come by law and testify to causality; and it is the business of science to find out what the causes are and by what laws they work. There is nothing accidental, nothing supernatural, in the impulse to do right or in the impulse to do wrong; both come by inheritance or by education; and science can no more rest content with the explanation which attributes one to the grace of Heaven and the other to the malice of the devil, than it could rest content with the explanation of insanity as a possession by the devil (*Responsibility*, 28).

Maudsley's comment that 'it is the business of science to find out what the causes are and by what laws they work' points to a significant shift from ideas of moral management, to the sense that insanity was something within the grasp of science. Again, this illustrates the shifting patterns of fin-de-siècle thinking and differing degrees of anxiety and confusion; in one sense, Maudsley's theories engendered greater security in that insanity could be seen as something to be cured but, on the other hand, they provoked greater anxiety, because they carried with them the obligation to at least attempt a cure.

Of particular interest to this book is the concept of partial insanity, whereby certain situations or thought patterns were believed to trigger an insane episode in an otherwise 'healthy' individual. Using such a theory, domestic murder could be defended as a temporary aberration from 'normal' behaviour, but it also meant that any apparently sane individual could become insane with startling ease. In 1871, the defence team for Christiana Edmunds (see Chapter 1, pp. 18–19 for a fuller discussion of her case) mounted a plea of insanity, arguing that 'about 12 or 15 months ago a great change came over her' (*Times*, 17 January 1871, 12); the following year a prosecution witness at the trial of the Reverend Watson for the murder of his wife conceded that a person suffering from extreme melancholia (as it was argued Watson did) 'might be liable to an outburst of passion and be quite himself again afterwards' (*Times*, 12 January 1872, 11).

As these cases illustrate, the concept of partial insanity was quite commonplace by the closing decades of the century and had, indeed, been part of scientific thinking for some time. The theory was first posited as long ago as 1830 by John Connolly, in his work *An Inquiry Concerning the Indications of Insanity, with Suggestions for the Better Protection and Care of the Insane*, a classic of nineteenth-century psychiatry. Connolly defined madness as a partial state, one that endured only so long as passion overturned reason: 'he ceases to be mad when he can correct the erroneous judgement of his excited mind; and not before' (qtd. in Taylor and Shuttleworth, 241). Although Connolly's theory of partial insanity was posited as early as 1830, it did not enter into the public debate concerning criminal culpability with any degree of consistency until the 1870s.

John Cowles Prichard's hugely influential work *A Treatise on Insanity and Other Disorders Affecting the Mind* (1835) developed Connolly's theory of partial insanity, dividing it into two distinct groups. The first of these, moral insanity, Prichard identified as

> madness consisting in a morbid perversion of the natural feelings, affections, inclinations, temper, habits, moral dispositions, and natural impulses, without any remarkable disorder or defect of the intellect or knowing and reasoning faculties, and particularly without any insane illusion or hallucination (qtd. in Taylor and Shuttleworth, 252).

Prichard's second sub-classification was intellectual insanity, one manifestation of which was monomania

> in which the understanding is partially disordered or under the influence of some particular illusion, referring to one subject, and involving one train of ideas, while the intellectual powers appear, when exercised on other subjects, to be in a great measure unimpaired (qtd. in Taylor and Shuttleworth, 252–3).

Jean Étienne Esquirol, in his work *Mental Maladies* (1845), made the specific connection between monomania and the passions:

> its seat is in the heart of man, and it is there that we must search for it, in order to possess ourselves of all its peculiarities. How many are the cases of monomania, caused by thwarted love, by fear, vanity, wounded self-love, or disappointed ambition! This malady presents all the signs which characterize the passions. The delirium of monomaniacs is exclusive, fixed and permanent, like the ideas of a passionate man (qtd. in Taylor and Shuttleworth, 257).

Essentially, then, moral insanity was 'a perversion of moral feelings which left the mental faculties unaffected', and intellectual insanity (or monomania) 'a form of insanity attached only to particular strains of thought' (Taylor and Shuttleworth, 229).

Building on the work of Connolly, Prichard and others, Henry Maudsley developed the concept of the 'borderland', a kind of hinterland where an individual was not technically insane, but carried within him or her the seeds of insanity or simply difference from the norm.[9] Maudsley argued that the

> moral responsibility of the unhappy people inhabiting this borderland will assuredly not be made until we get rid of the metaphysical measure of responsibility as well as of the theological notion that vices and crimes are due to the devil, and proceed by way of observation and induction to sound generalizations concerning the origin of the moral sentiments, the laws of their development, and the causes, course and varieties of moral degeneracy (*Responsibility*, 34).

Maudsley was at pains to argue that someone suffering from mental illness was not, as was commonly believed, someone who '"from himself is ta'en away," alienated from himself and from his kind, and ... something of a reproach to the nature of humanity' (*Responsibility*, 5). Rather, Maudsley suggested that a visitor to a mental asylum 'would not find a new world and a new race of beings; he would find man changed, indeed, but not transformed' (*Responsibility*, 2). Applying Maudsley's rationale, a murderer such as William Corder (who murdered his lover Maria Marten in 1827, and whose case is discussed in detail in Chapter 2) might no longer necessarily be deemed a devil, but possibly as one suffering from a mental illness which might respond to treatment. And, more significantly, all those who sought to condemn men such as Corder carried within them the potential for such a crime. By admitting kinship with the insane, the public was faced with the realization that this hitherto ostracized group exhibited exactly the same emotions and characteristics as 'normal' people: criminals were often now seen as products of their society or some defective physiology, rather than 'immoral' or 'evil' individuals.

Despite such attempts to classify differing forms of insanity through a more rigorous scientific approach, and although undoubtedly beginning to stabilize as a discipline by the close of the century, psychology shared much of the shifting nature of the fin de siècle. Although subject to new scientific thought and analysis – gesturing, in a sense, towards modernism – there was still a widespread belief

---

[9]   See also Forbes Winslow, *On Obscure Diseases of the Brain, and Disorders of the Mind*, 4th edn. (London, 1868) and Andrew Wynter, *The Borderlands of Insanity and Other Allied Papers* (London, 1875), both in Taylor and Shuttleworth. Winslow asked his readers to examine the darkest recesses of their minds, and acknowledge 'what a melancholy, degrading, and profoundly humiliating revelation most men would have to make of the dark corners, secret recesses, and hidden crevices of the human heart' (Taylor and Shuttleworth, 269). Wynter spoke of 'the vast army of undiscovered lunatics' (Taylor and Shuttleworth, 281).

that those suffering from insanity would betray it in their face and demeanour (even though physiognomy as a scientific discipline was on the wane), gesturing back partly to the moral transparency of melodrama and the earlier decades of the century, but also heavily influenced by concurrent developments in criminology. Lacey argues that

> the turn to psychology and subjectivity was far from complete ... for much of the nineteenth century mechanisms of legal responsibility-attribution remained both fundamentally evaluative and importantly trained on external markers of character. Instead of any radical discontinuity, in other words, what we see in the nineteenth century is rather a continuing negotiation between capacity/psychology and character/evaluation in the attribution of criminal responsibility (103).

This may seem less surprising if we consider that the development of criminology in the latter half of the nineteenth century had its roots in the earlier pseudo-sciences of physiognomy and phrenology. Physiognomy (the assessment of character from outward appearance, usually the face) is associated primarily with the work of Johann Kaspar Lavater, a Swiss theologian whose *Essays on Physiognomy* (first published in English in 1789) posited physiognomy as 'the science of knowledge of the correspondence between the external and internal man, the visible superficies, and the invisible contents'.[10] Phrenology, which posited the argument that character and behaviour could be determined by measuring the skull, had as its chief exponents the German Franz Joseph Gall and his Austrian assistant John Caspar Spurzheim. George Combe, an Edinburgh lawyer, founded Britain's first phrenological society in 1820 and this pseudo-science enjoyed its heyday in the 1820s and 1830s; although in decline by the middle of the century, 'the kind of assumptions on which both it and physiognomy were based continued to influence mainstream descriptions of the Criminal' (Davie, 41–2). By the 1850s and 1860s, 'it had become axiomatic ... that an individual's criminal character could be "read" from a "disproportionate" and/or "irregular" face', and this somatic reading of criminal intent or guilt is evident throughout the recording of criminal trials, as discussed in greater detail in Chapter 1 of this book.[11]

Changes in criminal policy, most notably the reduction of the death penalty and concurrent increase in imprisonment as a punishment, led to an important need to manage criminals who were now being released from prison, back into the community:

> The reduction of the death penalty and the implementation of imprisonment as a general mode of punishment produced a large population of prisoners who

---

[10]   Davie, 34, quoting from Lucy Hartley, *Physiognomy and the Meaning of Expression in Nineteenth-Century Literature* (Cambridge, 2001), 33.

[11]   Davie, 34, quoting Mary Cowling, *The Artist as Anthropologist: The Representation of Type and Character in Victorian Art* (Cambridge, 1989), 289.

needed to be reformed in order to be reintegrated into the community. Concern over the management of these criminals became a social issue which could serve as leverage in numerous and varied power struggles. An urgent *need to know* about criminals would be as strongly advocated by political and economic circles as by purely administrative ones (prison and police officials), thus increasing the issue's proliferation within social discourse (Leps, 23).

This was accompanied by a need to control the apparent rise in crime that occurred during the 1850s and 1860s, and such concerns gave rise to the emergence of criminology, defined by Neil Davie as 'the self-conscious application of scientific principles to the study of crime and criminals, embracing such issues as causation, correction and prevention' (29). The discipline of criminology was advanced by the publication in 1876 of Cesare Lombroso's *L'Uomo Delinquente* (*The Criminal Man*). Lombroso advocated what is now termed criminal anthropology, whereby 'the body carried inscribed upon it signs that betrayed its essential criminal character' (Thomas, 23). The links here with the earlier 'disciplines' of phrenology and physiognomy are obvious. Lombroso argued that

> up to 70% of criminals were, as it were, programmed from birth to commit crime; and that this "born criminal-type" (*delinquent-nato*) could be identified by the trained observer in the form of outward anatomical and physiological signs or "stigmata" (Davie, 130).

So, for example, Lombroso's view of the 'common murderer' was as follows:

> [They] ... have a glassy look, cold and immobile, but sometimes bloodthirsty and bloodshot. The nose is prominent, often aquiline or hooked, like one finds on a bird of prey. The jaw is robust; the ears long; the cheekbones wide; and the hair is frizzy, abundant and dark. Quite often there is no beard, the canine teeth are highly developed and the lips thin' (qtd. in Davie, 134).

In an age when 'the ingenuity and economic power of this, the first Industrial Nation, seemed capable of resolving any problem intellectual or practical', criminology seemed to present a solution to the one 'problem' that eluded a solution – criminal behaviour. With its scientific reliance on measurements, statistics and tabulation, criminology appeared to offer a means of not simply identifying 'the Criminal', but a chance to 'explore the very springs of crime itself' (Davie, 16, 15). What was also significant about Lombroso's work was

> his insistence on the need to seek explanations for crime through the systematic scientific scrutiny of *individual* criminals, rather than exploring the moral significance of different criminal acts.
>
> If the origins of the criminal act were to be found in a detailed study of the offender him- or herself, it followed that punishment needed to be tailored to the demands of each case. Perhaps *treatment* would be a better word than punishment in this context, for the criminal behaviour in question was considered to emanate

from constitutional urges or environmental pressures – or both – beyond the control of individual volition (Davie, 129).

The merging of these two burgeoning disciplines – psychology and criminology – starts to become evident here, as does the potential for greater understanding, if not sympathy for the criminal.

By the 1870s, with the advent of greater policing and control of the streets, and greater professionalization of both the police force and prisons, 'the threat of criminality seemed to ebb' (Wiener, *Reconstructing*, 215) and crime statistics appeared to drop, but this was accompanied by other anxieties. Whilst levels of street crime appeared to be on the wane, the growth of disciplines such as psychology and criminology led to a 'blurring of the stark moral certainties' of the earlier decades of the century, and attention turned 'from the streets to the home ... and in general from the unruly populace to persons and scenes of apparent respectability' (Wiener, *Reconstructing*, 244). What caused greater concern now was the extent to which criminality could be hidden beneath a veneer of respectability:

> On one hand, less fear of murder was expressed, and newspapers, popular pamphlets, and even street literature treated it in a less heated, melodramatic fashion than earlier in the century ... On the other hand, certain murders – planned, concealed ones – were gaining new interest as signs that lit up for a brief moment an unseen and opaque dark underside of modern life (Wiener, *Reconstructing*, 245).

Developments within the police force and the detection of crime which might have been thought to engender greater security, in fact sometimes achieved the opposite effect:

> Not only was society becoming more complex through population growth, urbanization, mobility and economic and technological development, but even, ironically, the very advance of knowledge, as it spread light into dark corners, at the same time seemed to heighten the sense that respectable social life was permeated by buried secrets (Wiener, *Reconstructing*, 246).

Increased policing was also increased surveillance, with the attendant possibility that people might become more skilled in concealing their misdemeanours, particularly within the family home. Such concerns were voiced in the Oscar Wilde trials of 1895, where

> the places mentioned in the court cases and newspaper reports were characterised in two main ways. On the one hand they were utterly separate from the middle-class domestic sphere and deemed somehow appropriate for such unspeakable sexual crimes. On the other hand they were well-known and 'respectable' sites which were hideously compromised by the homosexual activity which took place there ... A transition between the public and private was commonly

outlined – indicating the potential dangers to the unsuspecting of both the city street and of heavily curtained rooms (Cook, *Culture of Homosexuality*, 55, 59).

What was particularly disturbing to a Victorian public already concerned with what might pass behind the privacy of the closed front door was the fact that an individual suffering from some form of partial insanity could live in a community for years, and pass undetected. More complex understandings of identity and the psyche brought with them increased anxiety, particularly with regard to the potential instability within all of us. The literary trope of the 'evil other half' had been memorably employed earlier in the century by Collins in *Man and Wife* (1870), where Hester Dethridge is haunted by the apparition of an evil doppelganger, urging her to commit murder. This trope now recurred with increased anxiety in Robert Louis Stevenson's *The Strange Case of Dr. Jekyll and Mr. Hyde* (1886) and Oscar Wilde's *The Picture of Dorian Gray* (1891). Whereas Hester Dethridge in *Man and Wife* is essentially an unsympathetic character, and not the focus of the narrative, the shift in viewpoint with Stevenson and Wilde called into question the potential within all of us to nurse an evil alter ego. The location of these novels also crystallizes concerns voiced at the time about the potential offered by the city for anonymity and lack of culpability (discussed in Chapter 1). The instability of the figure of the insane and/or criminal individual reflected and fed into the overall lack of certainty that was characteristic of fin-de-siècle culture. With the self located within an interior space, and mental state increasingly difficult to 'read' from external signs (despite the claims of Lombroso and his followers), the difficulty of detecting whether one had 'crossed the border' meant that the boundaries between the law-abiding and those capable of committing transgressive acts were increasingly blurred. To believe in the concept of partial insanity or to follow developments in criminology was almost to compel an individual to have greater sympathy with those accused of crimes prompted by disturbed mental state. The 1890 case of Eleanor Pearcey illustrates the point perfectly.

On 24 October 1890, Frank Hogg visited his lover, Eleanor Pearcey (aka Mary Wheeler or Eleanor Piercey). Finding her not at home, he left her a short note, and returned home. Evidence suggests that while Frank Hogg was writing Eleanor this note, she was disposing of the dead bodies of his wife and child (both called Phoebe), which she transported in baby Phoebe's perambulator. Medical testimony remained unclear as to whether the baby had died from smothering, or from exposure to the cold, but the elder Phoebe's death was unquestionably murder – and a particularly brutal one, at that. The prosecution suggested that Pearcey struck her on the back of the head with a poker, causing convulsions. Finding that her first blow had not killed Phoebe, Pearcey allegedly then struck her three more times and finally slit her throat. Mr. Wells, the doctor called in when the body was found, testified during the trial that 'the head was practically severed from the body' (*Times*, 3 December 1890, 13).

The case was remarkable for the fact that, despite having been involved in an adulterous relationship with Frank Hogg, and despite having murdered Hogg's wife and young child (the former with a great degree of violence), considerable sympathy was expressed towards Pearcey both in the press coverage of the trial and in the public consciousness; nearly 2,000 letters of sympathy a week were sent to her counsel, along with sums of money for her mother. A *Times* editorial of 4 December spoke of the 'genuine and ardent passion' exhibited by Pearcey, and *Reynolds's Newspaper* argued that 'there is something in this case, brutal as all the circumstances are, that is calculated to awake public sympathy' (7 December 1889, 4). If we need any reminder of how far the public view of the domestic murderer had shifted from the start of the period under examination in this work, we need only consider how the public had responded to the arrest and trial of William Corder in 1828, discussed at length in Chapter 2. Corder's murder of Maria Marten was less violent in content, and did not involve the death of a child; and yet Corder was vilified by press and public alike, whereas Eleanor Pearcey aroused a considerable degree of public sympathy.

How do we account for the support expressed for Pearcey, and how might her case mirror the shifting configurations of the closing decades of the nineteenth century? Sympathy was partly engendered by the publication of her letters to Hogg, which were read in court and printed in full in the daily press. In one letter, dated 2 October 1888, Eleanor writes:

> My Dear F., – Do not think of going away, for my heart will break if you do: don't go, dear. I won't ask too much, only to see you for five minutes when you can get away: but if you go quite away, how do you think I can live? I would see you married 50 times over – yes, I could bear that far better than parting with you for ever, and that is what it would be if you went out of England. My dear loving F., you was so downhearted to-day that your words give me much pain, for I have only one true friend I can trust to, and that is yourself. Don't take that from me. What good would your friendship be then, with you so far away? No, no, you must not go away. My heart throbs with pain only thinking about it. What would it be if you went? I should die. And if you love me as you say you do, you will stay. Write or come soon, dear. Have I asked too much? From your loving, M.E.
>
> P.S. – I hope you got home quite safe, and things are all right, and you are well. – M.E.

Another letter, dated 18 October 1888, sees Eleanor pleading with Frank thus:

> Oh! Frank, I should not like to think I was the cause of all your troubles, and yet you make me think so. What can I do? I love you with all my heart, and I will love her because she will belong to you. Yes, I will come and see you both if you wish it. So, dear, try and be strong, as strong as me, for a man should be stronger than a woman.

A third letter, undated, continues in the same vein:

> Dear Frank, – You ask me if I was cross with you for only coming for such a
> little while. If you know how lonely I am you would not ask. I would be more
> than happy if I could see you for the same time every day, dear. You know I have
> a lot of time to spare, and I cannot help thinking. I think and think, till I get so
> dizzy that I don't know what to do with myself. If it was not for your love, dear,
> I do not know what I should really do, and I am always afraid you will take that
> away, then I should quite give up in despair, for that is the only thing I care for
> on earth. I cannot live without it now. I have no right to it, but you gave it to me,
> and I can't give it up. Dear Frank, don't think bad of me for writing this (*Times*,
> 2 December 1890, 13).

I have included these letters in such detail to convey the pathetic, obsessive
nature of Eleanor's devotion to Hogg, and to go some way to recreating a sense of
the experience of the jury at her trial (and the reading public who were following
events in the daily press), who were clearly swayed by the depth of her emotional
attachment to him. This potential for the readership to empathize with Pearcey was
reinforced by the visual representation of her (discussed in detail in Chapter 1),
where she was frequently portrayed in a sympathetic light. A *Times* editorial of
4 December suggested that the motive for the crimes was 'not jealousy of any very
simple kind', and went on to argue,

> whatever the mode may have been – whether premeditated attack or sudden,
> uncontrolled frenzy of jealous hate, the story is as strange as it is dreadful.
> The woman's character, known from her antecedents, is at variance with such
> ferocity. But this, perhaps, is only one more proof that no one can tell of what
> a human being may be capable until actual trial has been made (4 December
> 1890, 9).

Earlier in the century there is little doubt that Pearcey would have been
demonized by the press, with vigorous attempts to place a distance between her
and the 'normal' reading public. In 1848, Harriet Parker murdered her lover's
two children when she suspected him of infidelity; Robert Blake, Parker's lover,
was described by *Lloyd's* as of 'sober, industrious habits' in contrast to the 'most
dissipated' Parker, whom *Lloyd's* viewed as 'a dirty, repulsive looking woman'
(2 January 1848, 12). In Pearcey's case, not only was Frank Hogg's treatment
of her subject to criticism (despite him being ostensibly the innocent party), the
portrayal of Pearcey concurs to some extent with Maudsley's concept of the
borderlands, that 'no one can tell of what a human being may be capable until the
actual trial has been made.'

Despite the public sympathy, Eleanor Pearcey was hanged on Christmas Eve,
1890, with *Reynolds's Newspaper* using the occasion, as ever, to condemn the
class injustice inherent within Victorian society, comparing Pearcey's case with
that of Florence Maybrick, examined earlier in this chapter:

Mrs. Piercey [*sic*] is a woman poor and unfortunate, and no voice is likely to be raised on her behalf. Mrs. Maybrick, a "lady" – the daughter of a Baron – was, in the eyes of God, a criminal of deeper dye than Mrs. Piercey ... Mrs. Maybrick's life was spared because of the social position she had filled, though one of the vilest characters that has ever figured in the criminal courts. Mrs. Piercey, in all probability, will die (7 December 1889, 4).

Attempts were made before the hanging to mount a defence of 'epileptic insanity and hypnotic irresponsibility', suggesting that the crimes had been committed during an epileptic seizure and that Pearcey was unconscious of her actions at the time of the murder. Such defences were not uncommon at this time; epilepsy was viewed as a form of insanity during this period, and epilepsy was seen as offering 'a transformation in the afflicted's personality' not unlike that engendered by mesmerism or somnambulism (Eigen, 18). However, Pearcey's defence proved unsuccessful, largely because it only surfaced after she had been sentenced, and therefore smacked of desperation. An editorial in the *Illustrated Police News* just before Pearcey's execution highlights the fact that exploration of mental state was now a commonplace during criminal trials:

> even had it been represented by her legal advisers that, by reason of her poverty, experts could not be employed on her behalf to investigate her mental condition and give evidence in her favour, the plea of insanity could have been raised and duly debated in open court. Poverty should not – and, as a matter of fact, could not – be really disadvantageous to a prisoner in the critical position occupied by Mary Wheeler, while standing her trial for murder, because – if her counsel had boldly challenged the arraignment on that very account – some special inquiry into the state of her mind would assuredly have been undertaken by order of the Bench, or, at the very least, it would have been thrown on the prosecution to prove that the defence thus set up was not sound in itself (27 December 1890, 2).

Running parallel to this infiltration of psychology into trial proceedings is an interplay between the discourses of fiction and psychology. It is not uncommon to find fictional examples used in scientific works to demonstrate particular theories – for example, Shakespeare's Ophelia was commonly referred to when exploring theories of insanity. Marie-Christine Leps, in an examination of a scientific treatise, a newspaper report and a detective novel, all from the fin de siècle, notes 'the same images (birds of prey, animals, and dogs) are utilized to imply a threatening nature, embodied in immediately recognizable features' (5). Wiener, writing on this period, comments that 'the fiction of crime ... shared key images and tropes with factual writing, both the journalistic genre and the scientific body of writing known as criminology that emerged in this period. These different forms of constructing crime reveal in many ways similar concerns and similar procedures' (*Reconstructing*, 215). Such a cross-fertilisation of discourses occurred in the trial of Eleanor Pearcey, when Mr. Justice Denman commented on why anyone could conceive such a strong passion for a man like Hogg: *Reynolds's* responded in an editorial with the argument that 'a reperusal of the story of Bill Sikes and Nancy would change his views' (7 December 1889, 4). This use of fictional examples to illustrate scientific or legal tenets is again indicative of the epistemological instability of this period, with the sciences of psychology and criminology 'finding their way', and drawing upon whatever resources would render them comprehensible by the public. By the same token, novelists and playwrights were drawing upon the lexicon of psychology to explore the motivation and actions of their protagonists, adopting the tools of the psychiatrist to unveil the inner workings of the mind. This is not to say that fin-de-siècle novelists were the first to explore the psyche. As discussed in some detail in Chapter 3, as early as 1838 Dickens was making steps towards a psychologized analysis of Sikes's murder of Nancy.[12] What was different with these fin-de-siècle novelists was that the exploration of the psyche was more widely articulated, with the lexicon of psychology to support it.

Mona Caird's *The Wing of Azrael* (1889) and Thomas Hardy's *Tess of the D'Urbervilles* (1891) both provide evidence of this cross-fertilisation of disciplines. One of the most marked changes between these works and those from earlier in the century is in the portrayal of the domestic murderer. Where female protagonists commit murder in earlier works of fiction, they are portrayed with, at best, limited sympathy or as simply so far outside the realm of normal 'British' experience as to offer no threat to domestic stability.[13] The same cannot be said of these later works of fiction. Viola Sedley in *The Wing of Azrael* and Hardy's Tess are both portrayed with a great degree of sympathy and understanding. My argument in what follows is that the more sympathetic portrayal of these women is partly a manifestation of the perceived shift in relations between women (particularly middle-class women) and the domestic sphere in this period, and partly a reflection of developments in psychology and criminology, whereby the accused might be afforded a greater degree of understanding than in the earlier decades of the nineteenth century.

The Wing of Azrael, by Mona Caird, engages with contemporary debates about women and the domestic sphere, and the novel is an unashamed and obvious didactic platform for the author's political beliefs. Mona Caird was one of the most well-known of the New Woman writers, with her novel *The Daughters of Danaus* (1894) perhaps the best known of her works. She achieved particular notoriety when her essay entitled 'Marriage' was published in the *Westminster*

---

[12]   Sally Shuttleworth also writes of Brontë's attempts to 'unveil the concealed inner processes of the social body or the individual mind' in *Charlotte Brontë and Victorian Psychology*, 15.

[13]   Miami in *The Green Bushes* (1845) and the eponymous heroine of Sabine Baring-Gould's *Mehalah* (1880) are, respectively, a Native American Indian and a gipsy. The eponymous female protagonists of Thackeray's *Catherine* (1840) and Bulwer-Lytton's *Lucretia* (1846) are portrayed with little genuine sympathy. Mary Elizabeth Braddon's Lady Audley is conveniently found to be insane at the close of the novel. Hester Dethridge in Collins's *Man and Wife* (1870) may have her crimes 'explained' but she is portrayed as an intensely unlikeable, almost repellent character, whilst his earlier female murderer, Lydia Gwilt in *Armadale* (1866), meets a decidedly sticky end.

Review in August 1888. The essay was not anti-marriage *per se*, but rather argued for marriage as some form of private agreement, with greater equality on both sides. In response to Caird's view that modern marriage was not a success, the *Daily Telegraph* ran a letters column entitled 'Is Marriage a Failure?' with 27,000 letters received on the subject, a selection of which were published in the work *Is Marriage a Failure?* (1888), edited by Harry Quilter.

Mona Caird's novel *The Wing of Azrael* is a damning indictment of marriage and female subordination within the domestic space. Viola Sedley, the novel's heroine, has had the quality of 'meek and saint-like endurance' inculcated within her so firmly she agrees to sacrifice herself in a marriage to Philip Dendraith, to save her family from financial ruin (1:8). Viola's father regards her mother, Marian, as his 'possession' and argues with Viola when she initially refuses to accept Philip's marriage proposal: 'Do you know what a woman is who does not marry? I will tell you: she is a cumberer of the ground, a devourer of others' substance, a failure, a wheel that won't turn; she has no meaning; she is in the way; she ought never to have been born' (1:143).

Caird uses this disastrous marriage of Viola and Philip as part of a didactic framework for her condemnation of the restraints imposed upon women by the inequality of the marital state. In an early argument with Philip, Viola laments: 'Am I always to be *your wife*, never myself? I have not questioned your authority, but you ask for more than authority. You ask me to surrender my personality.' Philip's response to this outcry is to remind Viola that 'the world regards and criticizes you now as my wife, and nothing else. What else are you? You possess no other standing or acknowledged existence' (2:89). The ultimate message of the novel is that a loveless marriage means Viola 'might never be alone, never feel that she absolutely possessed herself. Her very thoughts were scarcely free. Freedom was an unknown word; the only words that ruled in that red-hot Purgatory were right, duty, submission' (2:169).

The few references that are made to the physical side of Viola's marriage are strongly suggestive of sexual abuse. Her five-month honeymoon is referred to simply as 'awful', and we are told that Viola now regards night-time as a 'living hell'; later in the novel, there is the suggestion that Philip is about to rape Viola, when he talks of overcoming her 'slight coldness' with his 'persistent devotion'. Viola comes to accept that the physical aspect of marriage is 'nothing less than an initiation into things base and unlovely, desecrating and degrading all that in her girlhood she had been taught to reverence and to cherish' (2:116, 169, 138).

What marks novels such as *The Wing of Azrael* out from the earlier sensation fiction of the 1860s and 70s is partly this direct condemnation of marriage. Although the heroines of sensation fiction may commit or contemplate murder, the novels do not critique marriage as such: Lady Audley's marriage is neither unhealthy nor unpleasant; and Lydia Gwilt has the potential to be happy with Ozias Midwinter, were she not so driven by her desire for revenge. The marriage plot may be problematized in the sensation novel, but marriage remains the ultimate aspiration of the female protagonists. Not so with this later work of fiction.

Viola is haunted by the existence of Sibella Lincoln, a woman who has left her unhappy marriage but who suffers social ostracism as a result. When Viola first sees Sibella, she is struck by the latter's good looks: 'how could a bad woman look like that?' (2:231). Viola's comment here could be seen as harking back to an earlier melodramatic mode, where guilt or innocence were visible as outward signs, suggesting a representational instability in fin-de-siècle culture, but it also shares echoes of criminal anthropology, and the attendant belief that moral character or a propensity for criminal activity could be 'read' in the face of an individual. Under Sibella's persuasion, Viola determines to leave her husband for her lover, Harry Lancaster. Discovered by Philip at the point of escape, in a 'horrible instant of blinding passion' she stabs him with a paper knife, in itself a particularly domestic weapon (3:201).

Having carried out the murder, Viola is initially unrepentant and declares that she would do it again. However, seeing a 'flicker of repulsion' cross her lover Harry's face, she realizes the enormity of her crime and shrinks away 'with a half-articulate cry ... of a spirit hurled from its last refuge, cut off from human pity and fellowship, cast out from the last sanctuary of human love' (3:205). It is Harry's revulsion that causes Viola to despair, perhaps suggesting here the limits of the feminist fight for independence, with Viola still turning to male authority to sanction or condemn her actions.

Caird leaves the reader in no doubt about Viola's fate; she is now a creature 'whose every breath had been cursed, who was stained and tainted through and through with shame and crime – for her was only a bottomless grave where she would fall and fall, weighted with her crime and her curse, through the darkness for ever and ever!'. Her inability to repent fixes an impassable gulf between her and Harry, and positions her as one who has 'nothing to do any longer with human feelings and passions'. Ultimately, Harry agrees that Viola's lack of repentance places her 'beyond the reach of salvation', and the novel closes with Viola drowning herself (3:205, 206, 222).

The rhetoric of these closing pages recalls the emotional excess of melodrama, grounded in a more modern moral outlook; Viola is condemned for Philip's murder, but not for her adultery. Similarly, when Viola and Harry are discovered by Viola's friend Dorothy, Dorothy uses the language of melodrama to berate Harry: 'It is all your fault; every bit of it. You are a villain – a black-hearted villain! I hate you! I believe you are the devil!' (3:147), but Harry's defence is far more modern and pragmatic in its approach: 'If you knew our story and understood things a little better ... you would perhaps come to see that your friend is true to herself in acting in defiance of the world' (3:147). Harry views Viola as 'a symbol of the troublous age in which she lived, a creature with weakened and uprooted faith, yet with feelings and instincts still belonging to the past, still responding to the old dead and gone dogmas' (3:82). This image of an individual caught between two epochs could equally apply to the novel as a whole, navigating a path between the polarities of melodrama and modernity. By the same extension, the work could be viewed as reflecting the conflicting ideologies at work in the closing decades of the century. This uneasy alliance of a melodramatic and a more modern moral outlook is one of the novel's weaknesses, and one which limits its effectiveness as an account of a woman's rebellion against domestic entrapment.

By the same token, the conflicting discourses of melodrama and psychology are also at work within the novel, and do not always sit comfortably together. Where the later stages of the novel increasingly lapse into the tropes of melodrama and the gothic (Philip has Viola watched and locked up, and he tries to make her believe she has seen a ghost), the earlier chapters do make genuine efforts to access Viola's troubled psyche. In her struggles to accept the role society wishes to impose on her, Viola draws on ideas of free will and determinism, and the concept of individual consciousness. Early in the novel the child Viola contemplates her own existence:

> she was, she *must* be real; a separate being called Viola Sedley, – with thoughts of her own, entirely her own, whom nobody in all this big world quite knew. *Viola Sedley*; – she repeated the name over and over to herself, as if to gain some clearer conception of her position in relation to the universe, but the arbitrary name only deepened the sense of mystery (1:3).

Her sense of herself as an individual 'with thoughts of her own' is what plagues Viola throughout the novel; ideas of identity, the unconscious mind, and the boundaries between sanity and madness were all concerns of nineteenth-century psychology, and these are all concepts with which Viola struggles. In particular, her struggle to determine her own individuality was one which would have resonated with a fin-de-siècle audience:

> technology and economic advances kept extending the scale and complexity of life, and as the natural sciences put forth new deterministic models of understanding the human world, the Victorian image of the individual weakened. Reflective persons were coming to feel dwarfed by their natural and social environment. At the same time, upper-middle-class discontent was growing as a result of the life-constricting repressiveness of triumphant respectability. Consequently, fears of a dam-bursting anarchy began to be replaced by opposite fears of a disabled society of ineffectual, devitalized, and overcontrolled individuals moulded by environmental and biological forces beyond their control (Wiener, *Reconstructing*, 12).

Unable to conform to societal expectations of her as a young woman, to conform to what Wiener has termed 'the life-constricting repressiveness of triumphant respectability', Viola's thoughts are constantly 'breaking the bounds of her teaching', particularly in the presence of her husband, Philip, when 'all that was hard and bold and reckless came to the surface; she could not believe as she ought to believe, she could not feel as she ought to feel' (2:107, 110). It is the existence of free will, these thoughts that contend so violently with what society demands of her, that causes Viola such distress, and leads Harry Lancaster to speculate 'would she act boldly and consistently, as she had resolved, or would she show herself the child of her circumstances, stumbling fatally under the burden of her sad woman's heritage of indecision, fear, vain remorse, untimely scruples?' (3:106). At times Viola's suffering is so great she questions her own sanity: 'if sanity has for its standard the condition of the average mind in similar circumstances, Viola must certainly have been pronounced to have gone far beyond that boundary-line' (2:137–8). Caird's employment of the 'boundary-line' draws heavily on Maudsley's concept of the borderland.

The competing discourses of melodrama and psychology rarely marry in the novel; the examination of Viola's wrestling with her own individual consciousness seems oddly detached from the melodramatic content of the novel, and too didactic in its approach. Caird's inability to marry these two discourses is, perhaps, symptomatic of the age in which the novel was written.

The Wing of Azrael is part of a sequence of New Woman novels that end with the suicide of the main protagonist and, while Caird's novel is undoubtedly a powerful critique of marriage, this sacrifice of Viola at its close clearly demonstrates the author's acknowledgement that murder cannot be sanctioned as a means of achieving release from marital restraint.[14] As Lucia Zedner has argued:

> the prescriptive ideology of femininity in Victorian England gave women an important moralizing role: not least the responsibility for maintaining the respectability of their family. As a result women's crimes contravened not only the law but, perhaps more importantly, their idealized role as wives and mothers. The high social costs attributed to criminality in women attracted considerable public anxiety and, as a result, female offenders were likely to be severely stigmatized (2).

Applying Zedner's thinking, it is a step too far to allow Viola to murder Philip *and* run away with Harry; she must be made to suffer for what is still the ultimate desecration of the domestic space. Although New Woman novelists, and those associated with the women's movement, were perceived as being critical of marriage, there is a sense in which they are unable to contemplate alternatives to it. As Sally Ledger argues: 'the inability to think beyond heterosexual marriage as the only available route to happiness and fulfillment for women also explains the pessimism of most New Woman novels which reach an impasse on the marriage question' (23). Murder in *The Wing of Azrael* and *Tess of the D'Urbervilles* offers a release from some form of domestic tyranny, to the extent that the crime becomes a defiant gesture of domestic empowerment. However, empowerment comes at a heavy price for these female protagonists.

The same is not always true of male domestic murderers in novels of the same period. The eponymous hero of *Dr. Phillips*, a novel by Frank Danby published in 1887, murders his wife. Although not successful in securing his ultimate aim of

---

[14]   Herminia Barton in Grant Allen's *The Woman Who Did* (1895) and Lyndall in *The Story of an African Farm* (1883) also end their own lives after a period of proto-feminist rebellion.

marriage to his mistress, and although his child dies, Dr. Phillips does 'get away with' murder. The close of the novel sees him nodding in front of the fire, his dead wife and child beside him in his imagination, and the tempting figure of Bessie the parlourmaid a pleasing reality:

> and they seem to him then as mother and child, caressing him, proud of him, the foremost sharers in his honours, the most enthusiastic of his worshippers.
>
> From this dream he wakes again to his loneliness, but Bessie is there with the coffee and the firelight flickers on her neat brown hair and saucy eyes, on her ruddy lips and white teeth, and Benjamin Phillips's loneliness has its consolations (285).

Despite Caird's notoriety following the publication of her essay in the *Westminster Review*, *The Wing of Azrael* was not particularly widely reviewed. Any critical attention the novel did receive was mixed. The *Graphic* found it 'a thoroughly unwholesome book, as well as an ignorant one' (15 June 1889); the *Glasgow Herald*, while conceding that it would be unfair to deny it the title of novel 'for it contains some clever character-drawing and ends with a murder and a suicide', still felt that the author had 'altogether overshot the mark. The husbands in the book are so hopelessly callous and selfish, the principal male fiend is so utterly inhuman, that they fail to point the very moral intended' (14 May 1889). The *Pall Mall Gazette*, whilst never exactly praising the novel's execution, did suggest that 'anyone who goes out to dinner and has to confess that he has not read "Azrael" will be at a disadvantage at London dinner-parties during the coming season' (26 April 1889, 1), suggesting that it was at least something of a middle-class sensation, and again perhaps emphasizing that the debates surrounding domestic entrapment and female emancipation were class-based.

This lack of enthusiasm on the part of the press can partly be explained by the novel's artistic merits. It is a polemic thinly disguised as a novel, and suffers as a result. But the *Graphic*'s comment on the unwholesomeness of the novel is of interest; one wonders whether the reviewer takes exception to Caird's dwelling on the physical element of marriage, to Viola's affair, or to the murder. Had Viola simply committed adultery, and fled with Harry at the end of the novel, would the work acquire a veneer of wholesomeness, or is it the murder that ultimately makes Caird's work so unpleasant? The issue of sexual conduct within marriage may also lie behind the reviewer's dislike of the novel; with the suggestion that Phillip has raped Viola, Caird is entering the social purity debate of the 1880s and 1890s, with women such as Elizabeth Wolstenholme Elmy campaigning for the legal recognition of marital rape.[15]

---

[15]   'From 1880 onwards Elizabeth Wolstenholme Elmy campaigned for the recognition of the wife's rights over her own person and for the legal acceptance of the offence of marital rape. These demands never received attention in Parliament' (Tosh, 155). However, as mentioned earlier in this chapter, the case of *Regina v. Jackson* in 1891 did mean that a husband no longer had the power to detain and imprison his wife.

Regardless of its contemporary reception, the novel has achieved little lasting success, and this is due as much to Caird's uncomfortable siting of a polemic within a more conventional narrative framework, as to the novel's uneasy alliance of psychology and melodrama. A similar interplay between these two discourses occurs in Hardy's *Tess of the D'Urbervilles*, but with a greater degree of success. Hardy moves towards a work of psychological veracity but there are still residual elements of melodrama in the novel and, more importantly, a deliberate distancing of the reader from Tess's psyche which may be a conscious act on Hardy's part to prevent too complete an identification with his female murderer.

Before exploring the extent to which Hardy enables any form of access to Tess's consciousness, it is important to understand the perception of female criminality at this point in the century. As Nicola Lacey argues:

> by the end of the nineteenth century, recorded female crime was at a relatively low level, amounting to less than one fifth of the more serious offences triable before a jury. Yet these low levels of recorded female crime were juxtaposed with significant late-Victorian fears of female criminality, and by a profusion of theories of female dangerousness, often projected onto images of sexually motivated or emotionally rooted crime (113).

Against such a backdrop of concern, Lacey argues that the fictional representation of female criminality often exemplified 'a form of mental incapacity, which is closely related to self-deception: absence of mind or multiple consciousness' (124). This is clearly evident in Tess's detachment from Alec's murder (examined later in this chapter), and can also be found in earlier novels, most notably Wilkie Collins's 1870 work, *Man and Wife*. In this novel Hester Dethridge has killed her abusive husband before the story commences, and murders the villainous Geoffrey Delamayn at the close of the novel before descending into insanity; throughout the novel Hester exhibits a 'deathlike tranquility' (113), and is visited by an apparition, her evil alter ego which urges her to kill again, and with which she does battle throughout the novel.

Lacey draws on the work of Peter Eigen, who has identified the emergence in the latter half of the nineteenth century of instances of 'unconscious crime'. Such crimes did not fall under the M'Naghten rules regarding insanity (in fact, 'medical witnesses expressly denied that the defendant was insane at all' [Eigen, 10]) but were, instead, exemplified by conditions such as automatism, sleep-walking, epilepsy, or loss of memory. As discussed earlier in this chapter, Eleanor Pearcey's abortive defence rested on the argument that she was suffering from a form of epilepsy when she committed the murder of her lover's wife and child. Eigen pinpoints the introduction in 1876 of the French medical term *vertigé épileptique*, which he classifies as 'a nonconvulsive form of epilepsy … described as rendering the defendant's actions "automatic"'. That same year, 'a verdict of "not guilty on the grounds of unconsciousness" was recorded for the first time at the Old Bailey, and those mounting such a defence were 'not deluded, not deranged, not delirious in the slightest, the defendant's action was involuntary because an *automaton* had committed the crime' (10). As Eigen goes on to argue, this 'morbid fascination with unconscious and uncontrollable behaviour' within a society so focused on the 'ethic of self-mastery', is tantamount to 'someone with an abject fear of snakes who, upon entering a zoo, makes his way immediately for the reptile house' (15). And yet, perverse as it may seem, the focus on unconscious action provides a means to exonerate some of the more disturbing crimes of the period, both within the courtroom and on the page. Eigen argues that 'the predominant paradigm for framing an episode of "absence" was the *trance*: an induced state of being in which the patient ... was suspended somewhere between consciousness and sleep' (15) and the trance provides a very convenient means of 'explaining' an unforgivable crime. Lacey, drawing on Eigen's research, argues that this focus on unconscious or distracted state of mind is particularly applicable to the fictional portrayal of *female* crime, 'which often takes place between the interstices of chapters, outside the reader's line of vision – perhaps symbolizing the unspeakable nature of female violence by this period' (125). Of course, the tendency to portray violent or criminal acts 'off stage', or to dwell on the altered state of the protagonist is not exclusively ascribed to female characters, if we consider such works as Stevenson's *The Strange Case of Dr. Jekyll and Mr. Hyde* (1886), Oscar Wilde's *The Picture of Dorian Gray* (1891), Franklin Blake's sleep-walking and theft of the diamond in Wilkie Collins's *The Moonstone* (1868) or even Angel's sleep-walking in *Tess*. For Lacey, 'female deviancy may have been rendered more palatable to the Victorian imagination when represented as coinciding with moments of suspended agency' (104), but I would suggest that both male and female deviancy needed to be 'explained' in some way, and the argument of 'unconscious crime' offered one such explanation.

Tess's 'absence' at several key moments in the novel, murder aside, has been commented on by a number of literary critics. Mitchell argues that at the heart of the novel 'is a blank space, an absent heroine ... Tess's "interiority" – her consciousness, in other words, – is deftly elided in a series of unobtrusive omissions' (190). For Kincaid, Tess 'struggles throughout the novel to bring herself into palpable being, and fails tragically' (13). At the most crucial moments of the narrative – the rape, the death of her child, the revelation of her story to Angel and the murder – Hardy avoids directly telling the story, allowing events to take place 'off stage' as it were. At the point of the rape, not only are we denied any direct account of the events, Tess almost ceases to have any corporeal form at all. The moon has set, rendering Tess 'invisible' in the wood. When Alec stumbles upon her the darkness has transformed her into 'a pale nebulousness at his feet, which represented the white muslin figure he had left upon the dead leaves'. Tess is reduced to a series of body parts and functions, not for the first time or the last.

The details of the murder are not given, all we are told is that Mrs. Brooks hears the floor boards creaking in the room above. All melodramatic discourse is at an end here, with a factual and bald account of Mrs. Brooks's discovery: 'she got upon the table, and touched the spot in the ceiling with her fingers. It was damp, and she fancied that it was a blood-stain'. Similarly, the discovery of Alec's body is treated with almost clinical detachment: 'the wound was small, but the point of the blade had touched the heart of the victim, who lay on his back, pale, fixed, dead, as if he had scarcely moved after the infliction of the blow' (369–70). Alec is now identified simply as 'the victim', and the act of murder appears almost accidental, with any suffering on Alec's part minimized.

When Hardy does allow events to have an impact on Tess, it is her outward appearance that reflects this. Rather than explore the traumatic death of her child through Tess's psyche, Hardy simply describes how it altered her physically: 'one day she was pink and flawless; another pale and tragical. When she was pink she was feeling less than when pale; her more perfect beauty accorded with her less elevated mood; her more intense mood with her less perfect beauty' (109). Critics have made much of the extent to which Tess is objectified, broken down into a series of body parts which invite lingering attention. Boumelha argues that 'the narrator seeks to enter Tess, through her eyes … through her mouth … and through her flesh' (120) while Kincaid suggests that

> others objectify her by separating her into parts, only to submit those parts to a curious blurring process and then to eroticise this blur as a wonderfully malleable or chameleon image. Tess takes on any shape for those she meets, but it is a conveniently empty shape, ready to be filled in and then longed for (13).

By focusing on the manifestation of emotions through physical externals Hardy is harking back to the earlier narrative mode of melodrama, and, as a consequence, seems consciously to withhold Tess's interior life from the reader's knowledge. Morgan argues that, set against the ideological positioning of women that dominated the nineteenth century, Hardy's heroines 'must have confused many readers caught with mixed feelings of admiration and alarm' (xiii); perhaps Hardy denies us a fuller level of access to Tess's consciousness for fear that the 'admiration' will outstrip the 'alarm', resulting in sympathy for or even identification with a female murderer.

Despite the perceived limits of access to Tess's interior life, the novel was perceived by contemporary critics as a work of great psychological depth. The *Pall Mall Gazette*, reviewing the novel on 31 December 1891, argued that Tess's verisimilitude 'is maintained throughout with a subtlety and a warm and live and breathing naturalness which one feels to be the work of a tale-teller born and not made. … After reading the book it is Tess who fills one's mind and haunts one's imagination'. The *Daily News* review on 26 January 1891 commented on the apparent paradox of declaring Tess a 'pure woman', but conceded that

> as we follow this moving presentation of one who sins deeply, we acknowledge that, to the last of her fatal and tragic life, she keeps the stainless heart of a child. The story is heartrending, beautiful, convincing … The fall of the girl is told with delicacy, tenderness, and reticence. She remains the innocent victim unsullied in soul … we think of her – a doomed instrument in the hands of Fate – as a child-woman, done to death by two blind forces, social law and the racial instincts stirring in her blood.

For the reviewer this was 'one of his finest, if not his finest novel', and the critic dwelt on Hardy as 'the prose epic poet of the labouring classes', revealing 'with a new poignancy the dullness [*sic*] and sordidness of their lot, the simplicity of their unenlightened minds.'

There are two issues to address in relation to the critical reception of the novel. Firstly, the *Daily News'* comment on the 'dulness and sordidness' of the labouring classes is significant. On the one hand, Hardy portrays Tess as a charming novelty, 'a pagan in her domination by the two over-powering passions of love and jealousy' (*Manchester Times*, 5 February 1892). But he also affords her a degree of innate gentility, much as Dickens did more than 60 years earlier with Nancy in *Oliver Twist*, creating some kind of hybrid class which enables the readership (whether working or middle class) to empathize with Tess, whilst not running the risk of fully identifying with her, and thereby in some way being culpable in her crime. This juxtaposition of the 'pagan' and the more genteel woman may also contribute to Tess's inaccessibility. Despite the critical acclaim Hardy received for his role as the 'poet of the labouring classes', it is precisely in this aspect that I feel Hardy's portrayal of Tess falters; ultimately, he is unable, or perhaps unwilling to access fully the consciousness of a working-class woman. Much has been made of the portrayal of Tess as a variety of cultural archetypes, but one wonders if Hardy were almost forced to render her thus through an inability to reveal her as she truly was.[16] Certainly, neither Alec nor Angel see her as she is: for Angel she is 'a visionary essence of woman – a whole sex condensed into one typical form'; for Alec she is simply every irksome woman who has ever demanded too much of him, and when she tells him that she was unaware of his sexual intentions towards her he replies, 'That's what every woman says' (135, 83).

Secondly, we need to address why the press regarded Tess's portrait as one of such psychological veracity. Hardy's portrayal of Tess is undoubtedly sympathetic, but he never truly accesses her psyche; in fact, almost the reverse is true. The reason the novel was read as a psychological work may have been partly to do with the relative infancy of psychology as a discipline; Hardy is employing some of the tools of psychology insofar as we are afforded access (albeit limited) to Tess's thoughts, and the mere fact that the reader is compelled to feel sympathy for a murderess might, in itself, have been deemed the result of psychological veracity. However, writers such as Dickens and Eliot were achieving similar effects a whole generation before; more significant in the critical acclaim enjoyed by the novel is the element of wish fulfillment. Passive for much of the novel, Tess harks back to an earlier model of feminine behaviour that Viola Sedley in *The Wing of Azrael* most resoundingly destroys. In the scene where Angel sleep-walks, and lays Tess in an empty stone coffin in the abbey grounds, Tess is entirely acquiescent in Angel's bizarre activities 'so easefully had she delivered her whole being up to him that it pleased her to think he was regarding her as his absolute possession,

---

[16]   Penny Boumelha has suggested that this representation of Tess as a variety of cultural archetypes 'indicates how complex and contradictory Tess is' (127).

to dispose of as he should choose' (243). One wonders if, for the critics at least, Tess's delivering her 'whole being' up to Angel harks back to an earlier time of woman as the more passive helpmate of man.

The *Pall Mall Gazette* felt that the novel could only be fully appreciated

> perhaps by a woman, in its intimate and profound interpretation of the woman's heart through the pure and beautiful and heroic Tess, doomed to many sorrows, done to death … by the tyranny of man, of nature, which makes woman emotionally subject to man, and of social circumstance (31 December 1891, 3).

In a similar vein the *Daily News* argued that 'the fall of the girl is told with delicacy, tenderness, and reticence. She remains the innocent victim unsullied in soul' (26 January 1892, 6). The fact that these reviews draw so heavily on the lexicon of melodrama – a 'pure … beautiful … heroic' heroine, 'doomed … by the tyranny of man', 'the innocent victim unsullied in soul' – is surely no coincidence. Casting Tess back several decades, and portraying her as the passive tool at the hands of man and nature enables the critics to fully feel for her plight; she presents no threat. Even though she kills Alec, he has been painted so clearly as the melodramatic villain that the audience can feel little sympathy for him, and showing the murder 'off stage' means we are never faced with an image of the murderous Tess.

Interestingly, the same is true of all but one of the stage versions of *Tess*. The novel underwent a variety of theatrical adaptations, with Hardy himself adapting the work in 1894–95 (although the play was not performed until 1924). Harry Mountford, the adaptor of, among others, Ellen Wood's *East Lynne*, wrote a version that premiered at the Grand Theatre, Blackpool, on 28 December 1899. The novel was also transformed into an opera, first produced at Teatro San Carlo, Naples, in March/April 1906; the first London performance was 14 July 1909 at Covent Garden. The most well-known adaptation was that of Lorimer Stoddard; the play debuted at the Fifth Avenue Theatre, New York, in 1897, with the celebrated US actress Mrs. Fiske in the title role, and was a huge success.[17]

Not surprisingly, all four plays make significant changes to the novel, most notably in the character of Joan Durbeyfield, who is shown as far more complicit in the deception of Tess than she is in the original novel, thus minimizing even further Tess's culpability. Given the censorship surrounding the representation of domestic murder on the Victorian stage (examined in detail in Chapter 2), it is no surprise that the Mountford version is the only one to show the murder on stage, and even here Tess appears to be acting in a semi-conscious state at times. During the selection of the potential murder weapon, an act which would seem to suggest a degree of deliberate and forward planning, Tess examines a poker 'quite

---

[17]   Stoddard, 73–129. Roberts's work provides a full examination of the theatrical history of the novel. Hardy's adaptation was first performed in Dorchester in 1924, and then in London on 7 September 1925. A version by H. A. Kennedy was also reviewed in the *Era*, 24 February 1900.

unconsciously' suggesting she is, perhaps, suffering from a degree of 'partial insanity' at this point in the proceedings (Mountford, 156–7).

However, despite Mountford's best efforts to suggest that Tess is somehow not in control of her actions, it is difficult to view Tess in quite such a sympathetic light as Hardy paints her, after witnessing the following exchange:

> *Tess has put chair in front of looking-glass on dressing table, and put razors at R. of table ...*
>
> Alec: And you really love me at last Tess?
>
> Tess: Can you doubt it now?
>
> A: My darling (*kisses her*). And you don't love Clare any more?
>
> T: Jealous! Jealous? Why how can I? Just look at yourself (*puts his arm round her waist*). Look at your dear face – why there is no mirror here. Come my love (*leads him into bedroom, puts him in chair*). Look there dear. Can't you see for yourself? How could I love anyone – how could I love Angel Clare when there is that bonny face close to me, shining from the glass. How pretty your hair is Alec (*runs her fingers thro' it and leans her cheek on it*). There. There! Put that nasty pipe down (*takes pipe away, and stands behind him*).
>
> A: Are you going to kiss me dear? It will be the first time you have ever given me one of your own free will.
>
> T: So it will darling, the very first. (*she takes razor in her right hand, out of his sight, and puts her right arm across his neck, as his head is resting on her shoulder – he is sitting in arm chair, and she is sitting on the right arm of it. She plays with his hair with her left hand*).
>
> A: And you will love me as long as I live.
>
> T: As long as you live – Close your eyes Alec, while I kiss you – (*he does so*) (*with sudden movement sweeps razor across his throat twice. His head drops on table and he falls off chair ...*)
>
> T: ... Free! Free!' (Act III, scene 3, pp. 157–9)

The stage directions which place Tess as the orchestrator of the scene (she 'leads' Alec into the bedroom and 'puts' him a chair) and her final victorious exclamative leave no doubt in any viewer's mind that this is a conscious act on Tess's part, an aspect of the crime which is downplayed in the novel, despite Lacey's assertion that 'the reader is left in no real doubt of the intentionality with which she commits the murder which condemns her to the gallows' (128).

The American reviews of Lorimer Stoddard's play merit some attention for the emphasis they place on the psychological element of both the original novel and the theatrical adaptation. Interestingly, several publications argued that the psychology of the novel was so pronounced, it almost rendered the work unsuitable for the stage. The *Brooklyn Daily Eagle* felt that Stoddard had 'eliminated the psychology which would seem to make the book utterly impossible for stage treatment' and the *Philadelphia Public Ledger* suggested that the play outraged 'one's sense of what should be the ethics of the stage', but conceded that 'the unpleasant passages in the story have not been put there merely for the purposes of sensation; they are part and parcel of a curious psychological problem'.[18]

This viewing of the psychological as unsuitable for the stage is curious, given the fact that melodrama (the dominant theatrical mode of the nineteenth century) relied heavily on the externalizing of thoughts through asides and soliloquies and through somatic gesture. It would seem that these critics are referring to something quite specific when addressing the 'psychological' elements of the novel, and this is, I believe, the potential to sympathize with the heroine. This is what causes such concern: that the audience might come to care for, even understand, the actions of a murderess. And whilst such actions might be deemed acceptable in a novel, on the stage they are far more powerful and have far greater potential to result in similar deeds, hence the concern that certain elements of the novel were 'impossible' to stage. The *Philadelphia Public Ledger*'s comment on the 'unpleasant passages' existing not 'merely for the purposes of sensation' also shows the marked development from the sensation fiction of the 1860s and 70s. There is little attempt on Mary Elizabeth Braddon's part to make us sympathize with Lady Audley, for example, but Hardy's heroine was, and remains, one of his best-loved creations. Because the reader is made to care for Tess, this was read by critics as an authentic psychological portrayal. And this, in turn, engenders enormous cultural anxiety. Linking back to Maudsley's concept of the borderlands, if we can feel sorry for such a character this might suggest an element of kinship with them.

In Stoddard's adaptation the murder is not shown on stage, but Tess's thoughts are externalized for the audience in a series of stage directions:

> *Tess hastily closes the door and walks madly up and down as if looking for something. She walks into a table, tries to put it aside, sees the carving knife, and becomes as rigid as a statue ... The idea grows in her face ... She goes madly about the room like a suffering animal trying to find something then tries to think. She finds a stain on the lace of her gown, tears it off carefully, but doesn't know what to do with it* (in Roberts, *Tess in the Theatre*, Act IV, scene 1, p. 127).

Several reviewers were particularly impressed with this scene, the *Chicago Chronicle* commenting on the 'realistic horror', and the fact that 'the thoughts in her blazing brain are right before us.'[19] For the *Cincinnati Enquirer* this moment of murder is when Tess generates the greatest sympathy in the audience: 'the

---

[18] *Brooklyn Daily Eagle*, 26 October 1897; *Philadelphia Public Ledger*, 18 January 1898, qtd. in Roberts, *Tess in the Theatre*, xxxvii, xxxix, xxxviii.
[19] *Chicago Chronicle*, 8 March 1898, qtd. in Roberts, *Tess in the Theatre*, p. xlvi.

femininity of her character, the gentleness of her nature is, even in that awful moment when she revenges cruel wrongs, not obscured. She is not a female fiend, and the audience loves and approves her act'.[20] Given the paucity of domestic murderesses on the Victorian stage, the only comparable character is that of Miami in *The Green Bushes* (1845), examined in some detail in Chapter 2. Madame Celeste's portrayal of Miami aroused enormous sympathy, but Miami is part Native American Indian, and presented throughout the play as 'other'.[21] For an audience to 'love and approve' the act of murder, committed by an English working-class woman, is a significant move forward, and suggests a greater willingness to understand the crime, if not necessarily to allow it to go unpunished. It is no accident, though, that Tess is mute during the lead-up to the murder and its immediate aftermath in Stoddard's adaptation, almost as if the murder happens in spite of herself, unlike the calculated actions of, say, Lady Audley. Full access to Tess's psyche through a vocalized monologue might carry with it the threat of knowing that the murder was, to some extent, premeditated, and thus divorcing her from the possibility of sympathy. To create a sympathetic character, at this point in the century, we must of necessity be denied full access to her psyche; part of her, at least, must still operate within the more familiar parameters of melodrama or sensation fiction, either as the victim of domestic abuse or subject to the vagaries of insanity.

---

[20] *Cincinnati Enquirer*, 30 November 1897, qtd. in Roberts, *Tess in the Theatre*, p. xlvi.

[21] As Lacey argues, within the realist literary tradition 'the madwoman, criminal or otherwise, is conspicuous by her marginality': Bertha Mason (*Jane Eyre*) is in the attic, Laure (*Middlemarch*) is both in the past and in continental Europe, 'and in the novels of sensation in which women like Lydia Gwilt ... occupy centre stage, we see a strong orientation to condemnation and punishment, as well as hints of mental instability peculiar to the Victorian imagination' (123–4).

Conclusion

> Whether valued as a nursery of civic virtues or as a refuge from the tensions of society, the family was worshipped throughout the Victorian period; it was more than a society institution, it was a creed and it was held as a dogma carrying all the force of tradition that family life distinguished England from less stable and moral societies (Wohl, 10).

> The house, once a workplace as well as a home, had become a self-contained, private, exclusively domestic space (Summerscale, 109).

The separation of the home from the workplace, and the attendant 'cult of domesticity' generated by the Victorians which elevated the home to an almost sacred space is now central to our understanding of Victorian sensibility, and a viewpoint which has underpinned much of this book and its examination of domestic murder. To create a clear sense of what the Victorian home stood for, it was defined by relation to its opposite, resulting in what Waters, among others, has identified as 'a series of binary oppositions through which the Victorians sought to order their world: outside and inside, work and home, public and private, male and female' ('Domesticity', 351). This opposition of public and private is partly what generated so much interest in the more notorious domestic murder trials examined in this book. The domestic space became so private that the opportunity to look inside and have the illusion of understanding what went on 'behind closed doors' proved irresistible to many Victorians. And this holds true not only for the trial coverage, but also for the treatment of the home within much nineteenth-century fiction: as Anthea Trodd has highlighted, 'the home as scene of crime appears in Dickens and Eliot and Trollope as well as in the sensation novels of Wilkie Collins and Mary Braddon' (2).

The privacy afforded by the home clearly had a darker underbelly, not simply offering a retreat from the cares of the working world, but also greater opportunity for deviance and secrecy. Rather than the idealized vision of home promulgated during the middle decades of the century at least, where individuals were encouraged to 'only come home, home to tea and fire and baby, home to Dickens, and there will be the reduction of tension, the achievement of balance, the security of enclosure, all part of the connotative reach of "comfort"', as the century progressed the domestic space increasingly came to resemble the 'uneasy cauldron of bliss' identified by Chase and Levenson (8).

Against this backdrop of unease regarding the domestic space, Trodd has highlighted the frequency of references in Victorian fiction and journalism to the demon Asmodeus from Alain-René Le Sage's *Le Diable Boiteux* (1707); rescued from an enchanted glass bottle, Asmodeus takes his rescuer on a series of journeys, lifting the roofs of houses to enable his rescuer to witness the secret goings-on therein. Trodd goes on to contend that these Asmodean allusions underpin two opposing images of the Victorian home: 'the innocent home which justifiably seeks to guard itself against the intrusions of a hostile world, and the guilty home which requires the attentions of some benevolent Asmodeus to expose it to daylight and sanity' (5). Certainly, much of the appeal of the murder trials examined in this work must have lain in the courts' Asmodean ability to 'lift the lid' on the intimacies of domestic life, revealing the inadequacies within. In 1871 Flora Davy was found guilty of the manslaughter of her lover, Frederick Moon, and sentenced to eight years in prison (Davy's case is discussed in Chapter 1). An editorial in the *Times* commenting on the case expressed anxiety about the extent to which deviant behaviour could pass unnoticed and unchecked, hidden within the domestic space:

> The frightful fate of poor Mr. Moon ... lifts the veil, or rather opens wide the window and door, and reveals a state of things too well known to a large part of the London world, too little known to the rest. Here are well-to-do persons, with abundant means at their command, in the pale of respectability, and only thought, perhaps, not quite accountable in their ways, spending their lives in a sort of quicksand of social confusion and moral corruption. Mr. Moon for years had been the chief frequenter and pecuniary mainstay of a house which externally was like any other house – well-dressed people going in and out, well-appointed equipages standing at the door. Within doors it was impossible to say what was what or who was who (17 July 1871, 11).

The lifting of the 'veil' here is significant; there is obvious titillation, a vicarious thrill, but also the suggestion that only a thin boundary exists between the 'respectable' world and the world of people like Moon and Davy.[1] The editorial also focuses on the physical construction of the home, opening 'the window and door' to reveal the true state of affairs within, a semantic field that found great currency with the advent of sensation fiction, and reinforces Trodd's discussion of the Asmodean influence. The privacy afforded by the domestic sphere is here presented as a threat, a means of cloaking one's true desires within an environment where nobody knew 'what was what or who was who'.

Six years later, the testimony offered in the Staunton case (examined in greater detail in Chapter 4) presents a particularly pertinent example of how an outwardly respectable domestic space could conceal all manner of aberrant behaviour. The room in which the victim Harriet Staunton slept at Woodlands was miraculously transformed when exposed to public scrutiny. Clara Brown, servant at Woodlands, said of the room:

---

[1]   The image of the veil also foreshadows the Cleveland Street scandal of 1889, when a homosexual brothel was uncovered by police in Cleveland Street, London; the *Star*, in its coverage of the case, 'announced that the time had come to break the silence, to lift the "veil" and "expose" the men involved "to the view of justice"' (Cook, *Culture of Homosexuality*, 63).

there was a bedstead in it – a chair-bedstead – and two boxes. There was no basin or jug, nor means of cleaning herself. I was present when the police afterwards examined that room. Other things had then been put into it. That was done after she was taken away.

Unreliable as Clara Brown's testimony proved to be on other points, in this instance she was correct, as corroborated by Frank Quested and Alfred Hollands, two police constables who visited the house on 10 May, after Harriet's mother had complained to the magistrate about being denied access. Frank Quested gave testimony at the trial that

there were two bedrooms in the house. The front bedroom was properly furnished, but the back bedroom was very dirty. There was no carpet on the floor, and a piece of board laid on two trestles formed a bedstead. A mattress laid upon that was very dirty, as was the pillow. There were no pillow-cases or bedclothes. There was no washstand. There were a chair and a box in the room; also a silk skirt hung up behind the partition. The floor was very dirty indeed, and looked as if it had not been cleaned for months.

But when Alfred Hollands returned on 20 May with Sergeant Bateman,

the back bedroom was properly furnished then. It had been cleaned and carpeted. There were a dressing table there and the ordinary appliances of a bedroom. There were a flock bed, two blankets, two sheets, and a counterpane. There were also chintz hangings round the bed and one chair (*Times*, 22 September 1877, 11).

The Stauntons clearly believed that, by an outward appearance of respectability, and the accoutrements of domesticity afforded by appropriate bed dressings, they could deflect attention away from any suspicion that they might have murdered Harriet.

The potential for the home to deliberately close itself up from the public gaze was echoed almost 20 years later, in the trials of Oscar Wilde:

Alfred Taylor's darkened, perfumed rooms were repeatedly evoked in court and described by the press ... Fresh air and light, the conduits of Victorian health and vitality, were absent, and the public gaze was shut out ... It was the antithesis of rooms described in a piece on Piccadilly in *Chambers's Journal* in 1892: 'Through the French windows travellers outside in the omnibus can catch a rapid sight of statuettes, a neat white bookcase well filled with bright volumes, a few pieces of choice French furniture – nothing approaching the palatial; but neat, tasteful and orderly, like the house of any English gentleman.' Here was a general standard to which the respectable Englishman could conform. It was orderly and neat, with nothing too lavish, and was, perhaps most significantly, unashamed of the public gaze (Cook, *Culture of Homosexuality*, 56–7).

As Cook highlights, the 'respectable' home was deemed to be 'unashamed of the public gaze' and yet Charles Booth, in *East London* (1889), the first volume of *Life and Labour of the People in London*, identified some of the distinguishing features of a 'respectable' neighbourhood as 'closed doors, lace curtains ... [an] almost empty street' as opposed to the 'open doors' of more disreputable parts of the East End (Walkowitz, 35). The respectable domestic space needed to close itself off from the outside world, and yet be unafraid of public scrutiny, a confusion of ideology that seems to optimistically hark back to the perceived certainties of earlier decades. It is certainly an idealized, almost unattainable ideal that was clearly at odds with the domestic realities revealed in the more celebrated domestic murder trials at the close of the century. By the 1890s, the ability to 'read' respectability and morality through dress and demeanour that once left the Victorian public certain of an individual's guilt or innocence was now a thing of the past. As Walkowitz argues, in her discussion of the fin-de-siècle shopping districts such as London's Regent Street, 'prostitutes ... could and did pass as respectable, while virtuous ladies wandering through the streets ... often found themselves accosted as streetwalkers' (50). The certainty with which William Corder could be labelled 'a cold-blooded villain' in 1828, subject to the vilification of press and public alike, was now replaced with a focus on the 'genuine and ardent passion' exhibited by Eleanor Pearcey in 1890 in her relationship with a married man, whose wife and baby she murdered. The 2,000 letters of sympathy that were sent to Pearcey's counsel every week would have been inconceivable just 60 years earlier, during the Corder trial.

The Spectacle of Murder

> Under the conditions of spectacle, everyday affairs change their aspect ... A shockingly public occurrence can create a widespread perception that some deep truth has been disclosed, but it remains part of the logic of spectacle that the significance of the truth is so often obscure. How fully do the actors in the sensational drama represent us, who gaze and chatter? (Chase and Levenson, 16).

Undoubtedly, all the domestic murders examined in this work, and to a large extent their fictional counterparts, were subject to the 'conditions of spectacle'. Subjecting such crimes to these conditions transforms what might seem the most familiar and 'everyday' of spaces – the domestic – into something more problematic. The apparent bedrock of Victorian society and ideology is revealed not as something 'fixed', but something open to change and question. The binary oppositions of public and private become blurred, with the home no longer offering a refuge from the cares of the world, but instead revealing its own set of problems, and being subject to the gaze of outsiders. For the nineteenth-century audience, the crimes committed by the likes of William Corder, Eleanor Pearcey, the Mannings and the Stauntons did indeed seem to make 'everyday affairs change their aspect', and to offer 'some deep truth'. How else can we explain the public interest in what were often seemingly commonplace murders?

This book has sought to understand the appeal of domestic murder to contemporaries, but also of interest is its appeal to us, the twenty-first-century public. Ultimately, why do these crimes still matter and why are we still so fascinated with the Victorians, and particularly Victorian crime? The first of these cases, the Red Barn Murder, took place more than 180 years ago, after all; and yet, the Moyse's Hall Museum in Bury St. Edmunds, Suffolk, centres its marketing around this case, suggesting an undiminished public appetite for such crimes.[2] The success of Kate Summerscale's *The Suspicions of Mr. Whicher*, Judith Flanders's *The Invention of Murder* and Kate Colquhoun's *Mr. Briggs' Hat*, to name but a few reveals a national, if not global appetite for Victorian murder. And a 2002 work of artist Freddie Robins entitled 'Knitted Homes of Crime' features knitted replicas of the homes of female murderers, among them Eleanor Pearcey and Christiana Edmunds.[3] What one critic has termed the 'uneasy juxtaposition of the macabre and the cosy' in Robins's work transforms the spectacle of sensational crime into art.[4]

Perhaps our interest in the Victorians, and Victorian crime in particular, lies partly with the fact that they were involved in the formative stages of ideas which now feel very much a part of 'who we are', particularly the concept of the home as a refuge and defence against the world. Although part of our focus on the domestic space may have shifted from gender relations to the positioning of the child within the home and wider society, we are no less concerned with the centrality of the home, and the sense in which we define ourselves nationally by the state of our domestic relations. There is something about the Victorian psyche that feels familiar to us, and yet also alien; and crimes which appear to undermine the apparently impregnable sense of individual and national self-worth associated with the Victorians speak to us because they reveal Victorian society as a fragile, contentious and troubled one – very much like that which we inhabit. We seek the security that the Victorians seem to exemplify, and yet we also find some sort of reassurance or even pleasure in witnessing its paradoxical fragility.

---

[2]   <http://www.stedmundsbury.gov.uk/sebc/visit/redbarn-intro.cfm>.

[3]   <http://www.freddierobins.com/work_current/knittedhomes.htm>.

[4]   Polly Leonard, 'Freddie Robins's Subversive Sweaters', <http://embroidery.embroiderersguild.com/2003-2/leonard.htm>.

Bibliography

Primary Sources: Books

An Accurate Account of the Trial of William Corder for the Murder of Maria Marten ... etc. London: George Foster, n.d.

Acton, William. *The Functions and Disorders of the Reproductive Organs in Childhood, Youth, Adult Age, and Advanced Life Considered in Their Physiological, Social and Moral Relations* (1857). 4th edn. *Embodied Selves: An Anthology of Psychological Texts 1830–1890*. Ed. Jenny Bourne Taylor and Sally Shuttleworth. Oxford: Clarendon Press, 1998.

Bos. *The Life and Adventures of Oliver Twiss, the Workhouse Boy.* London: E. Lloyd for J. Graves, 1839.

Boucicault, Dion. *The Colleen Bawn; or, The Brides of Garry Owen.* London: Thomas Hailes Lacy, n.d.

Buckstone, John Baldwin. *The Green Bushes; or, A Hundred Years Ago.* London: The National Acting Drama Office, n.d. Vol. 11 of *Collected Plays.*

Bulwer-Lytton, Edward. *Lucretia: or, The Children of the Night.* Ed. Juliet John. London: Routledge 1998. Vol. 3 of *Cult Criminals: The Newgate Novels 1830–1847.*

Caird, Mona. *The Wing of Azrael.* 3 vols. London: Trübner and Co., 1889.

Collins, Wilkie. *Basil.* Oxford: OUP, 1990.

———. *Man and Wife.* Oxford: OUP, 1995.

Connolly, John. *An Inquiry Concerning the Indications of Insanity, with Suggestions for the Better Protection and Care of the Insane. Embodied Selves: An Anthology of Psychological Texts 1830–1890.* Ed. Jenny Bourne Taylor and Sally Shuttleworth. Oxford: Clarendon Press, 1998.

Craik, Dinah Mulock. *John Halifax, Gentleman.* London: J. M. Dent, 1961.

Curtis, J. *An Authentic and Faithful History of the Mysterious Murder of Maria Marten ... etc.* London: Thomas Kelly, 1828.

Dallas, E. S. *The Gay Science.* London: Chapman & Hall, 1866.

Danby, Frank. *Doctor Phillips: A Maida Vale Idyll.* Cambridge: The Keynes Press, 1989.

Dickens, Charles. *The Adventures of Oliver Twist.* London: J. M. Dent, 1994.

———. *Our Mutual Friend.* Harmondsworth: Penguin English Library, 1971.

———. *The Mystery of Edwin Drood.* London: Penguin, 2002.

Donkin, H. B. 'Hysteria'. *A Dictionary of Psychological Medicine.* Ed. D. Hack Tuke. London: J. A. Churchill, 1892.

Esquirol, Jean Étienne. *Mental Maladies: A Treatise on Insanity. Embodied Selves: An Anthology of Psychological Texts 1830–1890.* Ed. Jenny Bourne Taylor and Sally Shuttleworth. Oxford: Clarendon Press, 1998.

Hardy, Thomas. *Desperate Remedies*. Oxford: Oxford World's Classics, 2003.

———. *Far From the Madding Crowd*. London: Penguin Classics, 2000.

———. *Tess of the D'Urbervilles*. Oxford: OUP, 1983.

Hone, William. *The Power of Conscience Exemplified in the Genuine and Extraordinary Confession of Thomas Bedworth*. London: W. Hone, 1815.

Hyatt, Charles. *The Sinner Detected. A sermon preached in the open air, near the Red Barn at Polstead, and at the Meeting-House, Boxford, Suffolk, and in the afternoon and evening of Sunday, the 17th of August, 1828, on occasion of the execution of William Corder, for the murder of Maria Marten, including particulars of his life never before published*. London: Westley and Davis, c. 1828.

Ibsen, Henrik. *Plays: Two*. Trans. Michael Myer. London: Methuen, 2006.

Jackson, William. *The New and Complete Newgate Calendar*. 6 vols. London: Alexander Hogg, 1795.

Knapp, Andrew, and William Baldwin. *The Newgate Calendar*. 4 vols. London: J. Robins, 1824.

Lewis, Alexis. *Grace Clairville; or, The Crime at the Symon's Yat*. London: John Dicks, n.d. Dicks' Standard Plays No. 951.

Maudsley, Henry. *Responsibility in Mental Disease*. 3rd edn. London: C. Kegan Paul, 1876.

Millingen, John Gideon. *The Passions; or, Mind and Matter. Embodied Selves: An Anthology of Psychological Texts 1830–1890*. Ed. Jenny Bourne Taylor and Sally Shuttleworth. Oxford: Clarendon Press, 1998.

Mountford, Harry. *Tess: An Adaptation of the Celebrated Novel 'Tess of the D'Urbervilles'*. Lord Chamberlain's Collection 53701. British Library, London.

The Newgate Calendar and the Divorce Court Chronicle. London: F. Farrah, 1872.

The Newgate Calendar or Malefactors' Bloody Register. 5 vols. London: J. Cooke, 1773.

The Newspaper Press Directory. London: C. Mitchell, 1870.

Pelham, Camden. *The Chronicles of Crime; or, The New Newgate Calendar*. 2 vols. London: Thomas Tegg, 1841.

Prichard, James Cowles. *A Treatise on Insanity and Other Disorders Affecting the Mind. Embodied Selves: An Anthology of Psychological Texts 1830–1890*. Ed. Jenny Bourne Taylor and Sally Shuttleworth. Oxford: Clarendon Press, 1998.

Quilter, Harry, ed. *Is Marriage a Failure?* London: Swan Sonnenschein, 1888.

The Red Barn: A Tale Founded on Fact. London: Knight and Lacey, 1828.

Ritchie, Robert P. *An Inquiry into a Frequent Case of Insanity in Young Men. Embodied Selves: An Anthology of Psychological Texts 1830–1890*. Ed. Jenny Bourne Taylor and Sally Shuttleworth. Oxford: Clarendon Press, 1998.

Ruskin, John. *Sesame and Lilies, Lecture II: Lilies, Of Queens' Gardens*. Lancashire: Hendon Publishing, 2000.

Smiles, Samuel. *Self-Help*. Oxford: OUP, 2002.

Stirling, E. *The Rose of Corbeil; or, The Forest of Senart*. London: J. Duncombe, 1838.

Stoddard, Lorimer. *Tess of the D'Urbervilles: Dramatization in Four Acts. Tess in the Theatre*. Ed. Marguerite Roberts. Toronto: University of Toronto Press, 1950.

Thackeray, William. *Catherine: A Story*. Ed. Sheldon F. Goldfarb. Ann Arbor: University of Michigan Press, 1999.

The Trial, at length, of William Corder ... etc. Bury St. Edmunds: T. C. Newby, c. 1828.

The Trial of William Corder, at the Assizes, Bury St. Edmunds ... etc. London: Knight and Lacey, 1828.

The Trial of William Corder for the Wilful Murder of Maria Marten ... etc. London: Dean and Munday, n.d.

Wilks, Thomas Egerton. *Michael Erle the Maniac Lover; or, The Fayre Lasse of Lichfield*. London: Thomas Hailes Lacy, n.d. Vol. 33 of *Lacy's Acting Edition of Plays*.

Winslow, Forbes. *On Obscure Diseases of the Brain, and Disorders of the Mind. Embodied Selves: An Anthology of Psychological Texts 1830–1890*. Ed. Jenny Bourne Taylor and Sally Shuttleworth. Oxford: Clarendon Press, 1998.

Wynter, Andrew. *The Borderlands of Insanity and Other Allied Papers. Embodied Selves: An Anthology of Psychological Texts 1830–1890*. Ed. Jenny Bourne Taylor and Sally Shuttleworth. Oxford: Clarendon Press, 1998.

Primary Sources: Newspapers and Periodicals

Athenaeum. 26 Oct. 1839: 804.

Atlas. 28 Dec. 1839: 829; 1 Feb. 1845: 73; 15 Sept. 1860: 749.

'Belles Lettres'. *Westminster Review* 30 (1866): 268–80.

Brooklyn Daily Eagle. 26 Oct. 1897. Rpt. in *Tess in the Theatre*. Ed. Marguerite Roberts. Toronto: University of Toronto Press, 1950.

Caird, Mona. 'Marriage'. *Westminster Review* 130 (1888): 186–201.

'Charles Dickens and His Works'. *Fraser's Magazine for Town and Country* (1840): 381–400.

Chicago Chronicle. 8 Mar. 1898. Rpt. in *Tess in the Theatre*. Ed. Marguerite Roberts. Toronto: University of Toronto Press, 1950.

Cincinnati Enquirer. 30 Nov. 1897. Rpt. in *Tess in the Theatre*. Ed. Marguerite Roberts. Toronto: University of Toronto Press, 1950.

Cobbe, Frances Power. 'The Morals of Literature'. *Fraser's* 70: 124–33.

Dickens, Charles. 'The Demeanour of Murderers'. *Household Words* 3 (14 June 1856): 505–7.

Era. 18 Nov. 1838: 9; 2 Feb. 1845: 6; 16 Sept. 1860: 10; 30 Sept. 1860: 19; 28 Oct. 1860: 10.

Examiner. 18 Nov. 1838: 723, 740; 15 Sept. 1860: 582–3.

'Hints for a History of Highwaymen'. *Fraser's Magazine for Town and Country* (1834): 279–87.

Illustrated London News. 1 Feb. 1845: 73–4; 15 Sept. 1860: 249.

Illustrated Police News. 22 Nov. 1890: 1; 27 Dec. 1890: 2.

'Literary Recipes'. *Punch.* 7 Aug. 1841: 39.

Lloyd's Weekly London Newspaper. 2 Jan. 1848: 12; 10 Aug. 1856: 12; 21 Jan. 1872: 1; 4 Aug. 1889: 3; 11 Aug. 1889: 1; 7 Dec. 1890.

Magnet. 3 Feb. 1845: 6.

Mansel, Dean. 'Sensation Novels'. *Quarterly Review* 113 (1863): 481–514.

Maudsley, Henry. 'Sex in Mind and in Education'. *Fortnightly Review* 15 (1874): 466–83.

'The Medical Evidence of Crime'. *Cornhill Magazine* 7 (1863): 338–48.

Morning Chronicle. 29 Jan. 1845: 5; 11 Sept. 1860: 6.

Morning Herald. 1 Jan. 1847: 6.

'Murder Madness'. *Sala's Journal.* 5 Nov. 1892: 649. Crime Folder 9. The John Johnson Collection. Bodleian Library, University of Oxford.

National Magazine and Monthly Critic (1837): 445–9.

Oliphant, Margaret. 'Novels'. *Blackwood's* 94 (1863): 168–83.

———. 'Novels'. *Blackwood's* 102 (1867): 257–80.

———. 'Sensation Novels'. *Blackwood's* 91 (1862): 564–84.

'Our Novels: The Sensational School'. *Temple Bar* 29 (July 1870): 410–24.

Philadelphia Public Ledger. 18 Jan. 1898. Rpt. in *Tess in the Theatre.* Ed. Marguerite Roberts. Toronto: University of Toronto Press, 1950.

'The Popular Novels of the Year'. *Fraser's* 68 (1863): 253–69.

Quarterly Review (June 1839): 83–102.

Reynolds's London Newspaper. 30 Mar. 1851: 6; 20 July 1856: 9; 21 Jan. 1872: 5, 6; 28 Jan. 1872: 5; 25 Aug. 1889: 5; 7 Dec. 1889: 4; 7 Dec. 1890: 4.

Saturday Review 30 (17 Sept. 1870): 369.

'Society's Looking-Glass'. *Temple Bar* 6 (1862): 129–37.

Spectator. 24 Nov. 1838: 1114–15.

Stack, Herbert J. 'Some Recent English Novels'. *Fortnightly Review* 15 (1871): 731–46.

Thackeray, William. 'Going to See a Man Hanged'. *Fraser's Magazine for Town and Country* (1840): 150–58.

———. 'Horae Catnachianae: A Dissertation on Ballads, with a few unnecessary remarks on Jonathan Wild, John Sheppard, Paul Clifford, and _____ Fagin, Esqrs.'. *Fraser's Magazine for Town and Country* (1839): 407–24.

Times. 24 Apr. 1828: 7, 'Murder at Polstead'.

———. 1 May 1828: 3, 'The Murder at Polstead'.

———. 8 Aug. 1828: 2, 'Trial of William Corder for the Murder of Maria Marten'.

———. 9 Aug. 1828: 3, 'The Trial and Conviction of William Corder'.

———. 12 Aug. 1828: 3, 'Conduct, Confession, and Execution of Corder'.

———. 15 Dec. 1831: 5, 'Winter Assizes'.

———. 3 Apr. 1837: 7, 'The Edgeware-Road Murder'.

———. 6 Apr. 1837: 5, 'The Edgeware-Road Murder – Final Examination and Committal of Greeenacre and Gale to Newgate'.

———. 13 Apr. 1837: 5, 'The Edgeware-Road Murder'.

———. 19 Apr. 1842: 7, 'The Roehampton Murder'.

———. 23 May 1842: 6, 'The Murderer Good'.

———. 19 Sept. 1843: 6, 'Further Particulars of the Arrival of Mrs. Gilmour at Paisley, from New York'.

———. 30 Dec. 1843: 7, 'Oxford Circuit'.

———. 20 Jan. 1844: 3, 'Case of Mrs. Gilmour'.

———. 28 Jan. 1845: 5, 'Adelphi Theatre'.

———. 2 Apr. 1845: 6, 'Horrible Murder in St. Giles's'.

———. 7 Apr. 1845: 6, 'The Murder in St. Giles's'.

———. 29 Mar. 1847: 7, 'Spring Assizes'.

———. 31 Mar. 1847: 7, 'Spring Assizes'.

———. 10 Jan. 1848: 6, 'The Golden-Lane Murder'.

———. 7 Feb. 1848: 6, 'The Murder in St. James's Park'.

———. 20 Aug. 1849: 6, 'The Murder at Bermondsey'.

———. 21 Aug. 1849: 8, 'The Murder in Bermondsey'.

———. 25 Aug. 1849: 5, 'The Bermondsey Murder'.

———. 27 Aug. 1849: 5, 'The Bermondsey Murder'.

———. 1 Sept. 1849: 5, 'The Bermondsey Murder'.

———. 17 Sept. 1849: 8, 'The Bermondsey Murder'.

———. 26 Oct. 1849: 4, 'The Bermondsey Murder'.

———. 27 Oct. 1849: 4, n.t.

———. 29 Oct. 1849: 5, 'The Bermondsey Murder'.

———. 14 Nov. 1849: 4–5, 'The Bermondsey Murder'.

———. 17 July 1871: 12, 'The Eltham Murder'.

———. 1 Sept. 1871: 9, 'The Alleged Poisoning at Brighton'.

———. 12 Oct. 1871: 5, 'Murder and Attempted Suicide'.

———. 11 Jan. 1872: 9, 'The Stockwell Murder'.

———. 12 Jan. 1872: 11, 'The Stockwell Murder'.

———. 17 Jan. 1872: 12, 'The Brighton Poisonings'.

———. 17 Jan. 1872: 11, 'The Case of Mr. Watson'; 12, 'The Brighton Poisonings'.

———. 19 Jan. 1872: 8, 'Homicidal Frenzy'.

———. 11 July 1877: 11, 'The Penge Case'.

———. 22 Sept. 1877: 11, 'The Penge Case'.

———. 27 Sept. 1877: 8, 'The Penge Murder'; 9, n.t.

———. 15 Oct. 1877: 9, n.t.

———. 13 Apr. 1886: 11, 'Central Criminal Court, April 12'.

———. 14 Apr.1886: 6, 'Central Criminal Court, April 13'.

———. 15 Apr. 1886: 3, 'Central Criminal Court, April 14'.

———. 19 Apr. 1886: 4, 'Central Criminal Court, April 17'.

———. 6 Aug. 1889: 9, 'The Liverpool Poisoning Case'.

———. 8 Aug. 1889: 7, n.t.

————. 10 Aug. 1889: 4, 'The Maybrick Case'.
————. 15 Aug. 1889: 5, 'The Maybrick Case'.
————. 2 Dec. 1890: 13, 'The Kentish-Town Murder'.
————. 3 Dec. 1890: 13, 'The Kentish-Town Murder'.
————. 4 Dec. 1890: 9, n.t.
Weekly Dispatch. 2 Feb. 1845: 56; 16 Sept.1860: 10.
Weekly Times. 16 Sept. 1860: 5.
Unidentified publication. 1 May 1842. Folder 3, Murder and Execution Broadsides.
　　John Johnson Collection. Bodleian Library, Oxford University.

Primary Sources: Murder and Execution Broadsides

'Apprehension of Daniel Good at Tonbridge for the Murder of Jane Jones, alias
　　Good'. Folder 3, Murder and Execution Broadsides. John Johnson Collection.
　　Bodleian Library, Oxford University.
'Apprehension of John Connor for the Murder of Ann Tape'. Folder 2, Murder
　　and Execution Broadsides. John Johnson Collection. Bodleian Library, Oxford
　　University.
'Full particulars of the Murder of Ann Tape, at a House of Ill Fame'. Folder 2,
　　Murder and Execution Broadsides. John Johnson Collection. Bodleian Library,
　　Oxford University.
'Treason and Murder. An account of the Behaviour and Execution of Margaret
　　Cunningham, alias Mason'. Crime 1: Murder and Execution Small Broadsides
　　A–P. John Johnson Collection. Bodleian Library, Oxford University.
'The Trial, Sentence and Execution of Joseph Connor'. Folder 2, Murder and
　　Execution Broadsides. John Johnson Collection. Bodleian Library, Oxford
　　University.
Untitled Broadside dated 17 November 1862. Folder 2, Murder and Execution
　　Broadsides. John Johnson Collection. Bodleian Library, Oxford University.

Secondary Sources

Adams, James Eli. *Dandies and Desert Saints: Styles of Victorian Masculinity*.
　　Ithaca: Cornell UP, 1995.
Altick, Richard. *Victorian Studies in Scarlet*. London: J. M. Dent, 1970.
Anderson, Patricia. *The Printed Image and the Transformation of Popular Culture
　　1790–1860*. Oxford: Clarendon Press, 1991.
Bailey, Peter. *Leisure and Class in Victorian England: Rational Recreation and
　　the Contest for Control, 1830–1885*. London: Methuen, 1987.
Bayley, John. 'Oliver Twist: "Things as they really are".' *Dickens and the
　　Twentieth Century*. Ed. John Gross and Gabriel Pearson. London: Routledge
　　& Kegan Paul, 1962. 49–64.
Booth, Michael. *English Melodrama*. London: Herbert Jenkins, 1965.

————. *Theatre in the Victorian Age*. Cambridge: CUP, 1991.

Boumelha, Penny. *Thomas Hardy and Women: Sexual Ideology and Narrative Form*. Brighton: The Harvester Press, 1982.

Boyle, Thomas. *Black Swine in the Sewers of Hampstead: Beneath the Surface of Victorian Sensationalism*. New York: Viking, 1988.

Brantlinger, Patrick. 'What is "Sensational" about the "Sensation Novel"?' *Nineteenth-Century Fiction* 37 (1982): 1–28.

Bratton, Jacky. *New Readings in Theatre History*. Cambridge: CUP, 2003.

Brooks, Peter. *The Melodramatic Imagination: Balzac, Henry James, Melodrama, and the Mode of Excess*. New Haven and London: Yale UP, 1976.

Cabot, Frederick C. 'The Two Voices in Thackeray's Catherine.' *Nineteenth-Century Fiction* (1974): 404–16.

Carter Wood, J. *Violence and Crime in Nineteenth-Century England: The Shadow of Our Refinement*. London: Routledge, 2004.

Chase, Karen, and Michael Levenson. *The Spectacle of Intimacy: A Public Life for the Victorian Family*. Princeton: Princeton UP, 2000.

Chernaik, Warren, Martin Swales, and Robert Vilain, eds. *The Art of Detective Fiction*. Basingstoke: Macmillan Press, 2000.

Cocks, H. G., and Matt Houlbrook. *Palgrave Advances in the Modern History of Sexuality*. Basingstoke: Palgrave Macmillan, 2006.

Cohen, Deborah. *Household Gods: The British and their Possessions*. New Haven: Yale UP, 2006.

Cohen, Ed. *Talk on the Wilde Side: Toward a Genealogy of a Discourse on Male Sexualities*. New York: Routledge, 1993.

Colby, Robert A. 'Catherine: Thackeray's Credo'. *The Review of English Studies* 15 (1964): 381–96.

Colebrook, Claire. *New Literary Histories: New Historicism and Contemporary Criticism*. Manchester: Manchester UP, 1997.

Colquhoun, Kate. *Mr. Briggs' Hat: A Sensational Account of Britain's First Railway Murder*. London: Little, Brown, 2011.

Cook, Matt. 'Law'. *Palgrave Advances in the Modern History of Sexuality*. Ed. H. G. Cocks and Matt Houlbrook. Basingstoke: Palgrave Macmillan, 2006. 64–86.

————. *London and the Culture of Homosexuality, 1885–1914*. Cambridge: CUP, 2003.

Cunningham, Gail. *The New Woman and the Victorian Novel*. London: Macmillan Press, 1978.

Davidoff, Leonore, and Catherine Hall. *Family Fortunes: Men and Women of the English Middle Class 1780–1850*. London: Hutchinson, 1987.

Davie, Neil. *Tracing the Criminal: The Rise of Scientific Criminology in Britain 1860–1918*. Oxford: Bardwell Press, 2006.

Davis, Jim, and Victor Emaljanow. *Reflecting the Audience: London Theatregoing, 1840–1880*. Iowa City: University of Iowa Press, 2001.

Disher, Maurice Willson. *Blood and Thunder: Mid-Victorian Melodrama and Its Origins*. London: Frederick Muller, 1949.

Donahay, Martin A. *Gender at Work in Victorian Culture: Literature, Art and Masculinity*. Aldershot: Ashgate, 2005.

Donohue, Joseph, ed. *The Cambridge History of British Theatre*, Vol. 2, *1660 to 1895*. Cambridge: CUP, 2004.

———. 'Theatres, Their Architecture and Their Audiences'. *The Cambridge History of British Theatre*, Vol. 2, *1660 to 1895*. Ed. Joseph Donohue. Cambridge: CUP, 2004. 292–308.

Dowling, Andrew. *Manliness and the Male Novelist in Victorian Literature*. Aldershot: Ashgate, 2001.

Earl, John. 'The Rotunda: Variety Stage and Socialist Platform'. *Theatre Notebook* 58/2 (2004): 71–90.

Eigen, Joel Peter. *Unconscious Crime: Mental Absence and Criminal Responsibility in Victorian London*. Baltimore: Johns Hopkins UP, 2003.

Federico, Annette. *Masculine Identity in Hardy and Gissing*. London: Associated University Presses, 1991.

Flanders, Judith. *The Invention of Murder: How the Victorians Revelled in Death and Detection and Created Modern Crime*. London: Harper Press, 2011.

Flint, Kate. *The Woman Reader 1837–1914*. Oxford: Clarendon Press, 1995.

Fulkerson, Richard P. '"Oliver Twist" in the Victorian Theatre'. *The Dickensian* 70 (1974): 83–95.

Gardner, Viv, and Susan Rutherford, eds. *The New Woman and Her Sisters: Feminism and Theatre 1850–1914*. New York: Harvester Wheatsheaf, 1992.

Gatrell, V. A. C. *The Hanging Tree: Execution and the English People 1770–1868*. Oxford: OUP, 1994.

Golz, Annalee E. 'Murder Most Foul: Spousal Homicides in Ontario, 1870–1915'. *Disorder in the Court: Trials and Sexual Conflict at the Turn of the Century*. Ed. George Robb and Nancy Erber. Hampshire: Macmillan Press, 1999. 164–85.

Goodlad, Lauren M. E. *Victorian Literature and the Victorian State: Character and Governance in a Liberal Society*. Baltimore: Johns Hopkins UP, 2003.

Gretton, Thomas. *Murders and Moralities: English Catchpenny Prints 1800–1860*. London: British Museum Publications, 1980.

Hadley, Elaine. *Melodramatic Tactics: Theatricalized Dissent in the English Marketplace, 1800–1885*. Stanford: Stanford UP, 1995.

Haining, Peter. *Maria Marten: The Murder in the Red Barn*. Plymouth: Richard Castell Publishing, 1992.

Hall, Catherine. *White, Male and Middle-Class: Exploration in Feminism and History*. Cambridge: Polity Press, 1992.

Hamilton, Paul. *Historicism*. London: Routledge, 1996.

Hammerton, A. James. *Cruelty and Companionship: Conflict in Nineteenth-Century Married Life*. London and New York: Routledge, 1992.

Hartman, Mary S. *Victorian Murderesses: A True History of Thirteen Respectable French and English Women Accused of Unspeakable Crimes*. London: Robson Books, 1977.

Heilmann, Ann. *The Late-Victorian Marriage Question: A Collection of Key New Woman Texts*. Ed. Ann Heilmann. 4 vols. London: Routledge, 1998.

———. *New Woman Fiction: Women Writing First-wave Feminism*. Basingstoke: Macmillan, 2000.

Hollingsworth, Keith. *The Newgate Novel 1830–1847: Bulwer, Ainsworth, Dickens and Thackeray*. Detroit: Wayne State UP, 1963.

Hughes, Winifred. *The Maniac in the Cellar: Sensation Novels of the 1860s*. Princeton: Princeton UP, 1980.

John, Juliet, ed. *Charles Dickens's Oliver Twist: A Sourcebook*. Abingdon: Routledge, 2006.

———. *Cult Criminals: The Newgate Novels 1830–1847*. London: Routledge, 1998.

———. *Dickens's Villains: Melodrama, Character, Popular Culture*. Oxford: OUP, 2001.

Jones, Jennifer. *Medea's Daughters: Forming and Performing the Woman Who Kills*. Columbus: Ohio State UP, 2003.

Jones-Evans, Eric. *Mr. Crummles Presents The Red Barn Murder or The Gipsy's Curse: A Dickensian Play in a Prologue and Three Acts*. Southampton: G. F. Wilson, 1966.

Kalikoff, Beth. *Murder and Moral Decay in Victorian Popular Literature*. Michigan: UMI Research Press, 1986.

Kelly, Gary, ed. *Newgate Narratives*. 5 vols. London: Pickering & Chatto, 2008.

Kilgarriff, Michael, ed. *The Golden Age of Melodrama: Twelve Nineteenth-Century Melodramas*. London: Wolfe Publishing, 1974.

Kincaid, James. '"You did not come": Absence, Death and Eroticism in *Tess*'. *Sex and Death in Victorian Literature*. Ed. Regina Barreca. Macmillan Press: Hampshire, 1990. 9–31.

Knelman, Judith. *Twisting in the Wind: The Murderess and the English Press*. Toronto: University of Toronto Press, 1998.

Lacey, Nicola. *Women, Crime, and Character: From* Moll Flanders *to* Tess of the D'Urbervilles. Oxford: OUP, 2008.

Ledger, Sally. *The New Woman: Fiction and Feminism at the Fin de Siècle*. Manchester: Manchester UP, 1997.

Ledger, Sally, and Roger Luckhurst, eds. *The Fin de Siècle: A Reader in Cultural History c. 1880–1900*. Oxford: OUP, 2000.

Leps, Marie-Christine. *Apprehending the Criminal: The Production of Deviance in Nineteenth-Century Discourse*. Durham: Duke UP, 1992.

Loesberg, Jonathan. 'The Ideology of Narrative Form in Sensation Fiction'. *Representations* 13 (1986): 115–38.

McLaren, Angus. *The Trials of Masculinity: Policing Sexual Boundaries 1870–1930*. Chicago and London: University of Chicago Press, 1997.

McWilliam, Rohan. *The Tichborne Claimant: A Victorian Sensation*. London: Continuum, 2007.

Mangham, Andrew. *Violent Women and Sensation Fiction: Crime, Medicine and Victorian Popular Culture*. Basingstoke: Palgrave, 2007.

Marks, Patricia. *Bicycles, Bangs and Bloomers: The New Woman in the Popular Press.* Kentucky: University Press of Kentucky, 1990.

Maunder, Andrew, and Grace Moore, eds. *Victorian Crime, Madness and Sensation.* Aldershot: Ashgate, 2004.

Mitchell, Judith. *The Stone and the Scorpion: The Female Subject of Desire in the Novels of Charlotte Bronte, George Eliot, and Thomas Hardy.* Westport: Greenwood Press, 1994.

Moody, Jane. 'The Theatrical Revolution, 1776–1843'. *The Cambridge History of British Theatre*, Vol. 2, *1660 to 1895*. Ed. Joseph Donohue. Cambridge: CUP, 2004. 199–215.

Morgan, Rosemarie. *Women and Sexuality in the Novels of Thomas Hardy.* London: Routledge, 1988.

Nead, Lynda. *Myths of Sexuality: Representations of Women in Victorian Britain.* Oxford: Basil Blackwell, 1988.

Nemesvari, Richard. '"Is it a man or a woman?": Constructing Masculinity in *Desperate Remedies'*. *Human Shows: Essays in Honour of Michael Millgate*. Ed. Rosemarie Morgan and Richard Nemesvari. New Haven: Hardy Association Press, 2000. 67–88.

Newey, Vincent. *The Scriptures of Charles Dickens: Novels of Ideology, Novels of the Self.* Aldershot: Ashgate Publishing, 2004.

Page, Norman, ed. *Wilkie Collins: The Critical Heritage.* London: Routledge & Kegan Paul, 1974.

Pick, Daniel. *Faces of Degeneration: A European Disorder c. 1848–c. 1918.* Cambridge: CUP, 1989.

Poovey, Mary. *Uneven Developments: The Ideological Work of Gender in Mid-Victorian England.* London: Virago, 1989.

Priestman, Martin, ed. *The Cambridge Companion to Crime Fiction.* Cambridge: CUP, 2003.

Pykett, Lyn. 'The Cause of Women and the Course of Fiction: The Case of Mona Caird'. *Gender Roles and Sexuality in Victorian Literature*. Ed. Christopher Parker. Aldershot: Scolar Press, 1995. 128–42.

———. *The 'Improper' Feminine: The Women's Sensation Novel and the New Woman Writing.* London: Routledge, 1992.

———. 'The Newgate Novel and Sensation Fiction, 1830–1868'. *The Cambridge Companion to Crime Fiction*. Ed. Martin Priestman. Cambridge: CUP, 2003. 19–39.

———, ed. *Reading Fin de Siècle Fictions.* Harlow: Longman, 1996.

———. *The Sensation Novel: From* The Woman in White *to* The Moonstone. Plymouth: Northcote House Publishers, 1994.

Ray, Gordon N. *The Letters and Private Papers of William Makepeace Thackeray.* 4 vols. London: OUP, 1945.

Richardson, Angelique, and Chris Willis, eds. *The New Woman in Fiction and in Fact: Fin-de-Siècle Feminisms.* Basingstoke: Palgrave, 2001.

Rimmer, Mary. *Introduction to Thomas Hardy, Desperate Remedies*. London: Penguin, 1998.

Robb, George, and Nancy Erber, eds. *Disorder in the Court: Trials and Sexual Conflict at the Turn of the Century*. Hampshire: Macmillan Press, 1999.

Roberts, Marguerite, ed. *Tess in the Theatre*. Toronto: University of Toronto Press, 1950.

Rodensky, Lisa. *The Crime in Mind: Criminal Responsibility and the Victorian Novel*. Oxford and New York: OUP, 2003.

Rowbotham, Judith, and Kim Stevenson, eds. *Behaving Badly: Social Panic and Moral Outrage – Victorian and Modern Parallels*. Aldershot: Ashgate, 2003.

Rylance, Rick. '"The Disturbing Anarchy of Investigation": Psychological Debate and the Victorian Periodical'. *Culture and Science in the Nineteenth-Century Media*. Ed. Louise Henson, Geoffrey Cantor, Gowan Dawson, Richard Noakes, Sally Shuttleworth and Jonathan R. Topham. Aldershot: Ashgate, 2004. 239–59.

Schoch, Richard W. 'Theatre and Mid-Victorian Society, 1851–1870'. *Cambridge History of British Theatre*, Vol. 2, *1660 to 1895*. Ed. Joseph Donohue. Cambridge: CUP, 2004. 331–51.

Sedgwick, Eve Kosofsky. *Between Men: English Literature and Male Homosocial Desire*. New York: Columbia UP, 1985.

Shellard, Dominic, and Steven Nicholson. *The Lord Chamberlain Regrets … : A History of British Theatre Censorship*. London: The British Library, 2004.

Showalter, Elaine. 'Desperate Remedies: Sensation Novels of the 1860s'. *The Victorian Newsletter* 49 (1976): 1–5.

Shuttleworth, Sally. *Charlotte Brontë and Victorian Psychology*. Cambridge: CUP, 1996.

Slater, Montagu, ed. *Two Classic Melodramas: Maria Marten and Sweeney Todd*. London: Gerald Howe, 1928.

Stearns, Peter N. *Be a Man! Males in Modern Society*. 2nd edn. New York: Holmes & Meier, 1990.

Stottlar, James F. 'A Victorian Stage Censor: The Theory and Practice of William Bodham Donne'. *Victorian Studies* 8 (1970): 253–82.

Stowell, Sheila. *A Stage of Their Own: Feminist Playwrights of the Suffrage Era*. Manchester: Manchester UP, 1992.

Summerscale, Kate. *The Suspicions of Mr. Whicher: or The Murder at Road Hill House*. London: Bloomsbury, 2008.

Surridge, Lisa. *Bleak Houses: Marital Violence in Victorian Fiction*. Athens: Ohio UP, 2005.

Sussman, Herbert. *Victorian Masculinities: Manhood and Masculine Poetics in Early Victorian Literature and Art*. Cambridge: CUP, 1995.

Swindells, Julia. *Glorious Causes: The Grand Theatre of Political Change, 1789 to 1833*. Oxford: OUP, 2001.

Taylor, Jenny Bourne. *In the Secret Theatre of Home: Wilkie Collins, Sensation Narrative, and Nineteenth-Century Psychology*. London and New York: Routledge, 1988.

Taylor, Jenny Bourne, and Sally Shuttleworth, eds. *Embodied Selves: An Anthology of Psychological Texts 1830–1890*. Oxford: Clarendon Press, 1998.

Thomas, Ronald R. *Detective Fiction and the Rise of Forensic Science*. Cambridge: CUP, 1999.

Tillotson, Kathleen. 'The Lighter Reading of the 1860s'. Introduction to Wilkie Collins, *The Woman in White*. Boston: Houghton Mifflin, 1969.

Tosh, John. *A Man's Place: Masculinity and the Middle-Class Home in Victorian England*. New Haven and London: Yale UP, 1999.

Trodd, Anthea. *Domestic Crime in the Victorian Novel*. Hampshire: Macmillan, 1989.

Walkowitz, Judith R. *City of Dreadful Delight: Narratives of Sexual Danger in Late-Victorian London*. London: Virago, 1992.

Waters, Catherine. *Dickens and the Politics of the Family*. Cambridge: CUP, 1997.

———. 'Domesticity'. *Charles Dickens in Context*. Ed. Sally Ledger and Holly Furneaux. Cambridge: CUP, 2011. 350–57.

Wiener, Martin J. *Men of Blood: Violence, Manliness and Criminal Justice in Victorian England*. Cambridge: CUP, 2004.

———. *Reconstructing the Criminal: Culture, Law, and Policy in England, 1830–1914*. Cambridge: CUP, 1990.

Williams, Raymond. *The Long Revolution*. London: Hogarth Press, 1992.

Wilson, Patrick. *Murderess: A Study of the Women Executed in Britain since 1843*. London: Michael Joseph, 1971.

Wohl, Anthony, ed. *The Victorian Family: Structure and Stresses*. London: Croom Helm, 1978.

Woodward, William R., and Mitchell G. Ash. *The Problematic Science: Psychology in Nineteenth-Century Thought*. New York: Praeger Publishers, 1982.

Worrall, David. *Theatric Revolution: Drama, Censorship and Romantic Period Subcultures 1773–1832*. Oxford: OUP, 2006.

Wynne, Deborah. *The Sensation Novel and the Victorian Family Magazine*. Basingstoke: Palgrave, 2001.

Zedner, Lucia. *Women, Crime, and Custody in Victorian England*. Oxford: OUP, 1991.

Online Sources

<www.bl.uk/collections/newspapers.html> [Accessed 17 May 2009].

<http://commons.wikimedia.org/wiki/File:Corder-broadside2.jpg> [Accessed 28 April 2013].

<http://commons.wikimedia.org/wiki/File:MariaMarten.jpg> [Accessed 28 April 2013].

<http://commons.wikimedia.org/wiki/File:WilliamCorder-awaitingtrial.jpg> [Accessed 28 April 2013].

Daily News, 26 January 1892, <www.bl.uk/collections/newspapers.html> [Accessed 18 February 2008].

<http://www.freddierobins.com/work_current/knittedhomes.htm> [Accessed 4 May 2009].

Glasgow Herald, 14 May 1889, <www.bl.uk/collections/newspapers.html> [Accessed 17 May 2009].

Graphic, 15 June 1889, <www.bl.uk/collections/newspapers.html> [Accessed 17 May 2009].

John, Juliet. 'Melodrama and Its Criticism: An Essay in Memory of Sally Ledger'. *19*, 8 (2009), <http://www.19.bbk.ac.uk/issue8/papers/john_final.pdf> [Accessed 17 May 2009].

Leonard, Polly. 'Freddie Robins's Subversive Sweaters'. <http://embroidery. embroiderersguild.com/2003-2/leonard.htm> [Accessed 11 June, 2009].

Manchester Times, 5 February 1892, <www.bl.uk/collections/newspapers.html> [Accessed 18 February 2008].

Pall Mall Gazette, 26 April 1889: 1, 31 December 1891: 3,<www.bl.uk/collections/ newspapers.html> [Accessed 18 February 2008].

<http://www.victorianweb.org/authors/craik/mitchell/3.html> [Accessed 29 September 2008].

<http://www.victorianweb.org/art/illustration/fildes/d190.html> [Accessed 27 April 2013].

<http://www.victorianweb.org/art/illustration/fildes/d4.html> [Accessed 27 April 2013].

<http://en.wikipedia.org/wiki/File:WilliamCorder-hanging.jpg> [Accessed 28 April 2013].

York Herald, 12 August 1889: 5, <www.britishnewspaperarchive.co.uk> [Accessed 19 February 2014].

Index

Page numbers in bold refer to illustrations.